THE BOOK OF THE
AKITA

THE BOOK OF THE
AKITA

Joan McDonald Brearley

Dedication

This book is dedicated to the great

HACHI-KO,

the dog that became a legend in his country
and forever in the breed because he epitomized
the loyalty and devotion of all dogs. It seems
only fitting that his statue at Shibuya Station in
Japan has remained a meeting place for lovers
in his native land.

Title page. Ch. Tsuyoi Inu's Toshi poses for this magnificent photo.
Owned by Barbara Cox, Cedar Hills Ranch, Placerville, California.
Page 7. Ch. Tamarlane's Sakurajima, C.D., owned by Bartley S.
Shaw of Wheat Ridge, Colorado.

ISBN 0-86622-048-8

© 1985 by T.F.H. Publications, Inc.

Distributed in the UNITED STATES by T.F.H. Publications, Inc., 211 West Sylvania Avenue, Neptune City, NJ 07753; in CANADA by H & L Pet Supplies Inc., 27 Kingston Crescent, Kitchener, Ontario N2B 2T6; Rolf C. Hagen Ltd., 3225 Sartelon Street, Montreal 382 Quebec; in ENGLAND by T.F.H. Publications Limited, 4 Kier Park, Ascot, Berkshire SL5 7DS; in AUSTRALIA AND THE SOUTH PACIFIC by T.F.H. (Australia) Pty. Ltd., Box 149, Brookvale 2100 N.S.W., Australia; in NEW ZEALAND by Ross Haines & Son, Ltd., 18 Monmouth Street, Grey Lynn, Auckland 2 New Zealand; in SINGAPORE AND MALAYSIA by MPH Distributors (S) Pte., Ltd., 601 Sims Drive, # 03/07/21, Singapore 1438; in the PHILIPPINES by Bio-Research, 5 Lippay Street, San Lorenzo Village, Makati Rizal; in SOUTH AFRICA by Multipet Pty. Ltd., 30 Turners Avenue, Durban 4001. Published by T.F.H. Publications Inc. Manufactured in the United States of America by T.F.H. Publications, Inc.

Contents

Acknowledgments

The author wishes to convey appreciation for the cooperation and enthusiasm expressed by so many devotees of the Akita breed during the creation of this book. Special thanks go to Nadene Fontano for general information and consultation on grooming; to James and Susan White for information on Search and Rescue Akitas; to Gerry Rose, Barbara Bouyet, Ms. Koehler, and Manan Vos for information on Akitas in Europe; Marion Sargent for the story of the breed in England; and all the other breeders who sent along facts and figures pertaining to

the breed. As always, a special thanks to Dr. Robert Shomer, V.M.D., for veterinary counsel, and support, over so many years. Since a book of this kind is never the work of one person alone, I hope all those who contributed to it in any way —and especially those who shared their photographs of their beautiful dogs—will enjoy some personal satisfaction and pleasure from it.

Joan Brearley
Sea Bright, New Jersey

About the Author

Joan Brearley is the first to admit that animals in general—and dogs in particular—are a most important part of her life. Since childhood there has been a steady stream of dogs, cats, birds, fish, rabbits, snakes, alligators, etc., for her own personal menagerie. Over the years she has owned over thirty breeds of purebred dogs as well as countless mixtures, since the door was never closed to a needy or homeless animal.

A graduate of the American Academy of Dramatic Arts where she studied acting and directing, Joan started her career as an actress, dancer, and writer for movie magazines. She studied ballet at the Agnes DeMille Studios in Carnegie Hall and was with an Oriental dance company which performed at the Carnegie Recital Hall. She studied journalism at Columbia University and has written for radio, television, and magazines, and she was a copywriter for some of the major New York City advertising agencies working on the accounts of Metro-Goldwyn-Mayer Studios, Burlington Mills, *Cosmopolitan* magazine, White Owl Cigars, and *World-Telegram & Sun* newspapers.

While a television producer-director for a major network Joan worked on "Nick Carter, Master Detective"; "Did Justice Triumph"; and news and special feature programs. Joan has written, cast, directed, produced and, on occasion, starred in television commercials. She has written special material for such personalities as Dick Van Dyke, Amy Vanderbilt, William B. Williams, Gene Rayburn, Bill Stern, Herman Hickman, and many other people prominent in the entertainment world. She has appeared as a guest on several of the nation's most popular talk shows, including Mike Douglas, Joe Franklin, Cleveland Amory, David Susskind and the *Today Show*, to name just a few. Joan was selected for inclusion in the *Directory of the Foremost Women in Communications* in 1969, and the book *Two Thousand Women of Achievement* in 1971.

Her accomplishments in the dog fancy include breeding and exhibiting top show dogs, being a writer and columnist of various magazines, and author of over thirty books on dogs and cats. For five years she was Executive Vice President of the Popular Dogs Publishing Company and editor of *Popular Dogs* magazine, the national prestige publication for the fancy at that time. Her editorials on the status and welfare of animals have been reproduced as educational pamphlets by dog clubs and organizations in many countries of the world.

Joan is just as active in the cat fancy, and in almost as many capacities. The same year her Afghan Hound Champion Sahadi Shikari won the Ken-l Ration Award as Top Hound of the Year, one of her Siamese cats won the comparable honor in the cat fancy. She has owned and/or bred almost every breed of cat. Many of her cats and dogs are Best In Show winners and have appeared in magazines and on television. For several years she was editor of the Cat Fanciers' Association Annual Yearbook, and her book *All About Himalayan Cats* was published in 1976.

In addition to breeding and showing dogs since 1955, Joan has been active as a member and on the Board of Directors of the Kennel Club of Northern New Jersey, the Afghan Hound Club of America, the Stewards Club of America, and The Dog Fanciers Club. She has been an American Kennel Club judge of several breeds since 1961. She has appeared as a guest speaker at many dog clubs and humane organizations crusading for humane legislation, and has won several awards and citations for her work in this field. She is one of the best-known and most knowledgeable people in the animal world. Joan is proud of the fact that her Champion Sahadi Shikari was top-winning Afghan Hound in the history of the breed for several years, and remains in the number two position today. No other breeder can claim to have bred a Westminster Group winner in the first homebred litter. She has also bred champion Yorkshire Terriers.

Joan has recently been made a Trustee of the Morris Animal Foundation, does free-lance publicity and public relations work, is a

Daughter of the American Revolution and the New York Genealogical Society. In her spare time she exhibits her needlework (for which she has also won prizes), haunts the art and auction galleries, and is a graduate auctioneer with the full title of Colonel.

This impressive list of activities doesn't include all of her accomplishments, since she has never been content to have just one interest at a time, but manages to dovetail several occupations and avocations to make for a fascinating career.

Joan lives with her dogs, cats, hamsters, guinea pigs, and twenty exotic birds in a townhouse on the oceanfront in Sea Bright, New Jersey, where she also serves as Councilwoman,

Secretary and active member of the First Aid Squad, and Trustee of both the Sea Bright Village Association and the Sea Bright Partnership.

Captions for pages 10-11.
1. M. Owens Hudson's portrait of Ch. Matsukaze's Holly-Go Litely, the "winningest" Akita in breed history. Three all-breed Bests in Show and a National Akita Specialty are just two of her accomplishments. She was #1 Akita in 1980 according to the Kennel Review System, #1 Akita 1981 all systems, and #1 Akita in 1982 for winning the most Group and Bests in Show in the breed. Bred by Gus Bell, owned by Bea Hunt, and handled during her show ring career by Rusty Short. 2. Water color portrait by Tamara Hall and owned by Dr. Sophia Kaluzniacki.

Chapter 1

Early History of Dogs

Many millions of years ago dinosaurs and other strange-looking creatures roamed the earth. As "recently" as sixty million years ago a mammal existed which resembled a civet cat and is believed to have been the common ancestor of dogs, cats, wolves, and coyotes. This animal was the long extinct Miacis (pronounced My-a-Kiss).

The Miacis were long-bodied, long-tailed, short-legged beasts that stalked and chased their prey, grasped it in their long, powerful, fanged jaws and gnashed their food with their teeth. Just fifteen million years ago the Tomarctus evolved from the earlier Miacis and provided an even truer genetic basis for the more highly intelligent prototype of the domesticated dog.

It is only fifteen to twenty thousand years since the first attempts were made to domesticate these ferocious tree-climbing animals. Archaeologists have uncovered the skeletal remains of dogs that date back to the age of the cave man, and co-existed with them as members of their families in several ancient civilizations.

There are several schools of thought among the scholars and scientists on the exact location of the very first creatures to live with man. Some contend that the continent of Africa was the original locale. Ancient remains unearthed near Lake Baikal date back to 9,000 years B.C. Recent diggings in nearby Iraq that are said to date back 12,000 years have produced evidences of what is called the Palegawra dog. Siberian remains are said to go back 20,000 years. The Jaguar Cave Dogs of North America have been dated circa 8,400 B.C. Others say Asia and claim the Chinese wolf to be the ancestor of the dog.

Advocates of the theory of the Chinese wolf point out that the language barrier was responsible for the Chinese wolf not being known or acknowledged in earlier comparisons. When scientists could not translate Chinese writing, they could not study or authenticate the early Oriental findings. Their theory is also based on the presence of the overhanging bone found in the jawbone of both the Chinese wolf and the dog. This is believed to be significant in the change from their being strictly carnivorous creatures to creatures that eventually become omnivorous carnivores.

When one considers the several breeds of Oriental dogs, ranging in size from the very small to the very large (Shih Tzu to Akita) it becomes a distinct possibility. We know that history relates the legends of shaggy toy breeds running around palace courtyards, and the huge Mastiff-type breeds guarding the walls of the ancient cities and following their masters into war.

While a prisoner in Genoa, Italy, the renowned Asian traveller, Marco Polo, dictated to another prisoner named Rusticiano the lengthy and detailed accounts of his travels in the Orient and throughout Asia. These tales of his journey comprised eighty to ninety manuscripts, the most important of them being in the possession of the Bibliotheque Nationale in Paris. In these manuscripts Marco Polo glorifies the life and times of Kublai Khan, grandson of Genghis Khan and a man he came to consider a friend before leaving China.

It was on his return to Venice in 1294 after years of service in the court of Kublai Khan at Shangtu, not far from Peking, that he began to take note of the great numbers of both small and large dogs. He was particularly so impressed with the Mastiffs that he wrote about his belief that a Mastiff could finish off a lion, should the occasion demand.

Whether it was the enormous Mastiff-type dogs that guarded homes and palaces and accompanied soldiers into war, or the chubby, middle-sized Chow Chow-type dogs bred to provide food for the masses, or the sturdy little lap and sleeve-size dogs that captured the fancy of the royal houses of Asia, the dogs from the Orient were destined to make their way into the hearts of dog lovers in the centuries that followed their early beginnings. Many of them found their way to foreign lands by way of sailors on trade ships, while others were given as gifts to visiting dignitaries and were taken home to other lands— and not always before many separate and individual breeds were established.

However, the general consensus of opinion among scientists dealing with prehistoric and archaelogical studies seems to settle on the likelihood that dogs were being domesticated in many parts of the world at approximately the same period in time. Since dogs were to become so essential to man's very existence, they were naturally absorbed into family life wherever and whenever they were found.

Climate, geography, and other environmental conditions all played a part in the evolution of the dog, and much later, the individual types and sizes and breeds of dogs.

The three most primitive types originated in three parts of the globe. While all bore certain very exact characteristics, the wolf-type seemed to evolve in southern Asia and Australia, the Pariahs in Asia Minor and Japan, and the Basenjis in Africa.

The Dingo found its way north to Russia and Alaska, across what is now the Bering Strait, into North America. The Pariahs moved far north and learned to pull sleds and developed into the various Northern breeds in the Arctic regions. The Basenjis and Greyhounds coursed the desert sands and hunted in the jungles of Africa when they weren't guarding royal palaces in Egypt. As dogs found their way across Europe, they served as guard dogs in the castles, rescue dogs in the Alps, barge dogs on the canals, and hunting dogs in the forests. The smaller dogs were bred down even smaller and became companions and pets for the aristocracy. Kings and Queens of the world have always maintained their own personal kennels for their favorite breeds.

BREED DEVELOPMENT

While the cave man used the dog primarily as a hunter to help provide meat and to provide meat themselves, he also made use of the fur as clothing and used the warmth from the dogs' bodies when sleeping. Dogs were to become even more functional as time went by, according to the dictates of their owners. Definite physical changes were planned and eventually would distinguish one dog from another even within the same geographical regions. Ears ranged in size from the little flaps that we see on terriers to the large upright ears on the Ibizan Hounds and the Akitas. Noses either flattened greatly as they did with Pekingese and Bulldogs, or they grew to amazing lengths as we see in the Borzoi. Tails grew to be long and plumey such as those we see on the Siberian Husky or the Akita, or doubled up into a curl such as those we see on the Pug. Legs grew long and thin for coursing Greyhounds or were short and bent for the digging breeds such as the Dachshunds and the Bassets. Sizes went from one extreme to the other, ranging from the tiniest Chihuahua all the way up to the biggest of all breeds, the Irish Wolfhound. Coat lengths became longer or shorter. There were thick, woolly coats for the northern breeds and smooth, short coats for the dogs that worked in the warm climates.

SENSORY PERCEPTION

As the dogs changed in physical appearance, their instincts and sensory perceptions also developed. Their sense of smell is said to be thirty million times keener than their human counterparts, allowing them to pick up and follow the scents of other animals miles in the distance. Their eyes developed to such a sharpness that they could spot moving prey on the horizon far across desert sands. Their hearing became so acute that they were able to pick up the sounds of the smallest creatures rustling in the leaves across an open field or in a dense forest.

All things considered, it becomes easy to comprehend why man and dog became such successful partners in survival and why their attraction and affection for each other is such a wondrous thing.

天明戊申晩夏寫
應擧

2

Chapter 2

The Akita in Japan

The Akita's ancestry dates back to 500 B.C. when they migrated from the mainland of China to the islands of Japan. In the twelfth century, dog fighting was a popular sport in Japan and some of the fighting dogs were said to have been introduced into the Akita lines of the Tosainu dogs. When interest in fighting waned, the Akita once again was relegated to guarding, hunting and herding duties.

Documentation on the Akita breed tells us that in the early seventeenth century a famous war lord, who had fallen from the Emperor's grace, was ordered to build a fortress on northern Honshu island, and to live out his life there as a provincial ruler. He greatly favored sporting dogs and used his newly acquired domain to compete in breeding the largest and most powerful dog Japan had ever seen. Bred with the huge Russian Laika dogs, there soon evolved a dog of superior size, keen hunting abilities and a tremendous spirit. So impressive were these dogs that for the next century they enjoyed much popularity and a place of honor among the aristocracy.

By the eighteenth century, however, political matters once again became of paramount interest and the breeding of great dogs fell into the background. The breed during the next two hundred years almost became extinct. But along about 1900, the Akita once again managed to come into its own. Since there were no firearms the dogs would down the prey and the hunters would spear or club it. While the dogs had always been used to hunt ducks, birds, small fur-bearing animals, deer, elk, antelope, monkeys, boar or bear, including the 800 pound Yezo bears, their owners began to see other ways in which their intelligence could be utilized. They eventually came to be used as cattle herders, seeing-eye dogs, military guard dogs, sled and draft dogs and as police dogs. They were also used in falconry. In fact, earliest written records were found in a Shogunate's hawkchambers, describing dogs working with hawks and falcons.

Because their webbed feet made them powerful swimmers and their thick coats made them able to withstand cold waters, they became useful to the fishermen. Fishing has always been a major Japanese industry with the thousands of miles of coastline on the islands. Akitas were found to be particularly good as baby-sitters and many children could be left with the family dog while the peasant women went out into the fields to work.

AN AKITA MYTH

Early on, the Akita was also considered to be a symbol of good health. Even today when a person is ill, or a baby is born, many Akita owners in Japan will send a small Akita statue to ensure their good health or a speedy recovery from illness of any kind.

THE NATIONAL TREASURE

In 1931, after three and a half centuries of selective breeding toward an ideal working dog, the Japanese government proclaimed the Akita the National Dog of Japan and thereby declared a National Monument. Also referred to as the Royal Dog of Japan, Akita champions have more recently been regarded as national art treasures and are subsidized by the government if their owners suddenly are unable to feed or care for them properly.

HOW THEY GOT THEIR NAME

The Akita takes its name from the northern prefecture of Akita, rugged, mountainous country where the winters are snowy and severe cold persists, and where this large, thickly-coated dog thrives. H. Saito, a recognized Akita authority, has unearthed and reconstructed bones from burial mounds of the emperors which bear out the ancient heritage of this breed. Clay images and other pieces of art work have since been discovered in the tombs which show this Chow/ Akita type dog with its erect ears and tail curled over its back.

THE AKITA BECOMES INDIGENOUS TO JAPAN

The Akita, referred to also as the Nippon Inu, is the largest of eight dogs regarded as being indigenous to Japan. Nippon, by the way, is the word for Japanese, and Inu is the word for dog. For years the Japanese took many precautions to be certain that their Nippon Inu did not leave their country. As with all the cherished Oriental breeds, the Japanese also preferred to keep the Akita as an exclusive gift to foreign dignitaries, royalty, or to be given under very special and extraordinary circumstances.

THE AKITA AND THE SAMURAI WARRIORS

Primarily the Japanese wished to keep their Nippon Inu dogs for the dog fighting events that proved so popular for so many years in that country. In fact, it is reported that dog fights were used to exemplify the ultimate in courage and bravery and all Samurai warriors attended them as part of their training sessions with this purpose in mind.

In the latter part of the 19th and early part of the 20th centuries dog fighting was still a favorite pastime, and with the Akita's natural aptitude for fighting, and taking its large size into consideration, fanciers became alarmed at the other diminishing qualities in the breed. So a Standard was written in 1938 which is very similar to the one still being used as the Japanese Standard today.

Some were being bred back to the Akita-Matagi, another of the Japanese hunting dogs, to try to recapture some of the old Akita qualities that were lost when breeders of fighting dogs concentrated on size and fierceness to the exclusion of all else. By 1940 all the crossbreeding for this stopped and the "modern" type Akita was perpetuated and established in the modern dog world, until its near extinction during World War II.

THE JAPANESE REGISTRY

Still on the island of Honshu, in the city of Odate, there remains the center of activity for the Akita breed. It is in Odate that the main headquarters for the registration body for the Akita in Japan is situated. From near extinction during the war years, the Akita today has prospered in the affluent society of Japan and there are literally hundreds of breeders and exhibitors in Japan. Among these are Dr. K. Shiguro, a veterinarian and a show judge, and Mr. Ichiro Ogasawara, who is also a member of the Akihi club.

THE STORY OF HACHIKO

We all have our favorite dog tales which prove unequivocably the loyalty and devotion of the dog. Perhaps the oldest, and best known of the Akita stories is the poignant story of the faithful dog Hachiko, or Hachi-Ko, as he is called by the Japanese. It has been told, and retold, by countless numbers of dog lovers from all over the world, and it even appears in some Japanese school books.

Hachiko was an Akita owned by Dr. Eisaburo Ueno, a professor at Tokyo University. Each morning the dog walked with his owner to the train station and each afternoon at 3 P.M. came back to meet him at the Shibuya Station platform. On May 21, 1925, the doctor boarded the train, as usual, but did not return. He suffered a stroke and died at the University, and that evening the dog sat among the priests and mourners. But the faithful Hachiko continued to return to the station each morning and each afternoon to wait for his master. All Tokyo came to know the dog and fed and cared for him while he kept his vigil. On the evening of March 7, 1935 they found Hachiko dead at the very spot where he had waited for so long for his owner to return. Everyone would ask, "Hachiko doko deska?" or "Where is Hachiko?" for many years to come.

In 1943 a small bronze statue of Hachiko was erected at the place where he had waited so patiently for ten years. But shortly after it was put in place, the government confiscated all statues to be melted down for arms during World War II.

In 1948 a son of Teru Ando, the sculptor who created the original statue of Hachiko, was commissioned to do another statue which was eventually erected in the same location. It has since become a meeting place for lovers, as well as an attraction—and meeting place—for dog lovers. But, we can be sure, Hachiko has become a legend. And a most fitting tribute that lovers meet there since Hachiko was waiting for someone he loved!

Captions for pages 18-19.
1. Kita Maru II, owned by Valerie Edmondson of Garden Grove, California. Maru has papers both here and in Japan, and he is pictured here at one-and-a-half years of age. 2. Echol's Midnite Lurch, C.D., is owned by Betty Hinson, Jonesboro, Arkansas. 3. An early Akita, Krug's Sotto, photographed by Creszentia Allen. Pictures of Sotto were also used on Akita stationery. 4. Ch. Echols White Tornado, an early champion once the breed was accepted in the United States. Cheryl Droste is handling.

2

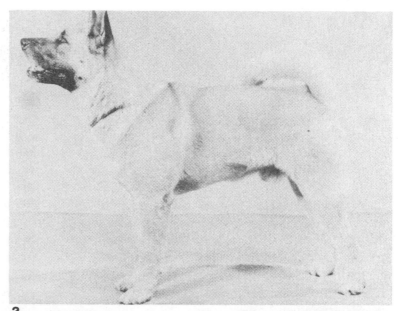

3

4

Chapter 3

The Akita Comes to America

It is generally agreed that the Akita came to America by the same route as many other Oriental dogs ... they returned with the American soldiers who went off to World War II. While, as we mention elsewhere in this book, the Japanese preferred to keep their dogs to themselves, several servicemen brought some of the Akitas back to the United States where interest in this magnificent breed took hold almost immediately.

While it was said that only some of the poorer specimens were allowed out of Japan, we can understand why some of the earlier dogs in this country were not up to the standards of those that remained in Japan. Once here, it became the favorite breed of many of the Japanese people who resided in this country, and helped to establish recognition here.

THE AMERICAN STANDARD

In 1955, a standard was drawn up for the breed in the United States. It was composed by interested American breeders with the assistance of the Director of the Japan Kennel Club. He wished to be sure the breed did not go too far afield from its original ideal and purpose in its native land. This project required a great deal of thought and communication since there were no fewer than four Akita clubs by this time, all of which had their own ideas about the breed's future and requirements.

After considerable deliberation a standard was accepted by the American Kennel Club and on January 1, 1956, the breed became eligible to be shown in the Miscellaneous Classes in the United States.

FIRST IN THE SHOW RING

The first Akita to be shown in this country under this new ruling was Fisher's Homare Maiku-Go, who won the Miscellaneous Class first prize at the Orange Empire Dog Club show on January 29, 1956, under judge Marie B. Meyer, a very famous judge and dog fancier.

THE AKITA AND HELEN KELLER

It was Helen Keller, the blind, deaf, and mute person who learned to speak and led an exemplary life, who brought the first Akita into the United States as her pet in the late 1930's. And after her remarkable pet Akita died, she imported another to take its place.

But it was through the servicemen who became acquainted with the breed while in Japan during World War II that the breed found its way into the American dog fancy. Since so many Akitas had died during the food shortages in Japan during the war, their numbers were greatly reduced, and the Japanese were reluctant to let them leave the country with their American owners for fear the breed might become extinct. However, many of the Americans were permitted to take their dogs out of the country and in spite of the fact that the animals were chosen originally as pets, those that were bred and can still be seen today do resemble the original Japanese Standard for quality.

As a matter of fact, with so many of today's breeders importing directly from Japan, this resemblance becomes even more obvious.

Size in the breed has become a questionable theory these days, with most dogs leaning toward the size larger than those found in Japan, where smallness means easier handling and housing in that over-crowded country.

SOME OF THE EARLY WINNERS

Most of the Akita activity back in the decade of the sixties was on the West Coast where imports from Japan were less costly. What with prices of travel, purchase price of the dogs, etc., an additional cross-country flight or transportation of any kind added considerably to the expense of importing.

Perhaps one of the first to come to mind was the impressive pinto Hozan, along with Akita Tani's Shoyo Go, Triple K Hayai Taka, and the Mexican Champion Kinsei Suna Nihon No-Taishi, C.D. It is interesting to note that while having to compete in the Miscellaneous Classes where no title could be attained, they did earn C.D. titles "way back then."

The bitches did well. The Goromaru line was represented by Shanpan and a bitch named Ginko, sired by a Mexican champion; Sakura Hime did well as did Meiyo and out of a good male named Terugide-Go imported from Japan.

We can only imagine how many champions would have been made during those early days, or how many first prize winners we would have racked up if there were a special Miscellaneous Class for Akitas only. But a debt of gratitude and thanks is due to those stalwart exhibitors who kept plugging away at the show rings to get the breed the exposure that led to their eventual popularity, success and acceptance in the American dog fancy.

THE 1970's

It was another Mexican champion, namely Fukumoto's Ashibaya Kuma that made a name for himself in the early seventies. Two imports also made their mark. They were brothers named Sakusaku's Tom Cat-Go and Tosko's Kabuki. Another Triple K dog named Tomo-Go, was winning as were Krug's Sotto and a dog named Imperial Ginzan.

The Triple K kennels had an entry named Chiyo, a brindle that was very good, and their Triple K Cho. Another was a pinto named Kikuhime. Another brindle bitch was Tusko's Star, an import that was to contribute to the breed through her excellent progeny. Sakusaku's Tiger Lily was a top bitch and a brindle import. The Imperial kennels also had a top bitch in their Fujihime.

AKITA PROBLEMS OF THE 1970's

Aside from the quality of the aforementioned dogs there was talk of the breeders' concern for the future of the breed. As the judges from Japan noted, there was a lot of work to be done in the breed. The short muzzle and wide flat head was in jeopardy, the colors were beginning to fade, loose skin, bad tail sets, hock problems and general physical fitness were beginning to show up, as some of the breeders began to push the dogs that were not totally according to the Standard but rather from their own kennels. It was up to the Akita Club of America to flourish and preserve what was good that they had already achieved and to steadily improve on as the day of recognition came closer to being a reality.

DAY OF RECOGNITION

In 1972 the Akita was accepted for registration in the American Kennel Club. On Wednesday November 1, the stud book was opened to them and the Akita became eligible to compete in the show rings for championship status, as of April 4, 1973.

The Akita had been competing in the Miscellaneous Class at the dog shows since 1956. In the Akita Club of America's stud book there were over twenty-five hundred Akitas registered with them, with most residing and competing on the West Coast. Naturally, the Akita joined the ranks of those competing in the Working Group.

TOP DOG FOR 1972

Just as the excitement grew over the prospect of recognition, the Akita Club of America show dog point system proclaimed Tusko's Kabuki as the Top Akita in America for 1972. This outstanding male was owner-handled by Pete Lagus of Alta Dena, California.

THE AKITA BOOM

As with most all good things, it wasn't long after recognition that the Akita "caught on" with the dog fancy. By 1983 not only was the quality of the Akita much improved in the show rings, but the general public, especially in New York City, created quite a "fad" for the big Bear dogs. It is believed that in excess of five hundred lived within the city and could be seen on the streets in every section of town.

Among those who succumbed to the Akita charm were such celebrities as Linda Ronstadt, Yoko Ono and famed dancer Judith Jameson. Articles appeared in newspapers lauding this newest "dog of the moment" and all its splendid "teddy bear" characteristics, and they could be seen at sidewalk cafes, and in city parks where their proud owners openly discussed the pros and cons of rearing in much the same manner as English nannies discuss their charges.

Captions for pages 22-23.
1. A consistent winner in the Miscellaneous Classes before the breed received A.K.C. recognition was Issei Riki Oji Go, first generation Japanese-American breeding for Lillian O'Shea, now Lillian Koehler. Riki was from the first litter from her Japanese imports, and a born showman. 2. Seisi Michiko Joeo Go, on the bench at a 1969 dog show. Owned by Lillian (O'Shea) Koehler of Hatboro, Pennsylvania, Michiko was one of the first Akita show dogs in the United States. 3. Ch. O'Shea Issei Shozo O Go winning final points for championship at a 1974 dog show. Clayton Fell handled for owner Lillian O'Shea (now Koehler) of Hatboro, Pennsylvania. Issei represents first generation American breeding for her kennel. 4. Ch. Triple K Tomo-Go, owned by Ted DePolo.

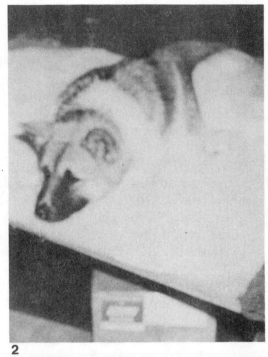

BEST OF
BREED

GILBERT PHOTO

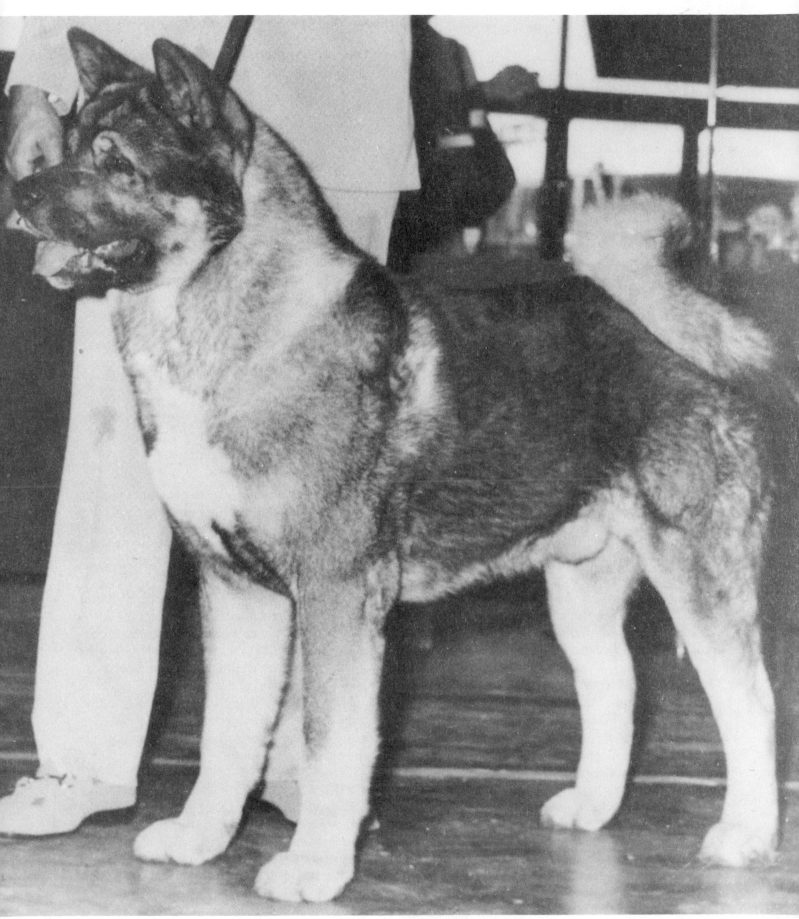

4

Chapter 4

The Akita Club of America

In June of 1956 a group of dedicated Akita fanciers banded together to form the Akita Club of America. It was their express purpose to form a club that would work toward improving and popularizing the breed in this country, and to work toward their recognition by the American Kennel Club.

As with each new breed seeking such recognition, it was necessary for them to serve as their own registering body. By 1970 their club boasted members in every state in the union, and had over 1300 Akitas listed in their Stud Book.

By 1970 they also had branched out as the need for local organizations formed. The oldest one was the Eastern Akita Club, which at that time pretty much covered the eastern coast. Two years later the Midwest Akita Club was formed and served the central states. In California, the Akitas of San Diego chapter followed by one year in the Southern California area and the Royal Akita Club was organized, serving Northern California.

Each club held a match show each year and membership continued to grow. The club produced a brochure telling the history of the breed, and to help educate the general public to this marvelous new breed to our country. Their main headquarters were located in Oakland, California.

THE AKITA REGISTER OF MERIT

The Register of Merit Awards are given by The Akita Club of America for outstanding producers of champions. This means a sire must produce ten or more American Kennel Club champions to be eligible and a dam must produce five or more to earn the title.

As of August 1983 when results were published in an article explaining the first ten years of the Register of Merit awards, 40 bitches and 23 males had earned "their letters." All these, and in just the few years since the breed has enjoyed AKC recognition! It is an established fact that many of the R.O.M. dogs and bitches have descended from other Akitas which have earned R.O.M. status.

Perhaps the most significant proof of this

comes from a litter whelped in April, 1960 in California at Camille Kam's Triple K kennels. The sire was a Japanese Grand Champion named Kinsho-Go and the dam of Gin Joo-Go of Triple K. Nineteen of the 23 R.O.M. sires at the time these statistics were compiled by Sophia Kaluzniacki, D.V.M., could trace their ancestry to one or more members of that litter. A proud tradition, to be sure.

THE SHOWDOGS RATING SYSTEM

In 1975 in the *Showdogs* magazine rating system no Akita made the list of Top Twenty Show dogs all-breeds, nor did they place on the list of Top Ten dogs in the Working Group. However, there were nine Akitas listed within the breed. Listing them one through nine they are as follows:

1. Brenwicks Gemini 664
2. Ch. Kazokus Riki Maru of Okii Yubi 653
3. Ch. Takis Akaguma Sakura 582
4. Matsu Kazes Kuro Kobito 509
5. Ch. Mitsu Kumas Tora Oji Go 491
6. Ch. Jamels Oso Cute 370
7. Sakusakus Hinode 272
8. Ch. Wanchans Akagumo 203
9. Takis Aite C.D. 188

The numbers following the names of the dogs, as in most dog show rating systems represent the number of dogs defeated during competition in the show rings. The figures represent breed and group successes from January 1, 1975 through December 31, 1975.

Following the 1975 statistics, rating systems were to come and go, but considering the initiation of this system and the numbers of dogs defeated, nine Akitas made a very good showing for themselves by winning over considerable entries in the breed.

However, one thing was certain . . . Akitas were here to stay and were destined to find their place in the winner's circle at shows all across the nation forevermore.

FIRST AKITA NATIONAL

October 17, 1976, was a red-letter day for the Akita Club of America. It was the first National Specialty show held in conjunction with the San Fernando Kennel Club show in California. Needless to say, it was a tremendous success, boasting 104 entries in the classes and 36 in the Sweepstakes. Nineteen Specials competed.

Mr. C.L. Savage was the judge for the Sweepstakes and the winner was Gaylee's Fonzi no

Kosetsu, co-owned and handled by Carol Foti. There was one brood bitch, five stud dogs in competition.

Mr. McMackin had been invited to judge this first major event but was unable to attend and J. Council Parker took over his assignment. His Best of Breed winner was Ch. Gaylee's Okami-naga, owned and handled by Leon Nogue. Club president Gus Bell presented the trophies along with Tiare Caudill, who was trophy chairman for this gala event.

Best of winners honors went to Susan R. Oekel's King's Nu Koya Kabuki Nisei, and Reserve Dog to Ryujin's Hotei, owned by E.L. and Barbara Weltlich. Winners Bitch was Takara's Miyuki, and Reserve was Cee Jay's Daddy's Ditto. Veteran Dog was Ch. Hozan of Matsu-Kaze. Best of Opposite Sex was Ch. Akita Tani's Kori of Kosho-Ki, owned by Everett and Marlene Sutton.

The host club for this National was the Akita Club of Greater Los Angeles, and local Chairperson was Mrs. Twyla Lusk who led the team of devoted members that made this event such a success.

OTHER EARLY CLUBS

In 1963, the American Akita Breeders organized in California. They saw and anticipated further the dangers that could lie ahead as the breed gained slowly, but surely, in popularity in this country and they set about trying to avoid the possible pitfalls that might be on the horizon. March 3, 1963, saw them organize and begin their work with a starting membership list of just twelve devoted owners. The club also was determined to begin the groundwork for having the breed accepted by the American Kennel Club. It would take them almost a decade to accomplish their desired championship title recognition.

The club proposed to encourage the breeding of the Akita to the Standard, to protect and advance the interest of the breed by encouraging competition within the realm of good sportsmanship, to hold yearly shows to bring the dog into the public eye in the dog fancy, and to maintain a registry of breeding required for American Kennel Club acceptance.

They also published *The Akita News*, a monthly publication dealing exclusively with the happenings in the breed, and produced a brochure about the Akita which featured many photographs, stories and historical pieces on the dog from any and all sources open to them at the time.

Shohi Kumiaj, a cooperative society for the preservation of the Akita, was formed in the spring of 1970 in Westminster, California, with its membership residing in states throughout our country. The society was dedicated to seeing that the Akita "retains its massiveness, intelligence, stable temperament, and roundness of structure as originally developed by the Japanese." It encouraged a free exchange among its members to trade experiences on health, care, breeding and selling practices as well.

The organization formulated a "Code of Ethics" which requires adherence by all members and absolutely prohibited outcrosses. Each puppy sold was to receive a signed registration paper, a four-generation pedigree and a signed bill of sale for its new owner. If the puppy was not "show" quality, no registration paper was to be given at all. A bill of sale for the dog was to be given stating the reason why registration papers were not available and a complete accounting of the conditions of sale.

Captions for pages 26-27.
1. Ch. Sakusaku's Perfect Pearl, R.O.M., a red and white pinto bitch whelped in 1973. She is co-owned by Barbara and B. J. Hampton of Las Vegas, Nevada. 2. Best in Sweepstakes at the 1981 Akita Club of America National Specialty show under judge Terri Arndt was Kuma Yama Kazan, owned by the Kuma Yama Kennels, Bonnie and Dean Herrmann, of Whitewood, South Dakota. 3. Ch. Oki Yubi's Sachmo of Makoto, owned by B. J. Andrews of Asheville, North Carolina. 4. Mitsu Kumas Tora Oji-Go, one of the 1971 Akitas. 5. 1974 Ch. Matsukaze's Kuro Tenno, black and tan Akita bred and owned by Gus D. Bell and handled for him by Rusty Cunningham Short.

1

2

3

4

The Code of Ethics further stated that any Akitas which were found to be entropoid, dysplastic, cryptorchid or monorchid, undersized, excessively short or excessively aggressive, flop-eared or which bore extremely hairy coats, had tufts of hair in the ears or feathering on the legs, shoulders or tail, were not to be used as breeding stock.

These strict, devoted clubs and their members laid the necessary responsible groundwork on which the breed eventually became accepted into the ranks of recognized breeds with the American Kennel Club.

THE NATIONAL AKITA DIRECTORY

The following is a list of Akita Clubs throughout the United States that are member clubs of the Akita Club of America, the parent club for the breed:

> Akita Club of Greater Houston
> Akita Club of Hawaii
> Akita Club of Las Vegas
> Akita Club of Long Island
> Akita Club of Puget Sound
> Akita Club of Tampa Bay
> Buckeye Akita Club
> Cascade Akita Club
> The Greater Baltimore Akita Club
> Great Lakes Akita Club
> Kin Ken Akita Club
> Squakheag Akita Club

Other clubs which are not associated with the parent club are the Akita Club of Canada and the following in the United States:

> Akita Club of Delaware Valley
> Akita Club of Indiana
> Akita Club of Western New York
> The Colonial Akita Club
> Diamond State Akita Club
> Gold Country Akita Club
> Golden Gate Akita Club
> River City Akita Club
> Rocky Mountain Akita Club

AKITA CLUB BY THE SEA

1983 saw yet another Akita Club come into being in California. This one is called the Akita Club by the Sea, serving San Diego and Imperial Counties. Their first All Akita Match Show was held in November of '83. President was Peter Lagus. Meetings are held in Poway, California. As with all the Akita Clubs, information can be obtained from the American Kennel Club listing of the current secretary of the parent club.

THE HOZONKAI SOCIETY

The city of Odate, Japan, which is located at the northern point of the main island of Honshu, is the chief location for interest in the breed and the main registering body for the Akita dog in that country. For centuries, and until 1928 the records for their Nippon Inu were kept there by the Japanese government.

It was here that the Hozonkai Society was formed by prominent citizens in the Tokyo area and they were responsible for preserving these marvelous Japanese dogs. They held the belief that the Akita developed from a medium-sized Japanese dog which was eventually crossed with larger Chinese and Korean breeds. While they admitted to the relationship with the Northern breeds, they also pointed out that the Akita differed in bone structure from such dogs as the Samoyed.

While the ravages of World War II seriously threatened the survival of the Akita in Japan, there were a few devoted breeders in Akita City and Odate who managed to keep their dogs alive by sharing their own food with them.

For several years in the early 1970's there was in the city of Los Angeles a group of Akita aficionados that held a special dog show called the Akita Inu Hozonkai. It was staged in conjunction with the Nisei Week celebration of the Japanese community in Little Tokyo. In addition to the usual tea ceremonies, judo matches, parades, etc., a Japanese judge was flown to Los Angeles to preside at this extra special Japanese Akita dog show event, at which the dogs were judged according to the Japanese Standard. Entries are unusually high with over 125 at the 1969 and 119 at the 1970 shows.

In 1969 when veterinarian Dr. Ichiro Ogasawara judged the show in Los Angeles he gave a critique stating that Akitas with black spots or stars on their tongues are shown in this pet class since such is considered a fault in the breed. He also stated that the American Akitas were about twenty years behind the Japanese in their breeding program. All of which gives credence to the theory that only the poorest specimens of the breed were allowed out of Japan with the American G.I.'s. He further stated that it has only been very recently that things have improved since more importing from Japan had taken place.

The 1970 judge, Mr. Hirazuni, was quoted in Joani Linderman's Akita column in *Kennel Review* magazine alluding to yet more problems with our American dogs at the time. He found

Lovely Akita head study featured on the emblem of the Akita Club of Puget Sound. It was designed by club member Kelle Clinton.

the color and brilliance in coat very much lacking. He went on to criticize facial traits: too many wrinkles, loose jowls, improperly shaped eyes and loose skin, weak hindquarters, and loose tails as the "predominant" faults. He added to this by stating that he felt the hair on the tails was not nearly long or full enough, and that there were not nearly enough white Akitas in this country. Apparently this is a favorite color in his native country and he took consolation only in the fact that our reds and brindle-colored dogs were good representations of the breed.

In 1971 Joani Linderman and her husband planned to attend the shows as they had the previous two years to take pictures of the dogs for interesting comparisons in the future.

It is interesting to note that in 1969 two Japanese-bred Akitas won Best and Best Opposite in Show and had won elsewhere in the United States as well. Progress apparently was made because an American-bred bitch was Best in Show in 1970 and Best Opposite Sex was the same male that was Best Opposite at the 1969 show.

Captions for pages 30-31.
1. A mother's watchful eye. . .Hodaha di Cambiano watches over her brood in Milano, Italy. Bred by Garabelli Maria Teresa, she is owned by Cornelis Koot of Milhese, Holland. Photographed by Manon Vos of Haren, Holland. 2. Asahi and friend Chiyoda-Ku at play in 1981 at the home of their owner Manon Vos of Haren, Holland. 3. A bitch living in Holland of the "new" type, typical of Japan and Italy. Photo by Manon Vos. 4. Samocho of Bandai Asahi, bred by B. Maas, Germany and owned by Van Veller of Holland. Photo by Manon Vos. 5. Father-daughter portrait of two Akitas owned by Manon Vos of Haren, Holland. The white male is Bsoetjimikado-go aus Chiyoda-Ku. The brown bitch is Asahi of Bandai Asahi. Photographed by their breeder-owner.

1   2

3   4

Ch. Tamarlane's Silver Star, owned by Dean and Bonnie Herrmann, Kuma Yama Akitas, and handled for them by Rusty Cunningham Short. Bred by Dr. Sophia Kaluzniacki, Star was the #1 Akita Bitch in 1979 and was chosen to represent the breed in the 1982 Standards edition of *Dog World* magazine.

Ch. The Real McCoy O'B.J., owned by Bill and B.J. Andrews of Asheville, North Carolina.

Left: Robert Santoli with Ch. Great River's Hoshi of Ginsan and Ch. Great River's Tsuki-Ko of Ginsan. "Star" and "Pumpkin" are two major influences at the Ginsan Kennels, Islip, New York. **Below:** Ch. Great River's Tsuki-Ko of Ginsan is pictured at ten months of age. "Pumpkin" was bred by Robert Player and is co-owned by Robert and Virginia Santoli of Islip, New York.

BEST OF WINNERS
TRENTON
KENNEL CLUB
1980
ASHBEY

Right: Golden Sun Seawood T'Siatko in a pensive mood at the Seawood Kennels of Alyce and Kelle Clinton in Lakebay, Washington. Taken in the Spring of 1981, this lovely headstudy is typical of the breed. The sire was Ch. Kodiak of Autumn Field ex Ch. Golden Sun's Taneha.
Below: Ch. Kuma Yama Ima Star and Ch. Silver Raider, shown by breeder-owners Bonnie and Dean Herrmann of Whitewood, South Dakota.

Ch. Marjo's Gin No Kiri Bukai is pictured winning at a 1981 dog show, with handler Marian Zak, under judge J. Council Parker. Owned by Lorraine Miller, Eljays Akitas, Westminster, Maryland. The sire was Ch. Yoi Nedon's Kata Uma ex Ch. Marjo's Inabikari, C.D.

Ch. Akiko's Walk'in Proud'N Tall, bred and owned by Patricia and Robert Berglund of Hampstead, Maryland. Whelped in October 1980, he is pictured winning at the 1983 Virginia Kennel Club show under judge Robert Thomas. The sire was Ch. Shibui's Tsuki Kage Boshi ex Aki's Sukoshi Odoroki.

Ch. Jamel's Oso Cute, O.F.A. and R.O.M., the # 1 Bitch in the United States for 1974 and 1975, is pictured with co-owner and handler Barbara Hampton at a 1973 show.

38

Ch. Tobe's Akritra Joy of Milor is pictured winning on the way to championship at a 1982 show. Bred by Tobe Kennels.

Ch. Great River's Galloping Gourmet with handler Sid Lamont. In just six months in the show ring "Acorn" won 53 Bests of Breed, 6 Group Firsts, and 19 more Placements. In 1983 he was rated # 1 according to the Akita Review System. Owned by Nadene and Bob Fontano and Robert Player.

All-white Akita Kin Hozan's Snow King of Daitan, bred by Bea Hunt and owned by Jim and Debbie Stewart, Daitan Akitas. King was handled during his show ring career by Rusty Cunningham Short, Ko-Fuku-No Akitas, Burbank, California.

Ch. Minkees Duke, owner-handled by N. Sailer, is pictured winning on the way to his championship.

Ch. Bar-BJ's Pretti Bare is pictured winning at a 1982 show under judge Dr. Richard Greathouse. Handled by Barbara Hampton, she is co-owned by Barbara and B.J. Hampton, Bar BJ Akitas, Las Vegas, Nevada. The sire was Bar-BJ's The Hustler.

Ch. Sparkle Like Kaito, 13-month-old Akita owned by Ruth and Wayne Zimmerman of Wilmington, Delaware. This bitch finished for her championship in eight shows, owner-handled from the Puppy Classes. The sire was Ch. Dragon Head's Emperor Kaito ex Yoo-Too's Phoenix of Bishamon.

Ch. Wotan's Command Performance, finishing for championship under Lester Mapes at the 1983 Crawford County Kennel Club show. "Eagle" was owner-handled by Peggy Casselberry, Wotan Kennels, North Canton, Ohio. The sire was Ch. Minkee's Arcturus Mekhan ex Renegade's Tasha of Deerhaven.

ND PLACE OBED
IN CLASS

ONONDAGA
KENNEL ASSOC. INC

LEIN   MAY 82

Kelly's Ray-Gin Bull of Frerose, C.D., with Diane Murphy handling for this Obedience win.

Right: Ch. Tamarlane's Capella, the 1983 top-winning Akita bitch in the United States. Co-owned by Carolyn Rennie and Dr. Sophia Kaluzniacki. Bred by Dr. Kaluzniacki, the sire was Ch. Akita Tani's Daimyo, R.O.M., ex Ch. Frerose's Sarah Lei, R.O.M.
Below: Ch. Eastwind Glacier Fox of Northland is pictured winning Best in Sweepstakes at the 1982 Akita Club of America National Specialty show, owner-handled by Loren E. Egland of Rochester, Minnesota. The judge is Jerry Hoskins, and Akita Club of America President James Sailer is presenting the trophy.

BEST IN SWEEPSTAKES

RAVENNA
KENNEL CLUB SHOW
AUG 1982
PHOTOS BY ALVERSON

The 1980 Westminster Best of Breed winner was Am. and Can. Ch. Big A's Stormy of Jobe, owned by Janet and Gary Voss of Hoffman Estates, Illinois. This win was under Dr. Richard Greathouse with handler B.J. Orseno. "Stormy" was the first bitch to win the breed at Westminster since the Akita became recognized.

Ch. Northlands Call of the Wild, finished for championship with 17 points from 5 major wins, and at just one year of age and in nine shows. Owner-handled by Loren Egland of Rochester, Minnesota. Sire was Ch. Sherigans Kondo ex Ch. O'B.J.'s Wild Alaska of Northland.

Chapter 5

The Akita Around the World

Even though the dog fancy in Europe is vast and dedicated to most all of the breeds, the population of the Akita there can still be considered sparse.

In Europe there are two "types" or "sizes" of Akitas. The large, heavy-boned variety is called, or referred to as the Dewa, while the smaller ones, comparable in size to the ones bred in Japan, are called, or referred to as the Tchinosaki. More recently there has been a trend to favor the very small and thinner type bred in Italy.

In Europe, as this book goes to press, there is only one Akita Club, called the Akita Inu Club, with its home base in Germany. Members come from various European countries since this is the only club, and it is the main source for keeping in touch with the progress the breed is making on the European continent. Hubert Finkennest was the founder of the Akita Inu Club and is one of the leading breeders in Germany. In the early 1970's Mr. Finkennest purchased several dogs from Mr. Hausler, who more than a quarter of a century ago imported several Akitas from Japan. Unfortunately, Mr. Hausler died in 1983.

Mr. Finkennest's bitch is a world champion and it is from his kennels that most of the best puppies are produced and are helping to establish the breed in Europe. Mr. Maas is also breeding and exporting quality puppies.

AKITA OWNERS IN EUROPE

Akita owners on the Continent are not too numerous and are widespread. While the number is growing slowly but surely, by the middle of the 1980's there were under fifty who were known to be devoted to the breed.

Some of these are Alois Abram, Karl-Heinz Behme, Gunter Bothe, Anneliese Braun, Brigitte Conrads, Dagmar Deininger, Margret Fingerhuth, Rudi Hardtmann, H-Allen Hellpap, Harald Hemsen, Cornelis Koot, Ulla Krudwig, Josef Marok, Ursula Mathis, Maria Muller, Dr. W. Jansen, Helmuth Kiecol, Harald Rausch, Sabine Marker, Klaus Miedl, Monika Oehl, Regine Frick, Klaus Eickhoff, Reiner Hoyer, Hans-Jurgen Sopp, Martin Schipper,

Norbert Schmerle, Inge Steinhauer, Ilse Schneider, Jurgen Wiegand, Friedrich Philipp, Fritz Stephani, Ulli Bruderlin, Dieter Klemm, Mrs. Franchomme, Marion Sargent, Gi Bowien, and Alfred Duff.

THE NETHERLANDS

There are few Akitas in Holland, though a lady named Manon Vos of Haaren, is active both in the German Club and in exhibiting at the dog shows in her country. She has purchased puppies from Mr. Maas of Germany and is showing her large, Dewa type Akita at dog events. Her Bsoetjimikado-go aus Chiyoda-Ku is all white, and is said to be one of the largest Akitas in all of Europe. Miss Vos sent photographs of him for this book. He is 72 centimeters in height and 60 kilos in weight.

This dog was her first male, and at one time was the only stud dog in Holland.

Miss Vos recently purchased from Mr. Maas a puppy that was sired by a Japanese-born stud out of a bitch from America. Miss Vos's kennel name is Kami Ken Tiphen.

Another member of the European club residing in Holland is Mr. Poppeil. He went to Japan early in the 1980's and brought back an Akita male, and within a year the Japanese breeders made him a gift of another 10-week-old puppy. So he is off to a good start with two impressive imports.

A Mrs. Muss, who also belongs to the Akita-Inu Club, also owns a male she purchased in Japan, as well as an Italian bitch that she intends breeding when they are old enough. Another breeding pair, purchased from Mr. Maas, are also new to Holland and their new owner has every intention of breeding.

Manon Vos cites many new contacts for those interested in Akitas and reports that their club holds mostly two-day meetings during which members exchange experiences, show photographs, and movies of their dogs, and frequently go to the shows together to spread the word about their favorite breed.

AKITAS IN GERMANY

Germany and Holland seem to be the two countries with the largest concentration of Akitas, though it can hardly be stated that there is a large concentration of them anywhere. However, there is a bonafide Akita Club in Germany, called the des Akita-Club von Deutschland with a membership of around twenty people. We will list the names since they seem to represent the avid breeders and/or exhibitors in that country. They are: Gerd-Lutz and Angelika Lammers, Rudolf and Renate Mub, Dr. Hilmar-Lutz Poser, Magdalene and Hubert Finkennest, Christine v. Mitzlaff, Alfred Breit, Rita Kreuchauff, Ingrid Neuburger, Heinz Schmidt, B.H. Vos, Joachim Popperl, Bernhard Maas, Erich Mauracher, Andre Forler, Guiliano Danesi, A. v.d. Linden, Karl-Walter Primm, Fritz Stephani, and the family van Veller. The van Veller family reside in Holland but are members of the club, which is sometimes the case when a breed is widespread geographically.

THE AKITA IN THE UNITED KINGDOM

1936 was the year that is said to have seen the first importation of an Akita into the United Kingdom. It was a bitch, and her name was Umako. She was followed by a dog named Isamu. It was also around this time that the breed was recognized by The Kennel Club and registered thereafter as Japanese Akitas. While the original two, Umako and Isamu, were bred, not much was heard from them and their progeny. It was quite some time before the breed surfaced publicly again in that country.

By the 1950's the breed once again came into the public eye when two Akitas were exhibited at the Crufts Show. But once again the breed failed to "catch on" and it wasn't until the 1970's when two were imported from North America, that the breed came into public notice, and shortly after their arrival they were sold to new owners in Scandinavia.

Early in 1980 Marion Sargent of the Tegwani Kennels, purchased a young puppy bitch from Canada. Her name was Davos Watakyshi Tomo-Dachi. Although she came out of quarantine that year she wasn't shown until 1981. While some of the shows held breed classes for Akitas (the first was in 1983) Akitas are still shown primarily in the Non-Classified classes. Marion Sargent's Tomo-Dachi represented the breed at Crufts in 1982 and won Best of Opposite Sex in the Not-Separately Classified Class at the show.

In the early 1980's a few more Akitas were being brought over from foreign countries. Two arrived from Japan, several more from the United States. Four bitches were mated but they all missed even though they were bred to different studs. Finally in 1983 the first puppies were born in quarantine, at the Littlecreek Kennels. They were sired by Ch. Krugs Red Cadillac. The first United Kingdom litter was born

soon after at Overhill Kennels. The bitch was American Champion Sachette No Okii Yubi. The sire was a dog now residing in Australia, O'B.J.'s Aces High.

Marion Sargent believes that the breed is destined to become very popular in England now that successful breeding and new interest has been expressed by several breeders and exhibitors.

SCANDINAVIAN AKITAS

Mr. F. Hillerstrom brought the first Akitas to Sweden in 1962 when his male Akikaze-Go, and a female, Uneko-Go arrived. Not too much ever came of them, as they and their only two puppies were used in a breeding program. Several years later, Mr. Taro Gadelius brought two Akitas from Japan to Sweden. Mr. G. von Platen purchased the male, Nero, who went on to

Captions for pages 52-53.
1. Two-and-a-half-week old Akita puppies photographed in October 1981 at their home in Holland. Their names are Beska, Bsoetjimikado, and Bushido. Beska now lives in Austria where she guards her owner's castle. Bsoetji lives with Manon Vos in Holland and Bushido lives in Germany with Gerd-Lutz Lammers. 2. Four-month-old Dutch Akita Asahi of Bandai Asahi, owned by Manon Vos of Haren, Holland. Whelped in December 1983, she was bred by B. Maas in Germany. 3. Akiro aus Chiyoda-Ku, whelped in 1977. The sire was Moro v. Schonbohen ex Ohura v Schonbohen, both from Japan. Akiro and the bitch Hodaho di Cambiano had the first Akita litter bred in Holland. Owned by Manon Vos. 4. Akai-Bara No Shiroma, imported from America by B. Maas of Germany. 5. A Canadian Import to Marion Sargent in West Haddon, England. She is from the Davos Kennels. Photo by Manon Vos of Holland. 6. The winner of the 1983 Akita Day was the 1½-year-old female from Norway, To-Tofu.

1

2   3

4   5

6

become an International and Swedish Champion and was still a handsome dog when he was ten years old.

Around the time Nero was imported to Sweden, Mr. I. Manum in Norway also imported two Akitas from Japan. They were Jiro, a male and Kiku-Hime, a female.

Almost ten years later, Mrs. E. Nisses-Gagner imported a bitch named Sakura from Japan. Sakura was mated with the famous Nero. Unfortunately, Nero died shortly after this breeding so it could not be repeated.

These four dogs, Nero, Sakura, Jiro and Kiku-Hime can now, more than two decades later—still be found in the pedigrees of most all of the Swedish, Norwegian and Finnish Akitas. In the early 1980's the sum total of Akitas in these countries is estimated to be approximately one hundred or more, including several that were imported during the late 1970's and early 1980's.

Of these one hundred or more Akitas, a few are used for hunting moose, others are used in obedience work, some travel to the dog shows, but most are said to be just companions and wonderful house pets.

THE SCANDINAVIAN AKITA CLUB

In 1976 an Akita Club was established in Sweden, and although there were only thirty Akitas at that time, the membership in the early 1980's has risen to 75 or more. These members are from Sweden, Norway and Finland, but there are also a few members from France and Great Britain. Each year the club arranges for a Nordic Akita Day with conformation judging, obedience trials, and every other year also included is a "mentality test." This show is the highlight of the season for Akita owners with members coming from great distances with their dogs for this annual event.

The Akita Bulletin, their quarterly magazine, keeps all members informed between these shows.

THE AKITA IN MEXICO

The Akita was a recognized breed in Mexico long before it came into its own in the United States, and once it was recognized in this country many California breeders travelled south of the border to earn championships for their dogs.

The first champion in Mexico was Triple K Hayai Take, owned by Camille Kam, who bred and showed the second Akita to attain Mexican championship. His name was Triple K Shina Ningyo, owned by Emma Jung.

Many Akitas have now earned their championships in both countries as the breed retains its popularity in Mexico.

DOGS AND DOG SHOWS IN RUSSIA

Little information comes out of Russia about the sport of dogs, but we do know that they have both local and national champions, and the regional titles can be won many times by the same dog, even though there is usually only one regional show each year. Every few years there is an event called the All National, and the national champion from this show is considered the top winning dog in the country. Dogs are rated Excellent, Very Good, Fair, Poor or Unacceptable, depending on both performance and conformation.

Russia held its first dog show in 1923, and shows have survived all regimes and political changes, though they are on a smaller scale than in other countries. As it is elsewhere in the world, the dedicated core of devoted breeders managed to preserve their important bloodlines during the hardships of the various wars.

In Russia if you wish to buy a dog you must do so through a local dog club, and the cost will depend on the quality and success of its sire and dam. You must register the dog with the club after receiving the dog's papers and if you wish to breed it you must consult with the Breeding Section of the same local club. Dogs which are permitted to be bred must have a show mark, or rating of "X" for Excellent, "V.G." for Very Good, for dogs, and at least a "G" for Good for bitches. The same ratings apply for obedience and utility degrees. Dogs are registered with three independent branch organizations under Toy, Hunting or Service Dog categories and then individually by breed. These service dog clubs can be found in all major cities in Russia and they are the central body overseeing all the activity under the name of the Federation of Service Dog Breeding.

There is no advertising of "puppies for sale" since there is always a demand for puppies. Therefore, the need to advertise is unnecessary. Russian show dogs are a healthy lot—since veterinary care is free!

During the researching for this book, no evidence was found that the Akita breed was represented in that country. That is not to say that they are not there. It is highly likely that with the geographical close proximity to Japan, they are in fact, a part of the dog scene in that country.

Top, left. Am., Mex., Int'l. Ch. Tobe's King of Kings, bred by Beverly Bonadonna and owned by Juan and Helen Lozada. King is shown winning at a 1982 show in Mexico. **Top, right.** Swedish Ch. Sakura. This white bitch is 6 years old. **Bottom.** Langan's Bearcat, imported from Canada and pictured at 7 months of age. Bred by S. Langan, the owners are Robert and Virginia Santoli of Islip, New York.

Captions for pages 56-57.
1. One-and-one-half-year-old Swedish Ch. Kinu-Yama, photographed in 1983. 2. Int'l. and Scan. Ch. Nero, photographed by Ake Wintzell when Nero was ten years old. 3. Swedish Ch. A-Chicara, photographed in September 1982. 4. Swedish sire A-Chikara with his 5-week-old daughter Shima-Too from Norway. 5. Three puppies bred in Sweden from newly imported Japanese Akitas. Zaome, a female, Zocho, a male, and Zogefuji, another female. 6. Two-year-old Swedish Akita named Asanagi. Akitas are used for hunting in Sweden.

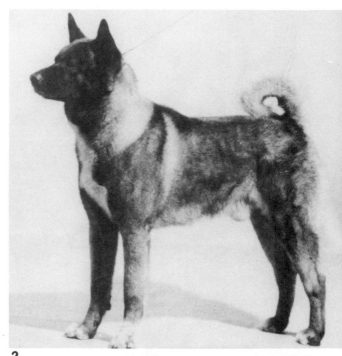

1

2

4

3 5

Chapter 6

The Akita As A Breed

THE AKITA STANDARD

Approved by the American Kennel Club April 4, 1973.

General Appearance—Large, powerful, alert, with much substance and heavy bone. The broad head, forming a blunt triangle, with deep muzzle, small eyes and erect ears carried forward in line with back of neck, is characteristic of the breed. The large, curled tail, balancing the broad head, is also characteristic of the breed.

Head—Massive but in balance with body; free of wrinkle when at ease. Skull flat between ears and broad; jaws square and powerful with minimal dewlap. Head forms blunt triangle when viewed from above. Fault: Narrow or snipy head.

Muzzle—Broad and full. Distance from nose to stop as to distance from stop to occiput as 2 is to 3. Stop well defined, but not too abrupt. A shallow furrow extends well up forehead.

Nose—Broad and Black. Liver permitted on white Akitas, but black always preferred. Disqualification: Butterfly nose or total lack of pigmentation on nose.

Ears—The ears of the Akita are characteristic of the breed. They are strongly erect and small in relation to rest of head. If ear is folded forward for measuring length, tip will touch upper eye rim. Ears are triangular, slightly rounded at tip, wide at base, set wide on head but not too low, and carried slightly forward over eyes in line with back of neck. Disqualification: Drop or broken ears.

Eyes—Dark brown, small, deep-set and triangular in shape. Eye rims black and tight.

Lips—Black and not pendulous; tongue pink.

Teeth—Strong with scissors bite preferred, but level bite acceptable. Disqualifications: Noticeably undershot or overshot.

Neck—Thick and muscular; comparatively short, widening gradually toward shoulders. A pronounced crest blends in with base of skull.

Body—Longer than high, as 10 is to 9 in males; 11 to 9 in bitches. Chest wide and deep; depth of chest is one-half height of dog at shoulder. Level back with firmly muscled loin and moderate tuck-up. Skin pliant but not loose. Serious faults: Light bone, rangy body.

Tail—Large and full, set high and carried over back or against flank in a three-quarter, full, or double curl, always dipping to or below level of back. On a three-quarter curl, tip drops well down flank. Root large and strong. Tail bone reaches hock when let down. Hair coarse, straight and full, with no appearance of a plume. Disqualifications: sickle or uncurled tail.

Forequarters—Shoulders strong and powerful with moderate layback. Forelegs heavy-boned and straight as viewed from the front. Angle of pastern 15 degrees forward from vertical. Faults: Elbows in or out, loose shoulders.

Hindquarters—Width, muscular development and bone comparable to forequarters. Upper thighs well developed. Stifle moderately bent and hocks well let down, turning neither in nor out.

Dewclaws—On front legs generally not removed; dewclaws on hind legs generally removed.

Feet—Cat feet, well knuckled up with thick pads. Feet straight ahead.

Coat—Double-coated. Undercoat thick, soft, dense and shorter than outer coat. Outer coat straight, harsh and standing somewhat off body. Hair on head, legs and ears short. Length of hair at withers and rump approximately two inches, which is slightly longer than on rest of body, except tail, where coat is longest and most profuse. Fault: Any indication of ruff or feathering.

Color—Any color including white; brindle; or pinto. Colors are brilliant and clear and markings are well balanced with or without mask or blaze. White Akitas have no mask. Pinto has a white background with large, evenly paced patches covering head and more than one-third of body. Undercoat may be a different color from outer coat.

Gait—Brisk and powerful with strides of moderate length. Back remains strong, firm and level. Rear legs move in line with front legs.

Size—Males 26 to 28 inches at the withers; bitches 24 to 26 inches. Disqualification: Dogs under 25 inches, bitches under 23 inches.

Temperament—Alert and responsive, dignified and courageous. Aggressive toward other dogs.

DISQUALIFICATIONS

Butterfly nose or total lack of pigmentation on nose

Drop or broken ears
Noticeably undershot or overshot
Sickle or uncurled tail
Dogs under 25 inches, bitches under 23 inches

AKITA APPEARANCE

It would be difficult to overlook an Akita when seeing one, whether you're at a dog show or merely walking down the street. The brisk gait and the alertness of the dog give it a commanding appearance that distinguishes it immediately. While it is very affectionate with its master and family, it can be counted on to defend its family when called upon.

The Akita's massive body and muscular conformation set it off as a thing apart. The head has an expression of dignity and character. The broad skull, while rather flat on top, has a stop and the ears are always erect and rather small with a broad base. While erect, they are still carried slightly forward over the eyes.

The Akita should have a level bite, a square muzzle of moderate length and very powerful jaws. The nose must be black, is large, and its eyes are medium in size, dark brown and triangular in shape. The neck, like the body, is muscular and without excessive dewlap. The chest is wide and reaches the elbows with the ribs well sprung. The back is level, with slight tuck up and firm loin. Bitches are sometimes slightly longer in loin than the dogs.

The Akita is a heavy-boned dog with straight, well set apart forelegs and powerful hocks bent but straight in line. The feet are said to be cat-like, slightly webbed with toes well arched and tight together.

The large, high-set plumey tail is carried over the back in a three-quarters full or double curl. When extended downward the tail tip should touch the hocks.

AKITA TEMPERAMENT

There have been some pretty wild stories reported about the Akita almost from the time they became recognized as an individual breed. They can't all be true, though every dog is different.

Generally speaking the Akita is loyal, protective, a family dog, who loves children. With exceptions to every rule and every dog, a lot depends on the people the dog lives with. If treated kindly the dog will be kind. If abused or mistreated, trouble will ensue.

It is a known fact that most male Akitas do not get along well with other male dogs, especially male Akitas. Plan accordingly and you will avoid trouble. Be careful when people—especially children—visit you and the dog is present. Proper introductions are in order after everyone is in and settled and the dog can take his time and his own way to make friends. Since they are such a large breed, extreme caution should be taken that they do not knock down older folks or children.

Common sense is the best answer. Just be sure that other breeds of dogs or cats or small animals are protected from them at all times. Often their size is the problem and not their disposition. Basically, Akitas love children, but someone else's children might be another story. Safety first!

Captions for pages 60-61.
1. Ten-year-old Fawn Ward with her one-year-old Akita, Wicca's Moonshadow of LeHi. Fawn is the vivacious daughter of Joel and Jeanette Ward, LeHi Kennels, Wescosville, Pennsylvania. 2. Playtime at Seawood Kennels in Lakebay, Washington. 3. Bar-BJ's The Hustler, brindle male bred and owned by Barbara and B. J. Hampton of Las Vegas, Nevada. Barb and "Grizz" are captured in an off moment in the ring at a 1981 Match Show where Grizz took a Group Second. 4. Peggy Gerry with her Sugi. . .enjoying the backyard at their Roslyn, New York home. Sugi's official name with the Japanese Kennel Club, American Kennel Club, and Akita Club of America is Jiro-Maru-no-Toyohashi. 5. Ch. Polyanna's Shady Lady, owned by Mr. and Mrs. J. A. Spiering, Jr., of Lower Burrell, Pennsylvania.

1

2

3   4

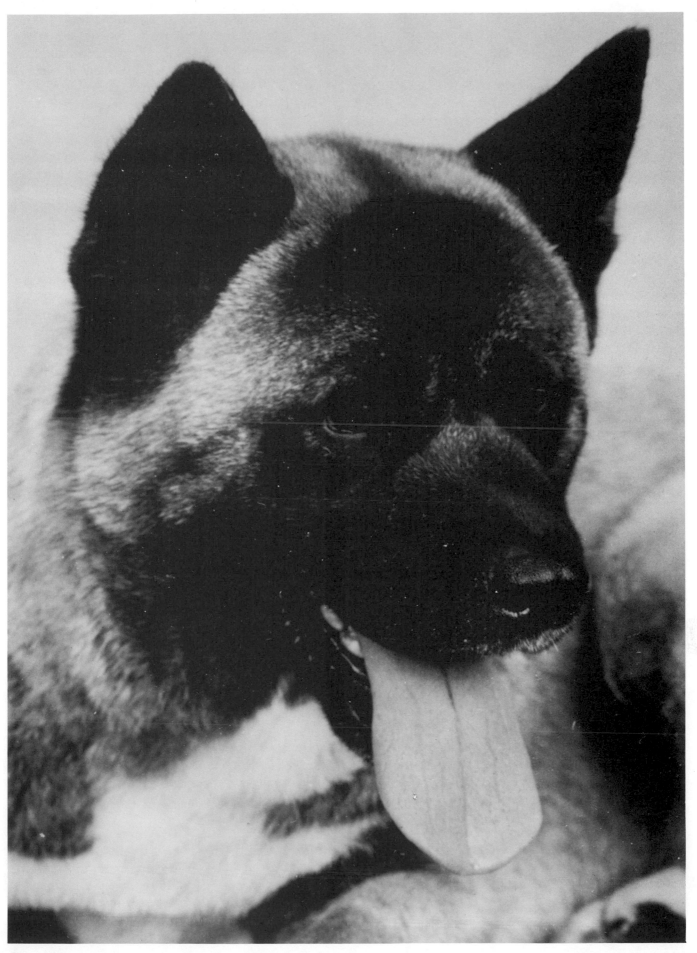

IS THE AKITA THE BREED FOR YOU?

You've decided that you think the Akita is a beautiful animal and you're entranced with their royal heritage in the Orient and you're convinced you want to share your life with one. Wonderful, but have you considered all aspects of the responsibilities and physical requirements for owning one?

Needless to say, if you want to proudly walk your grown Akita down the street are you physically able to handle yourself and the dog if you encounter another dog? Or can you restrain your dog if he wants to defend himself or even be the instigator in a dog fight?

Would other members of the family be physically able to restrain your dog if the situation were theirs? Can you and members of your family handle the dog walking down the aisles past other dogs at a dog show if you buy a show dog and exhibit? You must also ask yourself, if there is a danger within your home, are there elderly people or young children that the dog might knock down or jump on and injure, even playfully? You must presume that if you invest in an Akita it will be sharing your life for the next fifteen years or more and be aware of what problems might arise during that period of time.

We all think the Akita is a magnificent animal, and we all love to have beautiful things to look at and enjoy, but this is a large, living creature that must fit into our lives. A family discussion before your purchase, and a long informative talk with the breeder is essential if there are any doubts in your mind about your way of life and the part this dog would play in it. Don't buy a dog, get attached to it, and then find you've made a mistake. Preliminary planning is one of the most important parts of bringing a dog into your life.

THE AKITA COAT

Before deciding to buy an Akita, you might be wise to check your broom closet to see if you have a heavy-duty vacuum cleaner. When a dog the size of an Akita sheds—it really sheds! And it happens at least twice a year. Sometimes the females shed more often, but the winter-to-summer, and summer-to-winter coat changes can be a problem if you don't like hairs in clumps or individually all over you and your furniture.

Brushing helps of course, but when the dog needs to make room for a new coat to come in there is little you can do but clean up after the old coat comes out. Brushing would help stimu-late the new coat, while taking out the dead hairs and grooming your dog can be fun and a pleasant, intimate time together. Between sheddings a weekly brushing will keep the Akita in nice condition. Bathing and special care for show dogs is discussed further in our special chapter on grooming.

THE LONG-HAIRED AKITA

As with all dogs, every once in a while a litter of puppies will produce a "throwback." This throwback might take any of a number of different shapes or forms, but nonetheless, it is a foreign entry in what proves to be an otherwise normal litter.

Most experienced breeders will recognize these abnormalities, and take them into consideration if and when they cull. But others allow them to grow and mature and find homes for them, rather than destroy them, especially if the throwback is not of a dangerous or congenital nature.

With the Akita a number of long-haired, or long-coated Akitas have prevailed and can be seen. This long-coat is believed to be a throwback to cross-breedings with the Chow Chow, while others choose to declare it just a "fluke." No matter; there are occasional long-coated puppies in the best of litters, and while they are not frequent they do exist and are usually sold as pets to those who like them or to those who do not know they are not "preferred" with the serious, dedicated breeders. In fact, many breeders attempt to deny their own breeding when it comes to these long coats; or they will sell or place the puppies after neutering or spaying, withholding their registration papers. For those who just wish to enjoy the personality of the Akita these long-haired dogs are, or can be, the answer. And it sure beats destroying a beautiful animal just because the coat doesn't represent the desired length acording to the standard.

However, there is an obligation on the part of the breeder to make absolutely sure that the prospective buyer realizes that the coat is not what is called for and that it's "buyer beware."

HOW OLD IS YOUR DOG?

Until recently it was believed that for every year of a dog's life it was comparable to seven years of a human life. However, more recent research has proven this to be inaccurate. The one-year-old dog is more like a fifteen-year-old than a seven-year-old.

The following chart is a more reasonable comparison.

Human Age In Years	Dogs' Comparative Age In Years
15	1
24	2
28	3
32	4
36	5
40	6
44	7
48	8
52	9
56	10
60	11
64	12
68	13
72	14
76	15
80	16
84	17
88	18
92	19
96	20
100	21

So while there is a great aging process during the first three years of the dogs' life, once they reach three, it would be safe to say they age four human years, not seven, for every year of their lives.

AKITA FENCING AND HOUSING

More than one Akita breeder has told me that every Akita tries to dig its way back to China—or Japan—as the case may be. Even more than those few, all have suspected it or have had some experience with Akitas that love to dig holes. Akitas have been reported as chewing through 9-gauge cyclone fences, so any outdoor run should also have a top on it and cement blocks underground several feet deep around all the edges. Don't take chances with your dog. Not only might you lose it to traffic or the woods, but you are responsible for any damage or injury it might inflict on others. A safe, secure, sufficient fence is a good investment no matter how you look at it.

Akitas can do well living outdoors, even in very cold climates, if they have adequate housing. They must be sheltered against hot sun, cold winds, dampness and wet ground. Wood platforms in lean-tos are excellent. So are dog houses, and if in doubt, remember there are solar heated dog houses today also! Dog coats are not recommended for Akitas; they have magnificent coats of their own!

One of the most important aspects of housing more than one dog is adequate housing if you own a male and a female. When the bitch is in season you must have separate quarters for her or you will be having a litter you might not want. Consider a shelter for each dog or bitch you own *outside*, and separate quarters for each one *inside* the house.

CRATE TRAINING

When you are dealing with a dog of an Akita's size, space for running and playing and developing naturally is essential. However, if you are to have a show dog, which will be expected to travel to shows or which you expect to accompany you and your family on vacations, it is essential that it learn to ride in a car and travel well.

The introduction of a crate of proper size at an early age will introduce your puppy to his "house" so that it becomes a place of its own, rather than a confinement. Many owners feed

Chain-link fencing is suitable for an outdoor Akita run.

Ch. Tamarlane's Shogun Hepere, bred by Dr. Sophia Kaluzniacki and owned by Greg Smith.

First Am., Can., Bda. Ch. Kenjiko Royal Tenji, R.O.M., owned by Frederick Duane of the Frerose Kennels in Shohola, Pennsylvania. Jo-Jo's record includes more than 300 Bests of Breed and 49 Group Placements. He is a Register of Merit sire and was the first Akita to become a Canadian champion.

Left: Swedish-born Omamori-Hime, photographed at six months of age. **Below:** Two Swedish-born males used for sledding. The white is seven-year-old Fujimaru and the red is four-year-old Damishiro.

Right: The 1982 annual Akita Day winner was the female Akashi-Bara, a one-and-a-half-year-old Norwegian Akita. **Below:** Bsoetjimikado-go aus Chiyoda-Ku, bred by Hubert Finkennest in Germany and owned and shown by Manon Vos of Haren, Holland. The sire was Moro v. Schonboken-Nippon, and the dam was 1981 world champion Okura v. Schonboken-Nippon.

Left: Lovely head study of a white Akita owned by Manon Vos in Haren, Holland, and bred by Hubert Finkennest in Germany. Chyioda-Ku is pictured in Amsterdam at 14 months of age when he became best of his breed and youth winner in 1982.
Below: Asahi of Bardai Asahi, whelped in December 1983. This darling little bitch was bred by Bernhard Maas in Dorsten, Germany, and was sent to Manon Vos in Haren, Holland.

Right: Chow time at the Del Vento Kennels in Milano, Italy. Koishi del Vento is 2½ years old in this photograph. Owned by Bernhard Maas of Dorsten, Germany, and bred by Del Vento Divino of Milano, Italy. **Below:** A German Akita descended from Japanese parents.

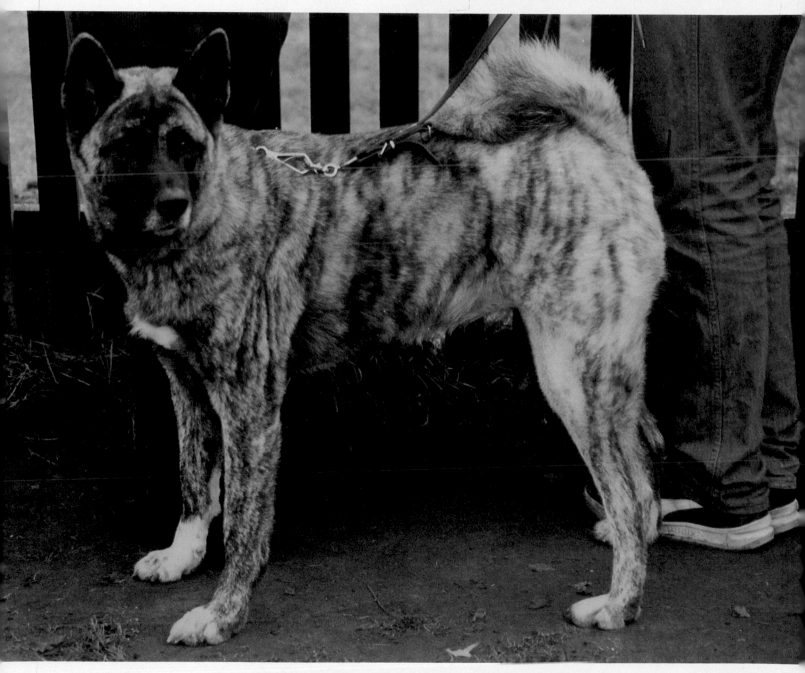

Am. and Can. Ch. Kim-Sai's Buster of Frerose, #1 Akita in Canada for 1982. Owned by Frederick O. Duane of Shohola, Pennsylvania.

Pictured **above** in front and rear views, and also **below** in side view, is "Mandy," owned by Barbara Bouyet. She shows the plush coat of the long-haired Akita. While many breeders choose to deny the breeding of these, they can crop up in any litter; although not the most desirable, they are still beautiful.

Kita Maru II enjoys a roll in the grass. Owned by Valerie Edmondson of Garden Grove, California.

Tamarlane's Happy Bear, a five-month-old puppy owned by Professor Max Bill of Zurich, Switzerland. Bred by Dr. Sophia Kaluzniacki, the sire was Ch. Tamarlane's Aldebaran ex Ch. Tamarlane's Akita Tani Ursula.

Swaneez Achu Aso, owned by Alyce and Kelle Clinton, Lakebay, Washington.

The three-and-a-half-year-old Swedish male, Kamikaze.

In this winning line-up, Ch. Cee Jay's Rocky Road of Kibo takes Best of Breed. Center is Ch. Bar-BJ's Pretti Bar E taking Best of Winners and Best of Opposite Sex on the way to her championship and Kuma takes Winners Dog, right.

Left: Miss Fawn Ward with three puppies named Wicca LeHi's Emeraude, Wicca LeHi's Shiseido (on Fawn's lap), and Wicca LeHi's Eau Sauvage. The LeHi Kennels of Joel and Jeanette Ward are located in Wescosville, Pennsylvania. **Below:** Ch. Kirabrans Mitsu No Jumbo takes a boat ride with Steve and Miriam Lisker of East Rockaway, New York.

Right: Miss Lynne Fontano was photographed in 1979 with a 5½-week-old Akita puppy bred by Nadene and Bob Fontano, Great River Akitas, Islip Terrace, New York. **Below:** Frerose's Yume v. Ingvar, photographed in Denmark in April 1979. Bred by Frederick Duane of Shohola, Pennsylvania.

A three-point major at her first show for future Champion O'B.J. Silver Chalice of Tomoko, owned by Marvin and Elaine Nussbaum of Greenbelt, Maryland. Tomo became a Champion at nine months of age with three majors. Her sire was Ch. Aitochi's Stinger of Sugar Run ex Ch. Okii Yubi's Dragon House Ko-Go, R.O.M.

BEST OF BREED
OR VARIETY

CLASSIC CITY
KENNEL CLUB SHOW
MAY 1983
HOTOS BY ALVERSON

Ch. O'B.J. Georgia Peach is pictured winning at a 1983 show. She is the foundation bitch at Rebecca Kestle's kennel in Athens, Georgia. Her owner claims she paved the way for the mismarked pinto in the show ring This 26½-inch bitch has placed in the Groups. She is a Sachmo daughter and a granddaughter of Ch. Sakuskus Tom Cat-Go.

Left: Ch. Hiryu Cloud Dancer and her little brother Smoke Dancer, owned by Chandra Sargent of Sun Valley, California. Cloud Dancer's sire was Ch. Conan the Conqueror ex Ch. Hiryu no Kogo-go, C.D. Smoke's dam was Kogo and the sire was Ch. Cee Jay's Rocky Road of Kibo.
Below: Am. and Can. Ch. Asahi Yama No Chiisai Takara, a bitch owned by Tom and Judy Clark of Edmonds, Washington.

Kosho Ki's Kodiak, owned by Barbara Bouyet of Thousand Oaks, California.

Annette Rivera and her doggy pal Emperor Genghis Banzai I, photographed by her dad, John Rivera, in 1980 at their home in Yonkers, New York.

Top, left. The Candy Man of Northwood, pictured here at four months of age, was owned by Ruth and Wayne Zimmerman of Wilmington, Delaware. **Top, right.** Three-year-old male Akita, Taisho Osama, owned by C. D. Crill of Placerville, California. **Bottom.** Mirage and his son, owned by Morris and Lil Lewis of Annandale, Virginia.

Captions for pages 82-83.
1. "Meeko," an 8-month-old long-coated Akita puppy owned by Judy and Henry Marx of Los Angeles, California. 2. Tiger's Eye Sun Raider, 9-month-old male long-coated Akita owned by Jerry Schumacher. 3. Mardell Denny's "Ben," a long-haired Akita, full grown. 4 and 5. Jeremy Denny with a 7-week-old long-coated Akita. 6. Jeremy and Jaime Denny with Ben. 7. A long-coated Akita male named Bear.

1   2

3

4

5

6   **7**

their dogs in their crates so they learn that it is a place for food, security, seclusion and a wonderful journey in the van or car. Others prefer that their dogs sleep all night in their crates as a part of housebreaking, and for safety. If your dog is to be a watch dog, this will not do, but if the crate is allowed to have the door remain open it is surprising how many puppies and grown dogs will automatically sleep, and relax, in their crates.

Early on take your puppy for rides in the car in the crate and he will accept it as a way of life. Whether it is an open or closed crate is a matter of choice, or perhaps climate. In hot climates when summer sun can be a danger, open crates provide the most air, but must be guarded against direct sunlight. Closed crates are warmer for cold climates and they must be shaded from direct sunlight also or they can become "hot houses." Good circulation of air is essential and no direct sunlight is the rule.

If there is a doubt in your mind about the proper size crate for your puppy, consult with the salesman at your pet store or supplier, so that he can provide the best dimensions for your car and for comfort for your Akita when it is full grown.

Needless to say, the crate should be washable, sturdy and have the proper flooring. A carpet is best for winter, along with a piece of blanket or a favorite cushion. In summer regular newspaper is adequate if the print doesn't rub off on the coat, or summer blanketing or a bath mat made of cotton is desirable.

A toy or an object to chew on can be provided to prevent boredom if the trip is long, or you can supply dry dog biscuits for nibbling once you have seen that your dog does not get car sick.

Hook your lead or leash to the handle of the crate for quick walks along the roadways, and carry water in a thermos for periodic drinks along the way.

Wherever you place the crate in your car make sure that there is not a direct current of air streaming into the crate. Even in hot weather the force of a direct draft can be harmful. There is no reason why a dog should not like traveling or sleeping or eating in his own private place if introduced to it properly. And it certainly will mean easier, safer driving for you.

OTHER AKITA TALENTS

The power and versatility of the Akita are well known and in many cases documented. We have seen and heard tales of their tremendous feats at weight-pulling meets, and their enthusiasm when pulling sleds or carts for fun and amusement of the families they belong to.

We also have heard of backpacking with an Akita. Specifically, Jerry and Linda Knarr who spent a vacation with their Akita, "Kato." Otherwise known as Paragon's Kato of Bojo, their adventures with their dog prove that it can be done and successfully. Even though the Knarrs claim the dog did not necessarily enjoy it, backpacking with an Akita sounds like a wonderful sport to investigate further. There are several backpacking clubs that hike with their dogs and enjoy the great outdoors with their animals.

THE AKITA IN ART

While the Akita-type dog was obviously around far before the Elizabethan era, primarily in the Orient, dogs of the large, thick, teddy-bear type were known. Mastiffs and other large breeds were frequently depicted in paintings down through the centuries, but few Akita look-alikes were captured on canvas by the masters.

However, people in the Orient were dog minded and had a great many teddy bear type dogs, i.e., the Chow, the Pomeranian, etc.; the likenesses of dogs which could be said to be Akitas do exist.

Perhaps one of the most popular ones dated 1788 and entitled "Puppies," a watercolor on silk was rendered by Japanese artist Maruyama Okyo. This was beautifully done during the lifetime of the artist (who lived from 1733 to 1795). "Puppies" and another of his pieces are reproduced in this book.

MODERN ART

There certainly can be no doubt in anyone's mind that the current Akita is not neglected in any of our many art forms. On canvas, pottery, jewelry,—name it, you'll find it—the Akita has found its niche in modern art. So many Akita fanciers have begun collections of ceramic figurines, etc., that the Akita is most assuredly here to stay "no matter how you look at them!"

AKITAS IN THE NEWS

It was inevitable that the powerful Akita would call attention to itself in New York City, where dog owners are always on the lookout for a rare and different breed. These remarkable dogs soon were making headlines in the big city.

A feature story on page 3 of the December 27, 1982, issue of the *New York Post* included some adorable pictures and quotations on price, temperament and characteristics by Kari Sherman. On

July 1, 1983, *The New York Times* featured an article on the continuing popularity of the breed, to which many Akita breeders took exception.

Perhaps the publicity which did nothing but praise the breed and highlight its desirable features frightened the fancy when it is remembered that usually the breed of dog that goes Best in Show at Westminster each year often ends up being much in demand by the public and is over-bred to meet the demands of the public wanting puppies "just like the one that won at the Garden."

A fad or trend in any breed can be like the kiss of death if unscrupulous breeders over-breed for monetary gains at the expense of the dogs. So while we love to praise our dogs to the skies, care must be taken that they do not become too popular.

THE AKITA REVIEW

With any luck at all, a breed will be fortunate enough to have a publication—either magazine or newsletter—all its own to herald the winning dogs as they climb to the top of the ladder of success in the show rings.

Indeed, the Akita is one of the most fortunate of all breeds to have just such a publication dedicated to their good and welfare. Its name is *The Akita Review*. This is a first-class magazine of the highest quality published every two months that labels itself "A Commitment to Excellence" in the breed. It is more than that. Its editors and publishers, Ed and Marlene Sutton of San Pedro, California, have done themselves and the breed proud with this most worthy publication. Color abounds and the features and statistics it presents are top drawer.

In addition to the usual departments, i.e., letters to the editors, book reviews, coverage of American Kennel Club doings, and a National Akita Directory, their ads and Kennel Listings, and foreign coverage which are exceptional, their statistics and feature articles and veterinary coverage leave nothing to be desired.

It is the policy of the author to recommend to those in *any* breed that if they are truly interested in the good and welfare of their dogs they not only belong to an all-breed and specialty club, but they subscribe to the very best publication available for their breed so that they may keep up to date with all the latest happenings and advances in it. Akita owners are most fortunate to have *The Akita Review* available to them. For further information write to P.O. Box 1337, San Pedro, California, 90731.

THE AMAZING DOG WORLD

Late in 1982 the Pet Food Institute released the findings of an extensive survey they had done on Americans and their pets. Their figures bore out the fact that Americans owned 49,000,000 dogs, 42,000,000 cats, 25,000,000 birds and 250,000,000 other animals of one kind or another. That adds up to more pets than there are humans in the U.S., Great Britain and Argentina combined.

It is even more amazing when you realize that approximately eight billion dollars a year is spent to care for these pets. Four billion goes for pet food, and nearly two billion to the veterinarians that care for them.

1982 was also the year that included the introduction of a soft-drink for dogs and water beds! We have long known about dog and cat psychiatrists and we can only imagine what kind of money is spent for pet sitters, pet cemeteries and pet advertising. In another chapter we get into what it costs to campaign a dog in the show ring today, costs of obedience training, and the like.

No matter how we feel about our indulgences we do know that we love our pets and that they return to us—a hundred fold—our love and affection and we know they are worth every cent we spend on them.

Captions for pages 86-87.
1. A particularly interesting Akita kennel stationery from Chandra Sargent's kennels in Sun Valley, California. 2. Pencil sketch rendered by Peter A. C. Pettersen of an Akita puppy, done in the likeness of the Santoli's Langan's Bearcat. 3. A rare print entitled "Puppies Among Bamboo in the Snow," painted in 1784 by Maruyama Okyo (1733-1795). This is a companion piece to the print "Puppies" and was submitted by Dr. Sophia Kaluzniacki of Green Valley, Arizona. 4. One of the bumper stickers that can be seen on Barbara Shanks's wagon in Williamsville, New York. 5. Stainless steel folding knife hand made by Steve Hoel of Pine, Arizona. Many of Steve's knives are in valuable collections all over the world. Engraving is done by Steve Lindsay of Kearney, Nebraska. 6. Peter A. C. Pettersen's pencil sketch of the Santoli's Ch. Great River's Tsuki-Ko of Ginsan. 7. "Crystal" has her "portrait" done in snow! Owned by Robert and Virginia Santoli of Islip, New York. 8. Ceramic figurine of an Akita by the Stone Brothers. It is a replica of Ch. Tamarlane's Silver Star, from the collection of Bonnie Herrmann of Whitewood, South Dakota.

KIRYU AKITAS

AKITA INU
MADE IN JAPAN

5

6

7

8

Chapter 7

Grooming Your Akita

Anyone who has ever admired a well-groomed, shiny Akita in the show ring must surely realize that a certain amount of grooming time is responsible for that handsome appearance. While we would all agree that good food and good health are largely responsible for good coat, we must also be realistic and grant that occasional brushing and a bath are also required to keep it looking like a respectable specimen of the breed.

Done on a regular basis, a brushing of any dog's coat will make the dog look better. With an Akita a daily light brushing is ideal. It will clean out the dead hair and keep the coat clean and shiny. Getting a dog used to being stacked on a table from the time it is a puppy will automatically make your grooming job easier throughout the rest of the dog's life. Since the Akita adapts to both warm and cold climates the coat is naturally thick and luxurious and the brushing will stimulate the hair growth as well as protect the dog's skin.

PREPARING TO GROOM

All dogs require steady footing in order to be comfortable on any given surface. A rubber mat on a grooming table is best, and if you can teach your dog to jump up and down off the table when the time comes to groom it will be easy for you. Just make sure both surfaces are not slippery! The sooner you get your Akita to stand still for grooming the easier it will be to prepare him for the "stand for examination" in the show ring also.

Make sure you have all your grooming equipment ready when the dog gets up on the table so you don't have to leave him standing there by himself, especially if you use a noose on a grooming pole. If the dog is left alone it may get bored and try to jump off while attached to the noose. Many a dog has done this and an owner has returned to find the dog dangling at the end of it, hanged!

Where you start to groom is your choice. Just make sure before you are through you have covered all areas of the dog and that all dead or loose hair is removed. This means being sure the bristles get all the way to the skin. Stimulating the skin with the brush will not only remove dead hair but will encourage the growth of the new hair.

AKITA SHEDDING

The Akita sheds twice a year . . . spring and fall. A daily or several times a week brushing will aid in the shedding process as well as stimulating the growth of the hair. Grooming every day during these shedding periods will help keep your furniture and clothing hair-free as well. During the peak of the shedding season a bath will also help remove the dead hair. These bi-annual shedding periods can usually be detected or forecast by sudden changes in the weather or temperature changes which would indicate a change in "coat" is due.

OTHER GROOMING REQUIREMENTS
Nails

On puppies and adult dogs it is necessary to keep the nails short. A good nail trimmer can be obtained at any petshop and should be a regular part of your grooming procedure. Have the breeder where you buy your puppy, or your veterinarian, show you the proper way to cut the nails so you don't "draw blood" every time you try cutting the nails. Dogs are naturally sensitive about their feet so you might as well learn to do it correctly right at the beginning so that you don't make nail trimming a traumatic experience for both you and your dog for the rest of its life. It must be done, so master the art as quickly as possible.

Ears

The lovely erect ears on the Akita which add so much to its alert expression should be held straight up, of course. A dog with dirt in the ear canals, or mites, or any other ear problem, is very likely to hold its ears at "half mast" or out toward the sides because of the sensation of itching or irritation as a result of any problem.

Check the ears at each grooming and if there is any build-up of dirt or wax, remove it with a little alcohol or baby oil on a piece of cotton, or a cotton swab. Extreme caution must be used when entering the ear or damage to the ear drum may result. Always keep in mind to be gentle, and never to "go around a corner." The ear canal generally speaking runs in a line parallel with the jaw bone. Keep this in mind and if the dog reacts badly stop at once. Wipe out the ear and outer ear with alcohol on a cotton ball. This should be sufficient care if there are no serious problems within the ear.

Eyes

The eyes should be clear at all times. Any other condition may be an indication of illness, but it can also be a temporary condition as a result of dust or pollen or seed that may have invaded the eye during the dog's excursions outdoors. If the matter cannot be wiped away with a tissue, or if it continues on a regular basis or is at all cloudy or makes the dog rub its eyes with its paws, immediate veterinary inspection is indicated. While it may indicate a temporary allergy, it may also indicate permanent eye damage that would naturally require more elaborate care and medication.

Teeth

Some dogs, like some people, have clean white teeth for all of their lives. Others, both dogs and people, are subject to varying degrees of tartar or plaque that builds up on the teeth and results in bad breath or cavities. Needless to say, this tartar build-up must be removed, especially if your dog is to be a show dog.

While veterinarians are well versed in the scaling of teeth, every owner should learn how to deal with this problem on his own so it never does get out of hand. If when the puppy is very young you start using a baby tooth brush with a little water in baking soda or salt made up into a paste you will accustom the dog to the cleaning of its teeth. You can also put this paste on a piece of gauze bandage and rub it over the surface of the teeth. This early care will minimize your problems in the future. Judges at the shows are required to check the bite of the dogs and the teeth must be clean. Also, it will help the dog to get used to having its mouth opened for inspection.

If your dog has bad breath from bad teeth, or any other reason, you will find improvement if you feed garlic powder in his food. Not garlic salt or cloves, but garlic powder. It will be just enough to sweeten the breath, and is believed by many people to also be a deterrent for worms. What have you got to lose?

GROOMING AIDS

The stores are filled with various kinds of grooming aids and coat conditioners that can help you keep your dog well groomed and smelling like a rose. They are on sale at all petshops and at the concession booths at all the dog shows. It is up to you to decide which is best suited to your particular dog and gives you the desired results. Consult the breeder of your dog if you have any questions, and learn what the professionals use if you are a newcomer to the fancy. For the most part, these coat conditioners are sprayed on with atomizers and then brushed into the coat to put on the finishing touch. However, it is wise to read, and re-read the instructions to make sure you are doing everything exactly right.

If your Akita is outdoors a great deal of the time or lives in a city where soot and excessive dirt plagues it, you will more than likely want to use one of the dry shampoos or lather dry bath preparations between tub baths. Do not expect miracles from these man-made preparations. They are only "aids" that will help maintain a clean, healthy coat which will be acceptable to live with.

There are also grooming "perfumes" for dogs available. These are also a matter of preference or necessity. If your dog is taken care of with regular grooming, and lives with you in your house most of the time, you will find he will be quite clean and smell like a dog should smell. Should he tangle with a skunk, a tomato juice rinse after a good bath is the solution!

Captions for pages 90-91.
1. Ch. O'B.J. Big Son of Sachmo, bred and owned by Bill and B. J. Andrews of Asheville, North Carolina. 2. Kinouk's Avalanche, eight-week-old son of Ch. Matsu Kaze's Key-Too Kinouk. Owned by Chandra Sargent, Sun Valley, California. 3. Yukii's Fire 'N Ice of E Oka takes a nice stretch on the cool grass at the E Oka Kennels in Peoria Heights, Illinois. She is a daughter of the top winning Am. and Can. Ch. Kakwa's Orca. 4. Three beauties from the Seawood Kennels of Alyce and Kelle Clinton in Lakebay, Washington. Photographed by Kelle Clinton in 1981, they are Golden Sun Seawood WaWa L'Wilac, Swaneez Achu Aso, and Golden Sun Seawood T'Siatko. 5. Nap time at E Oka Kennels for this 8-week-old Akita puppy. 6. Magnificent head study of Ch. Tamarlane's Kenji Akima, bred by Dr. Sophia Kaluznlackl of Green Valley, Arizona. The sire was Ch. Akita Tani's Daimyo, R.O.M., ex Ch. Frerose's Sarah Lei, R.O.M.

1   2

3

4

5   6

GROOMING THE WHISKERS

Trimming the whiskers on an Akita is a matter of preference. Many people prefer to see the whiskers since it represents the dog in its "natural state." Others prefer the "clean" look of the close trim and to see the muzzle clearly. For the show ring, most prefer the trim to show the judge the unobstructed outline of the face. Though there is nothing in the standard for the breed that either mentions or requires the whiskers to be trimmed, exhibitors for the most part allow the whiskers to grow between shows or once the dog is retired from the show ring.

GROOMING BEHAVIOR

If your Akita wriggles and squirms or backs off and fights you every bit of the way when grooming time rolls around, chances are you are being a little too rough. True enough, there are dogs that just never do get to like being groomed. These dogs require extra patience and, quite possibly, extra work, since they will employ every scheme known to canines to put you off and hamper your progress. But more than likely, if you meet resistance it's because the dog is genuinely uncomfortable.

The main tactic is to be gentle, especially in the sensitive areas around the groin, the feet, under the tail, around the eyes, the testicles, etc. The calmest of dogs will flinch when he sees the bristles of a brush or the shiny teeth of a steel comb flashing over head or about his eyes. You can be pretty brisk on the body and chest, but such fervor in the tender regions can resemble the Chinese torture!

Since we are dealing with a thick-coated breed, it will pay off later to get the dog accustomed to being groomed from the time he is a puppy . . . a newborn puppy. Grooming may never seem "easy," but it can be a gratifying experience for both dog and owner if approached with common sense and patience. Let your dog see that you take a definite pride in taking care of him. He will appreciate the interest, gentleness, and attention, and it will result in a closer communication between you and your dog through this time spent together. And he'll certainly look better for it!

Try starting the grooming process when the puppies are just a few days old. Play with their feet, singling out the toes, standing them briefly in show pose, propping up their tail, holding up their head, giving them a little scratching under the chin at the time. Repeat the words, "stay," and "good dog" as a clue to future ring procedure or praise. It all adds to a bright future and an outgoing personality.

Let your first grooming brush be a toothbrush, or nail brush, if it means getting used to brushing a puppy coat.

BATHING THE PUPPY

Puppies need be bathed only as required or for showing. Here again there are two schools of thought on the advisability of bathing the very young puppy. If you are an advocate of the bath, the same technique can be used for the puppy that is advised for the adult dog. Remember that drafts are very dangerous for puppies; *never* leave a puppy only partially dry, or put it outdoors in the cold while still damp.

If you believe a bath exposes and endangers a puppy unnecessarily, you might wish to use the dry shampoos we mentioned earlier in this chapter.

Bathing a dog can be hard work, and if you don't know a few of the tricks of the trade, it can be a disaster with a dog that has a heavy coat, with everyone and everything ending up equally and totally wet. We would suggest a rubber apron or an old, lightweight raincoat with the sleeves cut off at the elbows as proper attire, because sooner or later your dog is going to shake himself!

BATHING THE ADULT AKITA

There are probably as many theories on how, and how often, to bathe a dog as there are dog owners. There is, however, no set rule on frequency or method, although it is certain that show dogs, or dogs that spend a great deal of time outdoors in all kinds of weather, yet still spend time indoors with the family, will require a bath now and then.

Once you've made up your mind that the time for the bath has come, insert a wad of cotton in each of your dog's ears and perhaps a drop of mineral oil in each eye to prevent soap burning them. Have several heavy turkish towels close by and your shampoos and grooming brush and dryer and you are almost ready to begin—that is, if you have provided a rubber mat for steady footing in the bottom of the tub!

A rubber hose attached to the faucet for the wetting down and many rinsings will be a tremendous help. A pitcher for pouring the water over the dog will also do. Sufficient water pressure and a good sink drain is almost essential for the bathing of a dog, and will make your job easier.

Wet the dog—the entire dog—down thoroughly and make both first and second shampoos thick with lather that you rub right through the coat to the skin. The water should be warm, never hot, and you must rinse every last bit of shampoo out of the coat before drying. Soap that remains in the coat or on the skin will dry it and cause it to break off or be "gummy."

Start the rinsings and the soapings at the rear end of the dog. The noise and feel of the water will be more readily accepted if it is away from the face, and felt first on the more heavily coated areas of the body. Let a little water gather in the bottom of the tub so that the feet are well soaked, which will help melt away any heavy dirt that might be stuck to the pads or toes. When you get to the head, be sure to hold the head back and protect the eyes from any direct stream of water or soap. Cup your hands with water to wet the head, then gradually work up to the spray. Once you are sure that you have thoroughly rinsed the dog—do it again for good measure!

THE DRYING PROCESS

Let the water from the rinsings run off and make sure the feet have not gathered any of the soap or residue washing down the sink drain. Let the dog "drip dry" for a few minutes while you gently wipe down the coat with a towel. Then throw a dry towel over the dog for removing it from the tub, and getting it to the grooming table. While the dog is shaking itself under a towel, turn on the blow dryer and let it warm up. It will also let the puppy or dog get used to the sound of a dryer. We must remember that their hearing is much more acute than ours, and this must be a most unpleasant sound for them. How fortunate for those Akitas that live in hot climates and can dry naturally out of doors!

When the dryer has warmed up, gently start the brushing, usually in the opposite direction in which the coat grows, and with the dryer approximately a foot or more away from the coat. Try to dry the coat evenly all over the body and not just one spot at a time. In cold climates be sure the coat is dry to the skin, so make certain you do not bathe your dog unless you are fully prepared to take all the time necessary to dry the entire body.

Most Akitas take to the water readily, but there may be an occasional dog that does not, or who resents being placed in a tub. Be sure to talk to your dog and reassure it along the way. Make this time together a pleasant experience. Once you see how beautiful the dog looks when you are through, you will also see that the effort was worthwhile.

GROOMING THE AKITA FOR THE SHOW RING

If your Akita is to be a show dog, there are a few additional touches that can be added to the grooming procedure that will further enhance its coat and general appearance. Sooner or later every owner or handler arrives at what they consider to be the ideal way to present an Akita in the show ring, having achieved what they believe to be the perfect combination of shampoos, conditioners, etc., on the market today. This is not as simple as it may sound. All one has to do is pass a concessionaire's booth at a dog show and view the myriad grooming aids and products on display to realize how long it takes to give all of them a fair trial before settling on this "perfect" way to present the dog.

With so many procedures and combinations available, the entire process might seem to be one of trial and error. Since all products, with rare exception, are of good quality, the selection may be said to be "to each his own." Rather than working by the trial-and-error method, let the professionals groom your dog until you have procedures down pat. This will avoid damage to the coat, and display the proper technique in grooming the Akita. Watch the "pros" groom at the shows. You will almost be able to pick out the winners by the outstanding way the dogs are presented and the way they behave on the grooming tables. Do not expect the handlers to take time out to teach you while they are preparing to

Captions for pages 94-95.
1. Mitsu Kuma Toro, owned by Terry Wright, Lijo Kennels in Maryland. Toro made his championship in 1973 and was a Group winner in addition to over 60 times Best of Breed winner. 2. Close-up head study of Ch. Sachmo (1973-1981), owned by Bill and B. J. Andrews of Asheville, North Carolina. 3. Ch. Tobe's Remember Whiskey, owned and bred by Thomas and Beverly Bonadonna, Tobe Kennels. 4. Ch. Frerose's Dillon, bred by F. O. Duane, and pictured at eight months of age. Dillon is shown in action at the 1977 Staten Island Kennel Club show winning Puppy Class. 5. Best of Winners on the way to championship is Ch. Great River's Simon, winning under judge D. Bradley. Bred, owned, and handled by Bob Fontano, Great River Akitas. 6. Wotan's Dust Devil, bred and owned by Peggy Casselberry, North Canton, Ohio.

1

2   3

4

5

6

Willowdeen's Tamarlane Aria at four months of age knows when it's time for a walk. The sire was Ch. Tamarlane's Fuji Yama ex Ch. Parksway Oschi of Willowdeen. Co-owned by Dr. Sophia Kaluzniacki and Phyllis Graves.

go into the ring. But the breeder of your dog should be able to tell you how to go about learning for yourself or where to attend a grooming school. Otherwise you must learn by observation.

Assuming your dog has had its bath a day or two before the show, you will need your pin brush to go over it just before it enters the ring to make sure every hair is in place. Eyes, ears, nails and teeth should have been tended to, and for the show ring it is suggested that the whiskers be trimmed. It is essential that the dog be exercised before entering the ring and a light dusting of the feet with some non-slip product be applied if you are showing on an indoor slip-

pery surface. Nothing will throw off a dog's gait more than slipping on a turn around the end of a show ring. If your dog is shedding but has no bare spots, you may wish to exhibit if the shedding is not too severe.

For the most part you will find Akitas are clean dogs. Of course, one must forgive the puppy antics that carry the dogs through mud and leaves and water during the course of their play. This is all part of the growing-up process. But it is worth a little extra grooming care to watch them at play and see how very much they enjoy the outdoors and the good health that is a direct result of all your tender, loving care.

Chapter 8

Buying Your First Akita Puppy

In searching for that special puppy, there are several paths that will lead you to a litter from which you can find the puppy of your choice. If you are uncertain as to where to find a reputable breeder, write to the parent club and ask for the names and addresses of members who have puppies for sale. The addresses of Akita breed clubs can be obtained by writing directly to the American Kennel Club, 51 Madison Avenue, New York, N.Y. 10010. They keep an up-to-date, accurate list of breeders from whom you can seek information on obtaining a good, healthy puppy. The classified ad listings in dog publications and the major newspapers may also lead you to that certain pup. The various dog magazines generally carry a monthly breed column which features information and news on the breed that may aid in your selection.

It is advisable that you become thoroughly acquainted with the breed prior to purchasing your puppy. Plan to attend a dog show or two in your area at which you can view purebred dogs of just about every breed at their best in the show ring. Even if you are not interested in purchasing a show-quality dog, you should be familiar with what the better specimens look like so that you will at least purchase a decent representative of the breed for the money. You can learn a lot from observing the show dogs in action in the ring, or in a public place where their personalities can be clearly shown. The dog show catalogue is also a useful tool to put you in contact with the local kennels and breeders. Each dog that is entered in the show is listed along with the owner's name and address. If you spot a dog that you think is a particularly fine and pleasing specimen, contact the owners and arrange to visit their kennel to see the types and colors they are breeding and winning with at the shows. Exhibitors at the dog shows are usually more than delighted to talk to people interested in their dogs and the specific characteristics of their breed.

Once you've decided that the Akita is the breed for you because you appreciate its exceptional beauty, personality, and intelligence and you have a place in your home for an Akita, it is wise to thoroughly acquaint yourself by reading some background material on owning the breed. When you feel certain that this puppy will fit in with your family's way of life, it is time to start writing letters and making phone calls and appointments to see some puppies.

Some words of caution: don't choose a kennel simply because it is near your home and don't buy the first "cute" puppy that romps around your legs or licks the end of your nose. All puppies are cute, and naturally some will appeal to you more than others. But don't let preferences sway your thinking. If you are buying your Akita to be strictly a family pet, preferences can be permissible. If you are looking for a top-quality puppy for the show ring, you must evaluate clearly, choose wisely, and make the best possible choice. Whichever one you choose, you will quickly learn to love your Akita puppy. A careful selection, rather than a "love at first sight" choice will save a disappointment later on.

To get the broadest idea of what puppies are for sale and the going market prices, visit as many kennels as possible in your area and write to others farther away. With today's safe and rapid air flights on the major airlines, it is possible to purchase dogs from far-off places at nominal costs. While it is safest and wisest to first see the dog you are buying, there are enough reputable breeders and kennels to be found for you to take this step with a minimum of risk. In the long run, it can be well worth your while to obtain the exact dog or bloodline you desire.

Captions for pages 98-99.
1. Ch. Tamarlane's Arcturus, pictured here at four weeks of age. Owned by Gruelt Baker. 2. Seven-week-old Jade and brother Pogo at the Wotan Kennels, North Canton, Ohio. 3. One of Lillian Koehler's Akita puppies explores the great outdoors. 4. Sitting pretty is an Akita puppy named "Flyer," bred and owned by the Seawood Kennels, Lakebay, Washington. 5. Tiger's Eye Silverstorm Eoka, bred by Janet Vos and co-owned by Linda Henson and P. Brereton. 6. Six-week-old Toyo, bred by C. Bossert. 7. A typical O'B.J. Akita puppy, bred and owned by Bill and B. J. Andrews of Asheville, North Carolina.

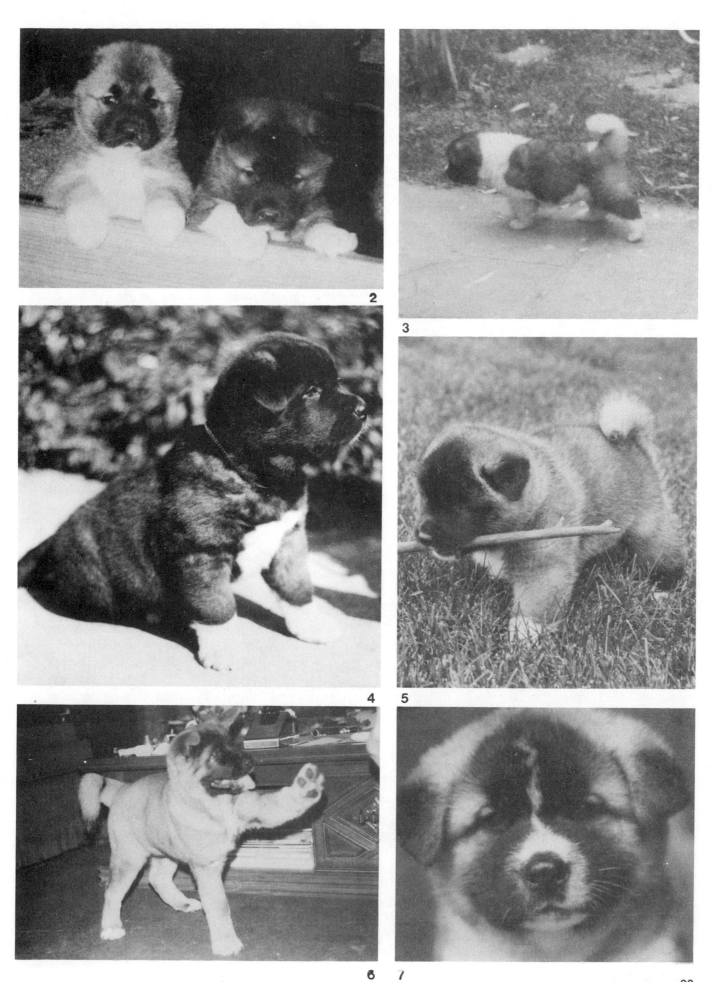

2

3

4

5

6 7

It is customary for the purchaser to pay the shipping charges, and the airlines are most willing to supply flight information and prices upon request. Rental on the shipping crate, if the owner does not provide one for the dog, is nominal. While unfortunate incidents have occurred on the airlines in the transporting of animals by air, the major airlines are making improvements in safety measures and have reached the point of reasonable safety and cost. Barring unforeseen circumstances, the safe arrival of a dog you might buy can pretty much be assured if both seller and purchaser adhere to and follow up on even the most minute details from both ends.

WHAT TO LOOK FOR IN AN AKITA

Anyone who has owned an Akita as a puppy will agree that the most fascinating aspect of raising the pup is to witness the complete and extraordinary metamorphosis that occurs during its first year of maturing. Your puppy will undergo a marked change in appearance, and during this period you must also be aware of the puppy's personality for there are certain qualities visible at this time that will generally make for a good adult dog. Of course, no one can guarantee nature and the best puppy does not always grow up to be a great dog. However, even the novice breeder can learn to look for certain specifics that will help him to choose a promising puppy.

Should you decide to purchase a six- to eight-week old puppy, you are in store for all the cute antics that little pup can dream up for you! At this age, the puppy should be well on its way to being weaned, wormed, and ready to go out into the world with its responsible new owner. It is better not to buy a puppy that is less than six weeks old; they simply are not ready to leave their mother or the security of the other puppies. By eight to twelve weeks of age you will be able to notice much about the behavior and appearance of the dog. Akita puppies, as they are recalled in our fondest childhood memories, are amazingly active and bouncy—as well they should be! The normal puppy should be alert, curious, and interested, especially about a stranger. However, if the puppy acts a little reserved or distant, don't necessarily construe these acts to be signs of fear or shyness. It might merely indicate that he hasn't quite made up his mind whether he likes you as yet! By the same token, though, he should not be openly fearful or terrified by a stranger—and especially should

not show any fear of his owner!

In direct contrast, the puppy should not be ridiculously over-active, either. The puppy that frantically bounds around the room and is never still is not especially desirable. And beware of the "spinners"! Spinners are the puppies or dogs that have become neurotic from being kept in cramped quarters or in crates and behave in an emotionally unstable manner when let loose in adequate space. When let out they run in circles and seemingly "go wild." Puppies with this kind of traumatic background seldom ever regain full composure or adjust to the big outside world. The puppy which has had the proper exercise and appropriate living quarters will have a normal, though spirited, outlook on life and will do its utmost to win you over without having to go into a tailspin.

If the general behavior and appearance of the dog thus far appeal to you, it is time for you to observe him more closely for additional physical requirements. First of all, you cannot expect to find in the Akita puppy all the coat he will bear upon maturity. That will come with time and good food, and will be additionally enhanced by the many wonderful grooming aids which can be found in pet shops today. Needless to say, the healthy puppy's coat should have a nice shine to it, and the more dense at this age, the better the coat will be when the dog reaches adulthood.

Look for clear, dark, sparkling eyes that are free of discharge. From the time the puppy's eyes open until the puppy is about three months old the eyes might have a slight blue cast to them. The darker the blue, the better are the chances for a good dark eye in the adult dog.

It is important to check the bite. Even though the puppy will cut another complete set of teeth somewhere between four and seven months of age, there will already be some indication of how the final teeth will be positioned. Too much of an overshot bite (top teeth are positioned too far *over* the bottom teeth) or too much of an undershot jaw (bottom teeth are positioned too far out *under* the top teeth) is undesirable as they are considered faults by the breed Standard.

Puppies take anything and almost everything into their mouths to chew on, and a lot of diseases and infections start or are introduced in the mouth. Brown-stained teeth, for instance, may indicate the puppy has had a past case of distemper, and the teeth will remain that way. This fact must be reckoned with if you have a show puppy in mind. The puppy's breath should be neither sour nor unpleasant. Bad breath can be a result of a poor mixture of food in the diet, or of eating meat of low quality, especially if fed raw. Some people say that the healthy puppy's breath should have a faint odor vaguely reminiscent of garlic. At any rate, a puppy should never be fed just table scraps, but should be raised on a well-balanced diet containing a good dry puppy chow and a good grade of fresh meat. Poor meat and too much cereal or fillers tend to make the puppy grow too fat. Puppies should be in good flesh, but not fat from the wrong kind of food.

Needless to say, the puppy should be clean. The breeder that shows a dirty puppy is one to steer away from. Look closely at the skin. Make sure it is not covered with insect bites or red, blotchy sores and dry scales. The vent area around the tail should not show evidences of diarrhea or inflammation. By the same token, the puppy's fur should not be matted with excretion or smell strongly of urine.

True enough, you can wipe dirty eyes, clean dirty ears, and give the puppy a bath when you get it home, but these things are all indications of how the puppy has been cared for during the important formative first months of its life, and can vitally influence its future health and development. There are many reputable breeders raising healthy puppies that have been reared in proper places and under the proper conditions in clean housing, so why take a chance on a series of veterinary bills and a questionable constitution?

MALE OR FEMALE?

The choice of sex in your puppy is also something that must be given serious thought before you buy. For the pet owner, the sex that would best suit the family life you enjoy would be the paramount choice to consider. For the breeder or exhibitor there are other vital considerations. If you are looking for a stud to establish a kennel, it is essential that you select a dog with both testicles evident, even at a tender age, and verified by a veterinarian before the sale is finalized if there is any doubt.

The visibility of only one testicle, known as monorchidism, automatically disqualifies the dog from the show ring or from a breeding program, though monorchids are capable of siring. Additionally, it must be noted that monorchids frequently sire dogs with the same deficiency, and to introduce this into a bloodline knowingly is an unwritten sin in the fancy. Also, a monor-

chid can sire dogs that are completely sterile. Such dogs are referred to as cryptorchids and have no testicles.

An additional consideration in the male versus female decision for the private owners is that with males there might be the problem of leg-lifting and with females there is the inconvenience while they are in season. However, this need not be the problem it used to be—pet shops sell "pants" for both sexes, which help to control the situation.

THE PLANNED PARENTHOOD BEHIND YOUR PUPPY

Never be afraid to ask pertinent questions about the puppy, as well as questions about the sire and dam. Feel free to ask the breeder if you might see the dam; the purpose of your visit is to determine her general health and her appearance

Captions for pages 102-103.
1. One of Lillian Koehler's Akita puppies. 2. An adorable 10-week-old Akita puppy, bred and owned by Peggy Casselberry, Wotan Kennels, North Canton, Ohio. 3. Fourteen-week-old puppy bitch named Krug's Zen's Daiji Yuki Fujin, sired by Ch. Krug's Aka Shogun Okami-Go out of Marjo's Kin No Fujin. "Yuki" was photographed in November 1982. Owned by Virginia Zwolinski of Hicksville, New York. 4. O'B.J. Michelin of Akitzu pictured at just four months of age. Bred by Bill and B. J. Andrews of Asheville, North Carolina. 5. The future top-winning Akita bitch in the United States for 1983, Ch. Tamarlane's Capella, is pictured at just four weeks of age. Bred by Dr. Sophia Kaluzniacki, she is co-owned by her and Carolyn Rennie. The sire was Ch. Akita Tani's Daimyo, R.O.M., out of Ch. Frerose's Sarah Lei, R.O.M. 6. A pair of three-week-old Akita puppies from the Wotan Kennels. 7. Jens Kathmandu, owned by Robert Miller, D.V.M., of Athens, Georgia.

101

1 2

3

4

5

6 7

as a representative of the breed. Ask also to see the sire if the breeder is the owner. Ask what the puppy has been fed and should be fed after weaning. Ask to see the pedigree, and inquire if the litter or the individual puppies have been registered with the American Kennel Club, how many of the temporary and/or permanent inoculations the puppy has had, when and if the puppy has been wormed, and whether it has had any illness, disease, or infection.

You need not ask if the puppy is housebroken ... it won't mean much. He may have gotten the idea as to where "the place" is where he lives now, but he will need new training to learn where "the place" is in his new home! And you can't really expect too much from puppies at this age anyway. Housebreaking is entirely up to the new owner. We know puppies always eliminate when they first awaken and sometimes dribble when they get excited. If friends and relatives are coming over to see the new puppy, make sure he is walked just before he greets them at the front door. This will help.

The normal time period for puppies (around three months of age) to eliminate is about every two or three hours. As the time draws near, either take the puppy out or indicate the newspaper for the same purpose. Housebreaking is never easy, but anticipation is about 90 per cent of solving the problem. The schools that offer to housebreak your dog are virtually useless. Here again the puppy will learn the "place" at the schoolhouse, but coming home he will need special training for the new location.

A reputable breeder will welcome any and all questions you might ask and will voluntarily offer additional information, if only to brag about the tedious and loving care he has given the litter. He will also sell a puppy on a 24-hour veterinary approval basis. This means you have a full day to get the puppy to a veterinarian of your choice to get his opinion on the general health of the puppy before you make a final decision. There should also be veterinary certificates and full particulars on the dates and types of inoculations the puppy has been given up to that time.

PUPPIES AND WORMS

Let us give further attention to the unhappy and very unpleasant subject of worms. Generally speaking, most puppies—even those raised in clean quarters—come into contact with worms early in life. The worms can be passed down from the mother before birth or picked up during the puppies' first encounters with the earth or their kennel facilities. To say that you must not buy a puppy because of an infestation of worms is nonsensical. You might be passing up a fine animal that can be freed of worms in one short treatment, although a heavy infestation of worms of any kind in a young dog is dangerous and debilitating.

The extent of the infection can be readily determined by a veterinarian, and you might take his word as to whether the future health and conformation of the dog has been damaged. He can prescribe the dosage and supply the medication at this time and you will already have one of your problems solved.

VETERINARY INSPECTION

While your veterinarian is going over the puppy you have selected to purchase, you might just as well ask him for his opinion of it as a breed as well as the facts about its general health. While few veterinarians can claim to be breed-conformation experts, they usually have a good eye for a worthy specimen and can advise you where to go for further information. Perhaps your veterinarian could also recommend other breeders if you should want another opinion. The veterinarian can point out structural faults or organic problems that affect all breeds and can usually judge whether an animal has been abused or mishandled and whether it is oversized or undersized.

I would like to emphasize here that it is only through this type of close cooperation between owners and veterinarians that we can expect to reap the harvest of modern research.

Most reliable veterinarians are more than eager to learn about various breeds of purebred dogs, and we in turn must acknowledge and apply what they have proved through experience and research in their field. We can buy and breed the best dog in the world, but when disease strikes we are only as safe as our veterinarian is capable—so let's keep them informed breed by breed, and dog by dog. The veterinarian can mean the difference between life and death!

THE CONDITIONS OF SALE

While it is customary to pay for the puppy before you take it away with you, you should be able to give the breeder a deposit if there is any doubt about the puppy's health. You might also (depending on local laws) postdate a check to cover the twenty-four hour veterinary approval.

If you decide to take the puppy, the breeder is required to supply you with a pedigree, along with the puppy's registration papers. He is also obliged to supply you with complete information about the inoculations and American Kennel Club instructions on how to transfer ownership of the puppy to your name.

Some breeders will offer buyers time payment plans for convenience if the price on a show dog is very high or if deferred payments are the only way you can purchase the dog. However, any such terms must be worked out between buyer and breeder and should be put in writing to avoid later complications.

You will find most breeders cooperative if they believe you are sincere in your love for the puppy and that you will give it the proper home and the show ring career it deserves (if it is sold as a show quality specimen of the breed). Remember, when buying a show dog, it is impossible to guarantee nature. A breeder can only tell you what he *believes* will develop into a show dog. . . so be sure your breeder is an honest one.

Also, if you purchase a show prospect and promise to show the dog, you definitely should show it! It is a waste to have a beautiful dog that deserves recognition in the show ring sitting at home as a family pet, and it is unfair to the breeder. This is especially true if the breeder offered you a reduced price because of the advertising his kennel and bloodlines would receive by your showing the dog in the ring. If you want a pet, buy a pet. Be honest about it, and let the breeder decide on this basis which is the best dog for you. Your conscience will be clear and you'll both be doing a real service to the breed.

BUYING A SHOW PUPPY

If you are positive about breeding and showing your Akita, make this point clear so that the breeder will sell you the best possible puppy. If you are dealing with an established kennel, you will have to rely partially, if not entirely, on their choice, since they know their bloodlines and what they can expect from the breeding. They know how their stock develops, and it would be foolish of them to sell you a puppy that could not stand up as a show specimen representing their stock in the ring.

However, you must also realize that the breeder may be keeping the best puppy in the litter to show and breed himself. If this is the case, you might be wise to select the best puppy of the opposite sex so that the dogs will not be competing against one another in the show rings.

THE PURCHASE PRICE

Prices vary on all puppies, of course, but a good show prospect at six weeks to six months of age will usually sell for several hundred dollars. If the puppy is really outstanding, and the pedigree and parentage is also outstanding, the price will be even higher. Honest breeders, however, will all quote around the same figure, so price should not be a strong deciding factor in your choice. If you have any questions as to the current price range, a few telephone calls to different kennels will give you a good average. Reputable breeders will usually stand behind the health of their puppies should something drastically wrong develop, such as hip dysplasia, etc. Their obligation to make an adjustment or replacement is usually honored. However, this must be agreed to in writing at the time of the purchase.

Captions for pages 106-107.
1. Kelly's Ray-Gin Bull of Frerose, C.D., pictured at three months of age, is owned by Frederick Duane of Shohola, Pennsylvania. 2. Four weeks old and ready for a ride to a show. Rusty Short's Oushi Skoshi. 3. Seven-week-old Harley, photographed in 1982 at owner Pat Castronova's kennels in Denver, Colorado. The sire was Ch. Kin Hozan's Mogami ex Meadow Lakes Michado Hime. 4. Nine-week-old future Ch. O'B.J. Silver Chalice of Tomoko, owned by Marvin and Elaine Nussbaum of Greenbelt, Maryland. 5. Peggy Casselberry and Wotan's Cassolai Royal Tenji at 3½ weeks of age. The sire was Pharfossa's Torro Chia Pao ex Wotan's Ming Jade Ojijo. 6. Seven-week-old "Brat" is ready for chow. His real name is Kisu's Miko Yama Akai, owned by Betty Hinson of Jonesboro, Arkansas. 7. Early show training for Wotan's Ami Akagane Hana at 3½ months of age. The sire was Ch. Bo Echols Ambec Minke ex River View's Perfect Ten.

1 2

3 4

5

6   7

Chapter 9

The Dog Show World

Let us assume that after a few months of tender loving care, you realize your dog is developing beyond your wildest expectations and that the dog you selected is very definitely a show dog! Of course, every owner is prejudiced. But if you are sincerely interested in going to dog shows with your dog and making a champion of him, now is the time to start casting a critical eye on him from a judge's point of view.

There is no such thing as a perfect dog. Every dog has some faults, perhaps even a few serious ones. The best way to appraise your dog's degree of perfection is to compare him with the Standard for the breed, or before a judge in a show ring.

MATCH SHOWS

For the beginner there are "mock" shows, called match shows, where you and your dog go through many of the procedures of a regular dog show, but do not gain points toward championship. These shows are usually held by kennel clubs, annually or semiannually, and much ring poise and experience can be gained there. The age limit is usually reduced to two months at match shows to give puppies four months of training before they compete at the regular shows when they reach six months of age. Classes range from two to four months, four to six months, six to nine months, and nine to twelve months. Puppies compete with others of their own age for comparative purposes. Many breeders evaluate their litters in this manner, choosing which is the most outgoing, which is the most poised, the best showman, etc.

For those seriously interested in showing their dogs to full championship, these match shows provide important experience for both the dog and the owner. Class categories may vary slightly, according to number of entries, but basically include all the classes that are included at a regular point show. There is a nominal entry fee and, of course, ribbons and usually trophies are given for your efforts as well. Unlike the point shows, entries can be made on the day of the show right on the show grounds. They are unbenched and provide an informal, usually congenial atmosphere for the amateur, which helps to make the ordeal of one's first adventure in the show ring a little less nerve-wracking.

THE POINT SHOWS

It is not possible to show a puppy at an American Kennel Club sanctioned point show before the age of six months. When your dog reaches this eligible age, your local kennel club can provide you with the names and addresses of the show-giving superintendents in your area who will be staging the club's dog show for them, and where you must write for an entry form.

The forms are mailed in a pamphlet called a premium list. This also includes the names of the judges for each breed, a list of the prizes and trophies, the name and address of the show-giving club and where the show will be held, as well as rules and regulations set up by the American Kennel Club which must be abided by if you are to enter.

A booklet containing the complete set of show rules and regulations may be obtained by writing to the American Kennel Club, Inc., 51 Madison Avenue, New York, N.Y., 10010.

When you write to the dog show superintendent, request not only your premium list for this particular show, but ask that your name be added to their mailing list so that you will automatically receive all premium lists in the future. List your breed or breeds and they will see to it that you receive premium lists for specialty shows as well.

Unlike the match shows where your dog will be judged on ring behavior, at the point shows he will be judged on conformation to the breed Standard. In addition to being at least six months of age (on the day of the show) he must be purebred for a point show. This means both of his parents and he are registered with the American Kennel Club. There must be no alterations or falsifications regarding his appearance. Females cannot have been spayed and males must have both testicles in evidence. No dyes or powders may be used to enhance the appearance, and any lameness or deformity or major deviation from the Standard for the breed constitutes a disqualification.

With all these things in mind, groom your dog to the best of your ability in the specified area for this purpose in the show hall and *exercise your dog before taking him into the ring!* Too many Akita owners are guilty of making their dogs remain on their crates so they do not get dirty, and the first thing the animals do when they start to show is stop to empty themselves. There is no excuse for this. All it takes is a walk *before* grooming. If your dog is clean, well groomed, *empty*, and leash trained you should be able to enter the show ring with confidence and pride of ownership, ready for an appraisal of your dog by the judge.

The presiding judge on that day will allow each and every dog a certain amount of time and consideration before making his decisions. It is never permissible to consult the judge regarding either your dog or his decision while you are in the ring. An exhibitor never speaks unless spoken to, and then only to answer such questions as the judge may ask—the age of the dog, the dog's bite, or to ask you to move your dog around the ring once again.

However, before you reach the point where you are actually in the ring awaiting the final decisions of the judge, you will have had to decide in which of the five classes in each sex your dog should compete.

POINT SHOW CLASSES

The regular classes of the A.K.C. are: PUPPY, NOVICE, BRED-BY-EXHIBITOR, AMERICAN-BRED, OPEN; if your dog is undefeated in any of the regular classes (divided by sex) in which it is entered, he or she is *required* to enter the Winner's Class. If your dog is placed second in the class to the dog which won Winner's Dog or Winner's Bitch, hold the dog or bitch in readiness as the judge must consider it for Reserve Winners.

PUPPY CLASSES shall be for dogs which are six months of age and over but under twelve months, which were whelped in the U.S.A. or Canada, and which are not champions. Classes are often divided 6 and (under) 9, and 9 and (under) 12 months. The age of a dog shall be calculated up to and inclusive of the first day of a show. For example, a dog whelped on January 1st is eligible to compete in a puppy class on July 1st, and may continue to compete up to and including December 31st of the same year, but is not eligible to compete January 1st of the following year.

THE NOVICE CLASS shall be for dogs six months of age or over, whelped in the U.S.A. or Canada which have not, prior to the closing entries, won three first prizes in the Novice Class, a first prize in Bred-by-Exhibitor, American-

bred or Open Class, nor one or more points toward a championship title.

THE BRED-BY-EXHIBITOR CLASS shall be for dogs whelped in the U.S.A. which are six months of age and over, which are not champions and which are owned wholly or in part by the person or by the spouse of the person who

Captions for pages 110-111.
1. Golden Sun Seawood WaWa L'Wilac is pictured winning a Group Placement at her first Match Show under judge Joanne Riley. Owned and handled by Kelle Clinton, Lakebay, Washington. The sire was Ch. Kodiak of Autumn Field ex Ch. Golden Sun's Taneha. 2. On the way to the top... future Ch. Tobe-Krug's Tai Fighter winning at a Match Show in 1981 at 4 months of age. Co-owned by the Tobe and Krug Akita Kennels. 3. Rusty Short's Ch. KoFuKu-No's Kuma Oso of Tormod at five months of age, winning at a Match Show. 4. Tiger's Eye Syoen, bred by Janet Vos and co-owned with Wendy Scott, is shown winning Best in Match at a Cascade Akita Club Match Show. The sire was Ch. Nan Chao's Rick-O-Shay ex Ch. Tiger's Eye Storm Warning. 5. Tobe's Jumbo Sun tops an entry of 900 dogs at three months of age to win Best in Match at the Mid Island Kennel Club show in 1983. Bred and owned by Tobe Kennels, Branchville, New Jersey.

1 2

SHO-FOTO

3

110

4

5

was the breeder or one of the breeders of record. Dogs entered in the BBE Class must be handled by an owner or by a member of the immediate family of an owner, i.e., the husband, wife, father, mother, son, daughter, brother, and sister.

THE AMERICAN-BRED CLASS is for all dogs (except champions) six months of age or over, whelped in the U.S.A. by reason of a mating that took place in the U.S.A.

THE OPEN CLASS is for any dog six months of age or over, except in a member specialty club show held for only American-bred dogs, in which case the class is for American-bred dogs only.

WINNERS DOG and WINNERS BITCH: After the above male classes have been judged, the first-place winners are then *required* to compete in the ring. The dog judged "Winners Dog" is awarded the points toward his championship title.

RESERVE WINNERS are selected immediately after the Winners Dog. In case of a disqualification of a win by the A.K.C., the Reserve Dog moves up to "Winners" and receives the points. After all male classes are judged, the bitch classes are called.

BEST OF BREED OR BEST OF VARIETY COMPETITION is limited to Champions of Record or dogs (with newly acquired points, for a 90-day period prior to A.K.C. confirmation) which have completed championship requirements, and Winners Dog and Winners Bitch (or the dog awarded Winners if only one Winners prize has been awarded), together with any undefeated dogs which have been shown only in non-regular classes; all compete for Best of Breed or Best of Variety (if the breed is divided by size, color, texture, or length of coat hair, etc.).

BEST OF WINNERS: If the WD or WB earns BOB or BOV, it automatically becomes BOW; otherwise they will be judged together for BOW (following BOB or BOV judging).

BEST OF OPPOSITE SEX is selected from the remaining dogs of the opposite sex to Best of Breed or Best of Variety.

OTHER CLASSES may be approved by the A.K.C.: STUD DOGS, BROOD BITCHES, BRACE CLASS, TEAM CLASS; classes consisting of local dogs and bitches may also be included in a show if approved by the A.K.C. (special rules are included in the A.K.C. Rule Book).

The MISCELLANEOUS CLASS shall be for purebred dogs of such breeds as may be designated by the A.K.C. No dog shall be eligible for entry in this class unless the owner has been granted an Indefinite Listing Privilege (ILP) and unless the ILP number is given on the entry form. Application for an ILP shall be made on a form provided by the A.K.C. and when submitted must be accompanied by a fee set by the Board of Directors.

All Miscellaneous breeds shall be shown together in a single class except that the class may be divided by sex if so specified in the premium list. There shall be *no* further competition for dogs entered in this class. Ribbons for 1st, 2nd, 3rd, and 4th shall be Rose, Brown, Light Green and Gray, respectively.

OBEDIENCE TRIALS

Some shows also offer Obedience Trials, which are considered as separate events. They give the dogs a chance to compete and score on performing a prescribed set of exercises intended to display their training in doing useful work.

There are three obedience titles for which they may compete: First, the Companion Dog or C.D. title; second, the Companion Dog Excellent or C.D.X.; and third, the Utility Dog or U.D. Detailed information on these degrees is contained in a booklet entitled *Official Obedience Regulations* and may be obtained by writing to the American Kennel Club.

JUNIOR SHOWMANSHIP COMPETITION

Junior Showmanship competition is for boys and girls in different age groups handling their own dogs or ones owned by their immediate family. There are four divisions: Novice A (10 to 12-year-olds) and Novice B (13 to 16-year-olds) for competitors with no previous Junior Showmanship wins, Open A (10 to 12-year-olds) and Open B (13 to 16-year-olds) for competitors with one or more JS awards.

As Junior Showmanship at the dog shows increased in popularity, certain changes and improvements had to be made. As of April 1, 1971, the American Kennel Club issued a new booklet containing the Regulations for Junior Showmanship which may be obtained by writing to the A.K.C. at 51 Madison Avenue, New York, N.Y. 10010.

DOG SHOW PHOTOGRAPHERS

Every show has at least one official photographer who will be more than happy to take a photograph of your dog with the judge, ribbons, and trophies, along with you or your handler.

These make marvelous remembrances of your top show wins and are frequently framed along with the ribbons for display purposes. Photographers can be paged at the show over the public address system, if you wish to obtain this service. Prices vary, but you will probably find it costs little to capture these happy moments, and the photos can always be used in the various dog magazines to advertise your dog's wins.

TWO TYPES OF DOG SHOWS

There are two types of dog shows licensed by the American Kennel Club. One is the all-breed show which includes classes for all the recognized breeds, and groups of breeds; i.e., all terriers, all toys, etc. Then there are the specialty shows for one particular breed which also offer championship points.

BENCHED OR UNBENCHED
DOG SHOWS

The show-giving clubs determine, usually on the basis of what facilities are offered by their chosen show site, whether their show will be benched or unbenched. A benched show is one where the dog show superintendent supplies benches (cages for toy dogs). Each bench is numbered and its corresponding number appears on your entry identification slip which is sent to you prior to the show date. The number also appears in the show catalogue. Upon entering the show you should take your dog to the bench where he should remain until it is time to groom him before entering the ring to be judged. After judging, he must be returned to the bench until the official time of dismissal from the show. At an unbenched show the club makes no provision whatsoever for your dog other than an enormous tent (if an outdoor show) or an area in a show hall where all crates and grooming equipment must be kept.

Benched or unbenched, the moment you enter the show grounds you are expected to look after your dog and have it under complete control at all times. This means short leads in crowded aisles or getting out of cars. In the case of a benched show, a "bench chain" is needed. It should allow the dog to move around, but not get down off the bench. It is also not considered "cute" to have small tots leading enormous dogs around a dog show where they might be dragged into the middle of a dog fight.

IF YOUR DOG WINS A CLASS

Study the classes to make certain your dog is entered in a proper class for his or her qualifications. If your dog wins his class, the rule states: *You are required* to enter classes for Winners, Best of Breed and Best of Winners (no additional entry fees). The rule states, "No eligible dogs may be withheld from competition." It is not mandatory that you stay for group judging. *If your dog wins a group,* however, *you must stay for Best In Show competition.*

Captions for pages 114-115.
1. Winning Best in Show is Am. and Can. Ch. Big A's Stormy of Jobe, the first Best-in-Show-winning Akita Bitch. The show was the 1980 Fort Bend Kennel Club event under judge Del Glodowski. Stormy also won the Breed at the Akita Club of America National Specialty Show the same day. 2. Best Junior Handler at the 1983 Akita Club of America National Specialty Show was Nanci Opel of Beltsville, Maryland, with Ch. Mill Creek Bozo Jo, C.D. Dick Woods presented the trophy. 3. Robert Grunder's Wotan's Royal Shoga Hime, winning Best of Breed, Best Puppy in Working Group, and Best Puppy in Match at the Carrollton Kennel Club show. "Sam" was shown by Mr. Grunder's daughter, Kelli. Kelli also won Best Junior Handler in the Match. 4. Ch. Oyen's Muy Macho takes the Breed at a 1975 dog show. Handled by Tom Bonadonna for owner Rosemary Aigner.

BEST IN SHOW

2 3

4

115

THE PRIZE RIBBONS AND WHAT THEY STAND FOR

No matter how many entries there are in each class at a dog show, if you place first through fourth position you will receive a ribbon. These ribbons commemorate your win and can be impressive when collected and displayed to prospective buyers when and if you have puppies for sale, or if you intend to use your dog at public stud.

All ribbons from the American Kennel Club licensed dog shows will bear the American Kennel Club seal, the name of the show, the date and the placement. In the classes the colors are blue for first, red for second, yellow for third and white for fourth. Winners Dog or Winners Bitch ribbons are purple, while Reserve Dog and Reserve Bitch ribbons are purple-and-white. Best of Winners ribbons are blue-and-white; Best of Breed, purple-and-gold; and Best of Opposite Sex ribbons are red-and-white.

In the six groups, first prize is a blue rosette or ribbon, second placement is red, third yellow and fourth white. The Best In Show rosette is either red, white and blue or incorporates the colors used in the show-giving club's emblem.

QUALIFYING FOR CHAMPIONSHIP

Championship points are given for Winners Dog and Winners Bitch in accordance with a scale of points established by the American Kennel Club based on the popularity of the breed in entries, and the number of dogs competing in the classes. This scale of points varies in different sections of the country, but the scale is published in the front of each dog show catalogue. These points may differ between the dogs and the bitches at the same show. You may, however, win additional points by winning Best of Winners, if there are fewer dogs than bitches entered, or vice versa. Points never exceed five at any one show and a total of 15 points must be won to constitute a championship. These 15 points must be won under at least three different judges, and you must acquire at least two major wins. Anything from a three to five point win is a major, while one and two point wins are minor wins. Two major wins must be won under two different judges to meet championship requirements.

PROFESSIONAL HANDLERS

If you are new in the fancy and do not know how to handle your dog to his best advantage, or if you are too nervous or physically unable to show your dog, you can hire a reliable professional handler who will do it for you for a specified fee. The more successful or well-known handlers charge slightly higher rates, but generally speaking there is a pretty uniform charge for this service. As the dog progresses with his wins in the show ring, the fee increases proportionately. Included in this service is professional advice on when and where to show your dog, grooming, a statement of your wins at each show, and all trophies and ribbons that the dog accumulates. Any cash award is kept by the handler as a sort of "bonus."

When engaging a handler, it is advisable to select one that does not take more dogs to a show than he can properly and comfortably handle. You want your dog to receive his individual attention and not be rushed into the ring at the last moment because the handler has been busy with too many other dogs in other rings. Some handlers require that you deliver the dog to their establishment a few days ahead of the show so they have ample time to groom and train him. Other handlers will accept well-behaved and trained dogs that have been groomed from their owners at ringside, if they are familiar with the dog and the owner. This should be determined well in advance of the show date. NEVER expect a handler to accept a dog at ringside that is not groomed to perfection!

There are several sources for locating a professional handler. Dog magazines carry their classified advertising. A note or telephone call to the American Kennel Club will also put you in touch with several in your area.

DO YOU REALLY NEED A HANDLER?

The answer to that question is sometimes yes, sometimes no! However, the answer that must be determined first of all is, "But can I *afford* a professional handler?" or, "I want to show my dog myself. Does that mean my dog will never do any big winning?"

Do you *really* need a handler to win? If you are mishandling a good dog that should be winning and isn't because it is made to look bad in the ring by its owner, the answer is yes. If you don't know how to handle a dog properly, why make your dog look bad when a handler could show it to its best advantage?

Some owners simply cannot handle a dog well and still wonder why their dogs aren't winning in the ring, no matter how hard they try. Others are nervous and this nervousness travels down the leash to the dog and the dog behaves accordingly. Some people are extroverts by nature, and these are the people who usually make excellent handlers. Of course, the biggest winning dogs at the shows usually have a lot of "show off" in their nature, too, and this helps a great deal.

THE COST OF CAMPAIGNING A DOG WITH A HANDLER

At present many champions are shown an average of 25 times before completing a championship. In entry fees at today's prices, that adds up to over $250. This does not include motel bills, traveling expenses, or food. There have been dog champions finished in fewer shows, say five to ten shows, but this is the exception rather than the rule. When and where to show should be thought out carefully so that you can perhaps save money on entries. This is one of the services a professional handler provides that can mean a considerable saving. Hiring a handler can save money in the long run if you just wish to make a champion. If your dog has been winning reserves and not taking the points and a handler can finish him in five to ten shows, you would be ahead financially. If your dog is not really top quality, the length of time it takes even a handler to finish it (depending upon competition in the area) could add up to a large amount of money.

Campaigning a show specimen that not only captures the wins in his breed but wins Group and Best in Show awards gets up into the big money. To cover the nation's major shows and rack up a record as one of the top dogs in the nation usually costs an owner between 10 and 15 thousand dollars a year. This includes not only the professional handler's fee for taking the dog into the ring, but the cost of conditioning and grooming, board, advertising in the dog magazines, photographs, etc.

There is great satisfaction in winning with your own dog, especially if you have trained and cared for it yourself. With today's enormous entries at the dog shows and so many worthy dogs competing for top wins, many owners who said "I'd rather do it myself!" and meant it became discouraged and eventually hired a handler anyway.

However, if you really are in it just for the sport, you can and should handle your dog if you want to. You can learn the tricks by attending training classes, and you can learn a lot by carefully observing the more successful professional handlers as they perform in the ring.

Model yourself after the ones that command respect as being the leaders in their profession. But, if you find you'd really rather be at ringside looking on, then do get a handler so that your worthy dog gets his deserved recognition in the ring. To own a good dog and win with it is a thrill, so good luck, no matter how you do it.

1 2

3

4

5

Chapter 10

Showing and Judging the Akita

Ever since I started judging dogs in 1961, I never enter a show ring to begin an assignment without thinking back to what the late, great judge Alva Rosenberg told me when we discussed my apprentice judging under his watchful eyes. His most significant observation I find still holds true for me today—that a judge's first and most lasting impression of a dog's temperament and bearing will be made the moment it walks into the ring.

It has always been a source of amazement to me the way so many exhibitors ruin that important first impression of their dog before the judge. So many are guilty of dragging their dogs along behind them, squeezing through the ringside crowds and snapping at people to get out of their way, just to arrive in the ring with a dog whose feet have been stepped on by people pushing to get closer to ringside and whose coat has been ruined by food and cigarette ashes. After all this, the dog is expected to turn on its charm once inside the ring, fascinate the crowds, captivate the judge, and bring home the silverware and ribbons! All this on a day that invariably is either too hot or too cold—or too rainy—not to mention the hours of standing rigidly on a crate, being sprayed in the face and all over their bodies with a grooming substance that doesn't smell or taste too good, and then brushed and trimmed until dry to their handler's satisfaction. Add this to the lengthy bath and grooming session the day before the show and the bumpy ride to the show grounds, and, well, Alva Rosenberg had a point! Any dog that can strut into the ring after what they regard as a 48-hour torture treatment *DOES* have to have an excellent disposition and a regal bearing. How fortunate we are that so many of our Akitas do have such marvelous temperaments in spite of our grooming rituals!

There is no reason an exhibitor cannot allow sufficient time to get to ringside with a few minutes to spare, in order to wait calmly somewhere near the entrance to the ring. They need only walk directly ahead of the dog, politely asking the people along the way to step aside with a simple statement to the effect that there is a "dog coming through." It works. I have seen spectators promptly step aside, not only to oblige this simple request when politely stated, but also to observe the beauty of the show dog passing by. Those who prefer to carry their dogs, and know how to do it without disturbing the coat, can make the same request for the same result.

The short waiting period at ringside also allows time for the dog to gain his footing and perspective and gives the exhibitor time to get his armband on securely so it won't drop down the arm and onto the dog's head during the first sprint around the ring. These few spare moments will also allow a great deal of the "nervousness" that travels down the lead to your dog to disappear as the realization that you have arrived at your class on time occurs to you, and you and your dog can both relax.

ENTERING THE RING

When the ring steward calls out the numbers for your class, there is no need for you to try to be first in the ring. There is no prize for being first. If you are new at the game, you would do well to get behind a more experienced exhibitor or professional handler where you can observe and perhaps learn something about ring behavior. The judge will be well aware of your presence in the ring when they make a small dot or a small check mark in their judge's book, as you enter. The judge must also mark all absentees before starting to evaluate the class, so you can be sure no one will be overlooked as they "count noses."

Simply enter the ring as quickly and calmly as possible with your dog on a loose lead, and at the first opportunity make sure you show your armband to the judge. Then take a position in the line-up already forming in the ring (usually at the opposite side from the judge's table). Set your dog up in the show pose so that once the judge has checked in all the dogs in the class he will have an immediate impression of the outline of your dog in show stance. This is also referred to as "stacking" your dog.

The judge will then go up and down the line of dogs in order to compare one outline with another, while getting an idea of the symmetry and balance of each profile. This is the time when you should see that your dog maintains the show stance. Don't be nervously brushing your dog, constantly adjusting his feet, tilting his head, primping his tail, etc. All of this should have been done while the judge was walking down the line with his eyes on the other dogs in the class.

By the time the judge gets to your dog it should be standing as still as a statue, with your hands off it if at all possible. Far too many exhibitors handle show dogs as if they were puppets with strings attached to all the moving parts. They are constantly pushing it in place, prodding it to the desired angle for the judge to see, placing the head and tail and feet according to their idea of perfection. More often than not their fingers are covering the dog's muzzle or they are employing their thumbs to straighten out a topline, or using a finger to tilt a tail to the proper angle. Repeatedly moving a dog's feet tends to make the judge believe the dog can't stand correctly by itself. If a dog is standing incorrectly the judge might assume that it just happened to be standing incorrectly at that moment and that the exhibitor couldn't imagine such a thing and therefore never noticed it!

Fussing over a dog only calls attention to the fact that the exhibitor either has to do a lot to make the dog look good or is a rank amateur and is nervously mishandling the dog. A free, natural stance, even when a little "off base," is still more appealing to the judge than a dog presented with all four feet barely touching the ground. All Akitas are beautiful on their own and unnecessary handling can only be regarded as a distraction, not as indulgence on the part of the exhibitor. Do not get the mistaken idea that if the judge thinks you are working hard with your dog you deserve to win.

MOVE THEM OUT

Once the judge has compared the outlines (or profiles) of each dog he will ask the exhibitors to move the dogs around the ring so that he might observe the dogs in action. This usually means two complete circles of the ring, depending on the size of the ring and the number of dogs competing in it. This is the time when the judge must determine whether the dog is moving properly or if it is limping or lame. The judge will check out the dog for proper gait and observe if the dog is moving freely on its own—not strung up on the end of a lead with the handler holding the head high.

Be careful not to hamper your dog in any way in the limited time and space you have to show the judge how your dog moves. This means

gaiting on a loose lead. Move next to your dog at a safe distance to the side so that you do not step on it going around corners or pull it off balance on turns. You must also keep in mind that you should not get too close to the dog ahead of you and that you must keep far enough ahead of the dog behind you so that your dog doesn't get spooked—or that you don't break the gait.

Once the judge has had the time to observe each dog in motion, the signal will be given to one person to stop at a specific spot in the ring, forming the line-up for closer inspection of each

Ch. Great River's Tana Kuma with handler Bob Fontano at the 1979 Staten Island Kennel Club show.

Captions for pages 122-123.
1. Poetry in motion. . .Ch. Tobe's Peking Jumbo, C.D., gives a good show of doing what comes naturally. Bred and owned by Tobe Kennels, Jumbo was #1 Akita in 1980 and is shown in action on the way to winning Best of Breed at the 1981 Westminster Kennel Club show. 2. Best Brace in Show at the 1979 Newton Kennel Club show was this beautifully marked pair of Akitas, bred, owned, and shown by Beverly Bonadonna, Tobe Kennels, Branchville, New Jersey.

121

NEWTON K.C.
SEPTEMBER 1, 1979
BEST
IN
SHOW
BRACE

dog individually. At the judge's discretion the individual evaluation can be done either in place or on a small table placed in the ring. Whether the judge chooses to evaluate each dog on the ground or on a table, the judge must go over the dog completely in order to evaluate it in accordance with the Standard for the breed.

JUDGING THE HEAD

As the judge approaches your dog, he will get his first close look at the expression. The judge will want to see the dark eye, will check the stop, the muzzle, the occiput, ear leather and set, and the head in its entirety for excellence. During this examination the exhibitor must make sure the dog remains perfectly still and in correct show stance. Since the dangers of the various virus infections and contagious diseases that can be passed from dog to dog at the shows has been made known to us, it is hoped the judge will ask that you show them your dog's bite. It is permissible, however, for the judge to open the dog's mouth to check out the bite, especially if the judge has reason to believe there is a fault. The judge will also evaluate the head from straight on as well as in profile.

Next the neck and shoulders will be checked. The judge will lift up the ears to see just how long the neck really is and how well placed the shoulders are. Shoulders play an important part in the proper placement of the front legs and pasterns. Running his hands down the front leg, the judge will go all the way to the foot, picking it up and checking the foot pads and nails, and paying particular notice to whether the dog puts its foot down correctly in place when released.

The judge will check the brisket and the tuck-up as well as the topline. At this point, with his hands going over the dog, the judge can determine the proper texture of the coat and the general weight of the dog. Tail structure and carriage are to be considered as well. Judging the hindquarters should prove the dog's legs are sturdy and well placed and strong enough to provide the strength for proper gait and movement. This is also the time when the judge will check to see that on the male dog both testicles are present and descended.

Once the judge has gone over the dog completely he will usually take a step or two away from the dog to give it a final over-all view, keeping a complete picture of it in his mind to make the comparison with the dog he has judged just before and will judge after yours. This is the time you must still keep your dog "on his toes" so that when the judge glances ahead or behind, your dog is not sitting down, chasing butterflies, or lifting his leg on the number markers. Remember, training is done at home—*performance* is required in the show ring at all times.

INDIVIDUAL GAITING

Once the judge has gone over each dog individually, he will go to the end of the ring and ask each handler to gait his dog. It is important at this point to pay strict attention to the judge's instructions as to how this is to be done. Some judges require the "T" formation, others the half-triangle. Further observation of your dog may bring a request for you to repeat the pattern, especially if your dog did not show well during the first trip. It is important that you hear whether the judge wants you to repeat the entire exercise or merely to gait your dog "down and back" this time.

When each dog has been gaited, the judge will want a last look at all of them lined up together before making his final decisions. Usually the procedure will be to once again present the left side of your dog as the judge weaves in and out of the line to check once more the fronts or rears or other individual points of comparison. Some dogs may be asked to gait a third time or to gait side by side with one of the other dogs should the judge want to "break a tie" as to which dog is the better mover. Because such deciding factors cannot be predicted or anticipated, it is necessary for the handler to always be ready to oblige once the request is given by the judge.

After the decisions are made, the judge will point to his four placements and those four will set their dogs up in front of the designated number markers on the side of the ring. Be ready at this point to show the numbers on your armband so that the judge can mark his judge's book. The judge then will present the winners with the appropriate color ribbons and any trophies won, and you may leave the ring.

Contrary to popular opinion it is not necessary or even correct to thank the judge for the ribbon. It is to be assumed that the dog *deserved* the ribbon or the judge would not have awarded it. Handing you the ribbon is part of the procedure and does not warrant a thank-you. The club, not the judge, is responsible for the donation of the trophies. It is not called for that the exhibitor speak to the judge, but if the win is significant enough so that you feel compelled to say *some-*

thing, a simple and not overly exuberant "I'm so pleased that you like my dog," or something similar is still more than is necessary.

The "thank-you" for the ribbon has on occasion become what some exhibitors like to think of as a "weapon." At ringside you can sometimes hear words to the effect that, "I didn't even thank him for that rotten red ribbon!" As if the judge had even noticed! However, it *is* expected that you take with you from the ring a ribbon of *any color*. To throw it on the ground or leave it behind in the ring so that the steward is obliged to call you back into the ring for the judge to hand it to you again is most unsportsman-like. You must play the game according to the rules. Your entry fee is to obtain the opinion of your dog by the judge. You must take the opinion and behave accordingly. If you do not like it, do not give them another entry, but you owe the judge the courtesy of respect for that title.

After this judging procedure is followed in the five classes for dogs, and Winners Dog and Reserve Winners Dog have been determined, the bitches are judged in this same manner. After Winners Bitch and Reserve Winners Bitch awards have been made, the Best of Breed judging follows. Class procedures here are discussed elsewhere in this chapter. Once the judge has completed his assignment and signed his judge's book, it is permissible to request any photographs that you may wish to have taken of your wins. At this time it is also permissible to ask the judge his motives in his judging of *your* dog. If you wish to, it should be done in a polite and calm manner. It must be remembered that the judge is not going to make comparisons rating one dog against another, but can, if he chooses, give a brief explanation as to how he evaluated your dog.

It is helpful to remember that "no one wins them all." You will win some and lose some no matter how good your dog is. Judges are human and, while no one is perfect, they have earned the title of "judge" for some mighty good reasons. Try to recall that this is a sport and it should be fun—tomorrow is another day.

THE GAMES PEOPLE PLAY

If you are new to the game of dog-show exhibiting there are a few things you should know about, such as how to protect yourself and your dog so that you do not get too discouraged and disillusioned right at the start.

There may be an occasion where your dog is winning a great deal and jealousy will arise from others competing in the ring with you. It has been known that some of these bad sports will try to get between you and the judge so the judge cannot see your dog at his best. Others may try stepping on your dog, breaking his gait so that he cannot be adequately judged, bringing bitches in season into the ring, throwing bait around to distract your dog, and so on. Needless to say, most judges are aware of these nasty tricks people play and will not tolerate them. Just be on your guard. Do not leave your dog alone or leave it in the care of others. Thefts have been known at dog shows, as well as poisoning and physical abuse. Watch your dog at all times, and be safe rather than sorry.

Captions for pages 126-127.
1. Ch. KoFuKu-No's Kuma Oso of Tormod, bred by Rusty Cunningham Short and pictured here winning at a California show in 1976. 2. Ch. Jamel's Terriaki is pictured winning a 4-point major from the Puppy Class at the 1976 Beverly Hills Kennel Club. Terriaki was co-bred and owned by Jackie and Mel Towbin and Barbara Hampton of Las Vegas, Nevada. The sire was Ch. Wanchan's Akagumo ex Ch. Jamel's Oso Cute. 3. Bar-BJ's The Swinger is pictured winning at a 1979 show from the Puppy Class under judge Connie Bosold. The Swinger is owner-handled by Janne L. Radcliffe-Tuck of Estes Park, Colorado. 4. Ch. Tobe's Obi-Wan Kenobi, C.D., and Ch. Tobe's Princess Leia Organa, C.D., getting ready to show as a brace. This multiple Best-In-Show-winning Akita Brace is owned and bred by Beverly and Tom Bonadonna, Tobe Kennels, Branchville, New Jersey.

1

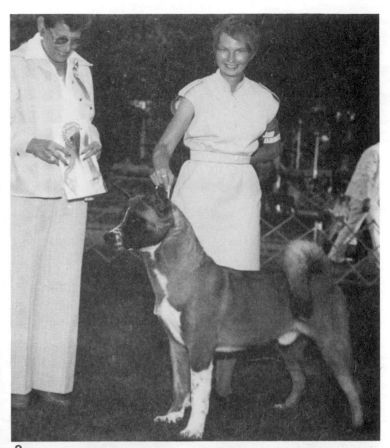

2   3

4

127

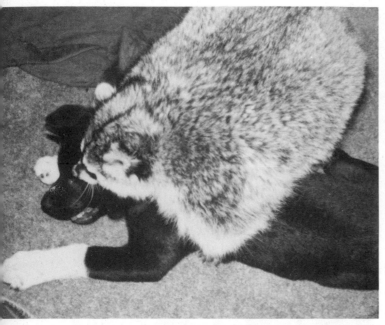

Top, left. Ninja and her best friend, a 50 pound raccoon. Both owned and enjoyed by Joseph and Pat Castronova of Denver, Colorado. **Top, right.** "Bug off!" Frerose's Tugger the Slugger and Charlie (the cat) seem to be having some sort of a standoff. Owned by Frederick Duane, Shohola, Pennsylvania. **Bottom.** Friend or foe? Twelve-week-old Polyanna's The Lady in Black doesn't seem too sure when she first meets Ginger. Owned by the J. A. Spierings of Lower Burrell, Pennsylvania.

Ch. KoFuKu-No's Yuki Ashi, photographed winning in 1975 with his breeder Rusty Cunningham Short, Burbank, California.

Am. and Can. Ch. Kim-Sai's Buster of Frerose, the # 1 Akita in Canada for 1982, is pictured winning under judge Glen Sommers at the 1978 Lackawanna Kennel Club show. Owned by Frederick Duane.

Ch. Echols Riki Kuma is pictured winning on the way to championship in 1975 under Thomas Gateley. Nancy Graulich owner-handled her dog to this win.

Ch. Krug Tobe's The Force of Elan. "Kristy" is pictured at seven months of age winning a four-point major from the Puppy Class at this 1981 show, owner-handled by Elaine Andiorio of Bernardsville, New Jersey. The sire was Ch. Tobe's Obi-Wan Kenobi, C.D., ex Ch. Okami's Kori of Krug.

Ch. Echols Ichi Ban Saki, owner-handled by L. Hickman to this win under judge Virginia Hampton.

Ch. Kikko Hime No Bar-BJ, owned by Tom Groves and Sherry Walsh, is pictured winning Best in Match, all-breed, at three months of age. Bred by Bar-BJ Akitas in 1977, the sire was Ch. Va-Guas Jamel the Mean Machine ex Ch. Sakusaku's Perfect Pearl.

Ch. Hiryu No Kogo-Go, C.D., is pictured winning Best of Breed under Japanese judge Hideo Ito, with breeder-handler Chandra Sargent of Sun Valley, California. Co-owned by Linda J. Nichols and Chandra Sargent. The sire was Jap. Gr. Ch. Rikimaru-Go ex Am. Ch. Forral's Party Doll.

A 1980 Group win for Ch. Tobe's Peking Jumbo, C.D. the #1 Akita in the United States for that year. Owner-handled by Beverly Bonadonna, Tobe Kennels, Branchville, New Jersey.

Right: Breed judging at the 1981 Westminster Kennel Club Show in New York City. **Below:** One of the early Champions in the breed was Ch. Shori's Daisan Banko Maru, owned by M. Keen of Marlborough, Connecticut, and pictured winning at a show in 1974.

Lijo's Big Jake, C.D., working on his C.D.X. exercises for the winter trials. Jake earned his C.D. at seven months of age. Owned by James and Susan White of Columbia, Maryland, the breeder was Lorea T. Wright.

Hot's Montana San, C.D.X., going through her paces on the way to her title. Owned by Andre Grasso, Garrison, New York.

Left: Ch. Tobe's Obi-Wan Kenobi, C.D., multiple breed winner and group placer. He was # 6 Akita in 1979, # 3 Akita in Obedience rating in 1979, and a member of the world's only multiple Best in Show Akita Brace. Owned by Bev and Tom Bonadonna, Branchville, New Jersey. Photo by the late Alton Anderson.
Below: Ch. Tamarlane's Sakurajima, C.D., owned by Bartley S. Shaw of Wheat Ridge, Colorado.

Am. and Can. Ch. Frerose's Mean Machine, Am. and Can. C.D., pictured winning the Breed at the 1977 Dan Emmett Kennel Club show. Owned by Frederick Duane, Frerose Kennels, Shohola, Pennsylvania. Mean Machine was the first American and Canadian champion to be first American and Canadian C.D. title holder also.

Another Working Group win as Best Brace for the Tobe Kennels' remarkable C.D. champions, Tobe's Obi-Wan Kenobi and Tobe's Princess Leia Organa. Bred, owned, and shown by Beverly Bonadonna, Branchville, New Jersey.

142

Ch. Mill Creek Bozo Jo, C.D., and Krug's Snowfire, owned by Howard and Judith Opel, Bearhold Akitas, Beltsville, Maryland.

Lijo's Big Jake, C.D., enjoys a romp with five-year-old Elizabeth White. Jake earned his C.D. just as he reached seven months of age, and at eleven months (in this photo) was working for his C.D.X. Bred by Lorea Wright, the owners are James and Susan White. The sire was Ch. Lijo's Grizzly ex Lijo's Haiku.

Ch. Eljay's Kibo No Zoge Hoshi, or "Hope," winning under judge Marie Moore at a 1982 show. Owned by Lorraine Miller, Eljay's Akitas, in Westminster, Maryland, the sire was Lijo's Zoge Hoshi Go ex Ch. Marjo's Tsugi Hagi Hagikko. Handled for owner by Marian Zak.

CHILDREN IN THE SHOW RING

No one is more approving than I of children learning to love and to care for animals. It is beautiful to see a child and an animal sharing complete rapport and companionship or performing as a team in the show ring. Those of us who have been around dog shows for any length of time have all been witness to some remarkable performances by children and their dogs. Junior Showmanship is one example; dogs caring for or standing guard over babies and infants is another example.

However, there is nothing "cute" about a child being allowed to handle a dog where both the welfare of the child and the general public are in danger. Dogs have been known to pull children to the ground with resulting injury to either child or dog, or both. I have seen frightened children let go of leashes or become tangled up in them in the middle of dog fights that left all three participants injured.

If a child shows the natural desire to exhibit a dog after having attended handling classes where they are taught how to properly show a dog, they must also be taught ring procedure. It is not fair to expect other exhibitors to show patience while a judge or the steward informs the child where to stand or waits for them to gait the dog several times before they do it in the formation requested. Lack of knowledge or repeated requests delay the judging, look bad to the ringside crowds, and certainly don't make the dog look good.

If necessary, parents might stay after the dog-show judging and actually train the child in an empty ring. Parents should also sit ringside with the children to explain the judging procedures to them so they will know what to expect when they enter the ring. Many match show appearances should precede any appearance in a point show ring also. Certainly no parent could possibly expect a judge to give them a win just because they are a cute pair—even though they are!

BAITING

No matter how one feels about baiting a dog in the ring, we must acknowledge that almost everyone at one time or another has been guilty of it. Certain breeds are particularly responsive to it, while others show little or no interest with so much going on all around them.

There is no denying that baiting can be an aid to basic training. But in the show ring some judges consider it an indication that the training of the dog for the show ring is not yet complete. It becomes obvious to the judge that the dog still needs an incentive to respond to what other dogs are doing in the name of performance and showmanship.

Frequently, squeaky toys will work as well. Using conversation and pet nicknames in trying to encourage the dog is inappropriate.

DOUBLE HANDLING

You can be sure the competent judge becomes aware of any double-handling to which some of the more desperate exhibitors may resort.

Double-handling is both distracting and frowned upon by the American Kennel Club. Nonetheless, some owners go to all sorts of ridiculous lengths to get their apathetic dogs to perform in the ring. They hide behind trees or posts at ringside or may lurk behind the ringside crowd until the exact moment when the judge is looking at or gaiting their dog and then pop out in full view perhaps emitting some familiar whistle or noise or wave a hat or whatever in hopes that the dog will suddenly become alert and express a bit of animation.

Don't be guilty of double-handling. The day may come when you finally have a great show dog, but the reputation of an owner guilty of double handling lives on forever! You'll be accused of the same shady practices and your new show dog is apt to suffer for it.

APPLAUSE, APPLAUSE!

Another "put-on" by some of our less secure exhibitors is the practice of bringing their own cheering section to applaud vigorously every time the judge happens to cast an eye on their dog.

The judge is concentrating on what he is doing and will not pay attention to this or will not be influenced by the cliques set up by those trying to push their dogs to a win, supposedly by popular approval. The most justified occasions for applause are during a Parade of Champions, during the gaiting of an entire Specialty Best of Breed Class or during the judging awards for Stud Dog, Brood Bitch, and Veterans Class. At these thrilling moments the tribute of spontaneous applause—and the many tears—are understandable and well received, but to try to prompt a win or stir up interest in a particular dog during the normal course of class judging is amateurish.

If you have ever observed this practice, you will notice that the dogs being applauded are sometimes the poorest specimens whose owners seem to subconsciously realize they cannot win under normal conditions.

SINS WHEN SHOWING DOGS

* DON'T forget to exercise your dog before entering the ring. Do it before grooming if you are afraid the dog will get wet or dirty after getting off the grooming table.

* DON'T ever take a dog into the show ring that isn't groomed the very best you know how.

* DON'T take a dog into the ring if you have any indication it is sick or not *completely* recovered from a communicable disease.

* DON'T drag the dog around the ring on a tight lead that destroys its proud carriage or disposition or chances of becoming a show dog in the future if not that particular day.

* DON'T talk to the judge in the ring. Watch the judge closely and follow instructions carefully. Don't speak to those at ringside, or to your dog in an excessive or loud manner.

* DON'T strike or in any way abuse your dog before, during, or after the judging. The time and place for training and discipline is at home, not in public. Always use the reward system, not punishment, for the most successful method of training a dog.

* DON'T be a bad loser. You can't win 'em all, so if you win today, be gracious; if you lose, be happy for the dog who won.

* DON'T shove your dog in a crate or leave him on the bench alone until it's time to leave the show grounds. A drink of water or something to eat and a little companionship will go a long way toward making dog shows more enjoyable for him so that he will show even better the next time.

STATISTICS AND THE PHILLIPS SYSTEM

As Akitas continued to grow in popularity it was only natural that the entries at the dog shows continued to swell and competition was keen. The larger the entries, the more coveted the wins. In 1956 when Irene Phillips created her Phillips System of evaluating show dogs, Akita fanciers fell right in line with her point system and began keeping records of their dogs'

wins to compare them not only with other Akitas, but with other Working dogs, and even other dogs of all breeds.

At the beginning of the 1980's, a quarter of a century later, dog fanciers are still keeping score on the top winners in the breeds, and while many a "system" of making it to the top of a winner's list has been recorded and publicized, there is no denying that they are all based on the most popular, fairest, and most recognized of all systems for naming the top winning dogs in the country.

True, records are made to be broken, and we can all look forward to the day when another magnificent Akita will come on the show scene and cut a path through the crowds of show dogs to triumph as the newest top-winning dog in our breed. There is always room for another great dog to bring additional glory to the Akita and just as naturally as night follows day, we all hope that extra special specimen will be our own.

Captions for pages 148-149.
1. Best in Match at a recent Akita Club of Long Island show was three-month-old Tobe's Gentle Ben. Ben was bred and handled by Beverly Bonadonna, Tobe Kennels, to this win under judge Will Brumby. 2. Ounce of Bounce wins Best of Breed at a Fun Match show. Owned by Pat Castronova of Denver, Colorado. 3. Ch. O'B.J. Big Son of Sachmo is pictured winning the Working Group at the 1982 Griffen Kennel Club show. Owner-bred by Bill and B. J. Andrews of Asheville, North Carolina. 4. Eight-month-old Gaylee's Arctic Fury of Northland, owned by Loren Egland of Rochester, Minnesota. 5. Ch. Cee-Jay's Yukon is pictured going Best in Match at the Great Lakes Akita Club in 1981. Owner-handled by Loren Egland of Rochester, Minnesota. 6. Ch. O'BJ Kye Kye-Go of E Oka moves out to show one of the reasons she was rated in the Top Five bitches in 1982 and Number One bitch in 1983. Owned by Linda Henson and Peggy Brereton.

1

2

3

4

5

6

Chapter 11

The Akita in Obedience

Dog shows and conformation classes had a tremendous head start on obedience in the United States. It was in 1933 that the first obedience tests were held in Mount Kisco, New York. Mrs. Helene Whitehouse Walker inaugurated these initial all-breed obedience tests which she had brought from England. Along with Blanche Saunders, her kennel maid at that time, she was responsible for the staging of the first four obedience tests held in the United States.

Obedience training and tests for dogs were an immediate success from the moment those first 150 spectators saw the dogs go through their paces.

Mrs. Walker was instrumental in getting the American Kennel Club to recognize and even sponsor the obedience trials at their dog shows, and her discussions with Charles T. Inglee (then the vice president of the AKC) ultimately led to their recognition. In 1935 she wrote the first published booklet on the subject, called simply *Obedience Tests*. These tests were eventually incorporated into the rules of the AKC obedience requirements in March 1936. It developed into a twenty-two page booklet that served as a manual for judges, handlers, and the show-giving clubs. The larger version was called *Regulations and Standards for Obedience Test Field Trials*.

Mrs. Walker, Josef Weber (another well-known dog trainer), and Miss Saunders added certain refinements, basic procedures, and exercises, and these were published in the April 1936 issue of the *American Kennel Gazette*.

On June 13 of that same year, the North Westchester Kennel Club held the first AKC-licensed obedience test in conjunction with their all-breed show. There were twelve entries for judge Mrs. Wheeler H. Page. The exercises for Novice and Open classes remain virtually unchanged today—half a century later. Only Tracking Dog and Tracking Dog Excellent have been added in the intervening years.

By June of 1939, the American Kennel Club realized that obedience was here to stay and saw the need for an advisory committee. One was established and chaired by Donald Fordyce, with enthusiastic members from all parts of the country willing to serve on it. George Foley of Pennsylvania was on the board. He was one of the most important of all men in the fancy, being superintendent of most of the dog shows on the eastern seaboard. Mrs. Radcliff Farley, also of Pennsylvania, was on the committee, along with Miss Aurelia Tremaine of Massachusetts, Samuel Blick of Maryland, and Frank Grant of Ohio, as well as Josef Weber and Mrs. Walker.

A little of the emphasis on the dog obedience was diverted with the outbreak of World War II, when talk switched to the topic of dogs serving in defense of their country. As soon as peace was declared, however, interest in obedience reached new heights. In 1946, the American Kennel Club called for another obedience advisory committee, this time headed by John C. Neff. This committee included Blanche Saunders, Clarence Pfaffenberger, Theodore Kapnek, L. Wilson Davis, Howard P. Claussen, Elliott Blackiston, Oscar Franzen, and Clyde Henderson.

Under their leadership, the obedience booklet grew to forty-three pages. Rules and regulations were even more standardized than before, and there was the addition of the requirements for the Tracking Dog title.

In 1971, an obedience department was established at the American Kennel Club offices to keep pace with the growth of the sport and to review and give guidance to show-giving clubs. Judge Richard D'Ambrisi was the director until his untimely death in 1973, at which time his duties were assumed by James E. Dearinger, along with his two special consultants, L. Wilson Davis for Tracking and Reverend Thomas O'Connor for Handicapped Handlers.

The members of the 1973 committee were Thomas Knott of Maryland, Edward Anderson of Pennsylvania, Jack Ward of Virginia, Lucy Neeb of Louisiana, William Phillips of California, James Falkner of Texas, Mary Lee Whiting of Minnesota, and Robert Self (co-publisher of the important *Front and Finish* obedience newspaper) of Illinois.

While the committee functions continuously, meetings of the board are tentatively held every other year unless a specific function or obedience question arises, in which case a special meeting is called.

During the 1975 session, the committee held discussions on several old and new aspects of the obedience world. In addition to their own ever-increasing responsibilities to the fancy, they discussed seminars and educational symposiums, the licensing of tracking clubs, a booklet with suggested guidelines for obedience judges, Schutzhund training, and the aspects of a Utility Excellent Class degree.

Through the efforts of succeeding advisory committee members, the future of the sport has been insured, as well as the continuing emphasis on the working abilities for which dogs were originally bred. Obedience work also provides novices an opportunity to train and to handle their dogs in an atmosphere that provides maximum pleasure at minimum expense—which is precisely what Mrs. Walker and Blanche Saunders intended.

When the advisory committee met in December 1980, many of the familiar names were among those listed as attending and continuing to serve the obedience exhibitors. James E. Dearinger, James C. Falkner, Rev. Thomas V. O'Connor, Robert T. Self, John S. Ward, Howard E. Cross, Helen F. Phillips, Samuel W. Kodis, George S. Pugh, Thomas Knott, and Mrs. Esme Treen were present and accounted for.

As we look back on a half century of obedience trials, we can only surmise that the pioneers—Mrs. Helene Whitehouse Walker and Blanche Saunders—are proud of the progress made in the obedience rings, founded on their original ideas and enthusiasm. Therefore, everyone was delighted when Mrs. Walker received the 1983 Gaines Obedience Fido Award. She was honored for her contribution to the dog fancy and for 50 years of interest in the obedience field. The award was presented to her by Mr. Steve Willett, Director of Professional Services for Gaines at their Dog Care Center in White Plains, New York. The citation read in part, ". . . for outstanding service and contributions to the advancement of obedience training and competition."

Mrs. Walker also received a framed engraved scroll presented to her by William Stifel, president of the American Kennel Club.

It was noted that Mrs. Walker and Blanche Saunders drove more than 10,000 miles in 1937 in a car and trailer giving exhibitions in obedience all across the country. It is interesting, too, that in that year 95 dogs received their Companion Dog titles, and by 1982 more than 8,000 dogs had earned this title. Catherine Riley, a protege of the late Blanche Saunders, arranged the affair which culminated in a standing ovation for Mrs. Walker, which was both fitting and proper!

THE OBEDIENCE RATING SYSTEMS

Just as the Phillips System mushroomed out of the world of show dogs, it was almost inevitable that a "system" or "systems" to measure the successes of obedience dogs would become a reality.

By 1974, Nancy Shuman and Lynn Frosch had established the "Shuman System" of recording the Top Ten All Breed Obedience Dogs in the country. They also listed the Top four in every breed, if each dog had accumulated a total of fifty or more points according to their requirements. Points were accrued on a scale based on qualifying scores from 170 and up. Eventually Akitas were to place among the winners.

AKITAS IN THE DELANEY SYSTEM

In 1975 *Front and Finish, The Dog Trainer's News* published an obedience rating system in their newspaper compiled by Kent Delaney to evaluate and score the various obedience dogs which had competed during the previous year. This system was devised primarily to measure the significance of a win made over a few dogs against those made over many dogs.

Points were given for both High in Trial or Class Placements, as recorded and published in the *American Kennel Gazette* magazine. The dog that scores highest in the trial receives a point for each dog in competition, and first place winner in each class receives a point for each dog in the class. The dog placing second receives a point for each dog in the class less one, third

1

2 **3**

4

5

6

7

place winner a point less two, fourth place winner a point less three.

In 1975 there were four Akitas that qualified for the system within the breed. Number One was S. and C. Balsbaugh's Oyoro Kobi, C.D. Second was Sabaku Kazes Ginghis Khan, owned by G. Leahy; Third was Kazoku No Nikko, owned by W. Nevers; and Fourth was Yuko Mitsus Momo Hime, owned by M. McKenzie.

1976

In 1976 there were seven listed in the Delaney System along with their points. First was Diaruss Hime Kiko of Kiku, 74 points, and owned by D. Duncan. Second was Krugs Friendly Bear of Tobe, 70 points, and owned by B. Bonadonna. Third was Magokoro Kuma Taro, 20 points, owner B. and C. Endo. Four and Five tied with ten points each; they were B. Hinson's Echols Red Delight and M. Hanley and B. Lea's Okki Yubis Snow Jo. Sixth was S. and G. Pinel's Cho Jos Erai Kibo No Skiki with nine points; and Seventh place with eight points went to Inugoyas Kage No Kuma, co-owned by W. and S. Glenn and M. Koplaski.

1978

In 1978 no Akita placed in the Top Ten all-breed or the Top Ten Working Group lists, but three made it in the breed. D. and R. Rutledge's Okamis Rambo Hana Go, C.D., scored 69 points. In second place with 46 points was Yuki Hime Go, owned by R. Sewake; and in third place was Magokoro Kuma Taro, C.D.X., with 12 points.

1979

Almost a full ten rated the breed list in 1979. Saburos Kuma Go earned 68 points. The owner was C. Weatherman. Second was Tada Tamashi No Hinata Tani, 33 points, owned by S. Osborne. Third was Ch. Tobes Obi Wan Kenobi, owned by B. Bonadonna and winner of 23 points. Fourth was Adai Na Kuma, owned by S. Bailey, with eighteen points. Fifth was Ch. Okki Yubis Snow Jo, C.D.X. and T.D. with seventeen points and co-owned by M. Hanley and B. Lea. Sixth place with fourteen points was J. Mitchell's Ch. Charismas Miko Go No K Mikado, also a C.D.X. and T.D. titlist. Seventh place went to Mr. and Mrs. J. Skellington's Akita Tanis Bronco, with nine points. Also a winner of nine points was S. Yost's Freroses Tara Kolbitos. D. and R. Rutledge's Akai Kashi No Aka Tora had eight points.

1980

The decade of the eighties still found no Akitas in the Top Ten all-breed list or Top Ten Working Breeds. But eight Akitas qualified within the breed. First was S. and M. Penel's Shikis Hoshi with 27 points. Second was L. Nichol's Akagumo Akiha, C.D., with 21 points. Third was Remwoods Tiger By The Tail with 20 points and co-owned by T. Duncan, S. Bobowiec and E. Woods. Fourth was S. Yost's Freroses Tara Robita with fourteen points. Number Five was Chojo Miru, owned by R. and S. Engle with eleven points. Sixth was Pashans Watashi Fujin, nine points, and owned by G. Francis. Seventh place went to Ch. Charismas Miko Go No K Mikado, U.D.T., owned by J. Mitchell. Number Eight was Gin Gins Tabi San Go with five points, owned by E. Parker.

1983

By 1983 an Akita had placed in the Top Twenty-five Working Dogs in their points system. At 23rd place was the Ch. Great Rivers Galloping Gourmet, owned by N. Fontano and R. Player. This, of course, made him the Number One dog in the Top Ten Akitas list, followed by Ch. Kakwas Orca, owned by T. Tyler and B.J. Andrews. Third place was B. and B.J. Andrews' Ch. O'BJ Big Son of Sachmo, with B. Loe and R. Shaw's Ch. O'BJ Abaddon of Dune. Number Five went to Ch. Mike Truaxs Royal Tikara Pal, owned by C. Truax. Ch. Hots Mos Barnaby Jones was in Sixth place, owned by J. Dalesslo, and K and K. Baron and W. and B. Littschauager's Blue Maxs Chikara Buichi was Number Seven. The Blaisdel's Ch. Cee Jays Rocky Road of Kibo was in Number Eight spot, followed by R.L. Musisca's Ch. Jakura's Pharfossa Michael in Number Nine position. Number Ten was Ch. Sherisan Keystone of Kintaro, owned by G. Saweikis and L. Hickman.

It is good to see that we are filling the entire Top Ten lists with winning dogs!

THE AKITA IN OBEDIENCE

To say that Akitas take well to obedience training is putting it mildly. While you will occasionally come across a "stubborn" one, or one that is slow to learn, this is the exception to the general rule. As with most dogs, Akitas love to please their owners, and when trained properly they make excellent obedience workers. More and more of them are attaining their titles every year.

THE FIRST U.D. AKITA

The first Utility Dog title holder in the United States was Mexican Champion Imperial Rikimaru-Go. Born on April 23, 1966, his sire was Kinsei Suna Nihon-No Taishi, C.D., also a Mexican champion and obedience dog, and his dam was Nakkusu's Shirobushi.

On April 28, 1968, his owners, Mr. and Mrs. D. McElrath, entered him in a Utility Obedience Class at the San Gabriel Kennel Club show in California. This was the first Akita ever to appear in obedience in the United States. A strikingly beautiful black and white brindle dog, Rikki really did himself proud on all scores. Judge Marian Mason Hodesson of Tucson, Arizona, awarded him a qualifying score of 195 out of the possible 200 points. The McElraths, owners of the Kamakura Akita Kennels, also had other Akitas in obedience, wanting to prove the versatility of their dogs.

By 1983 Akitas were well established in the obedience rings. They had come a long way since 1968. For the year 1982 there were seven outstanding obedience winners that were listed in the Delaney System and published also in *The Akita Review.* These were Uchidas Sashiki, owned by J. Ushida, Number Two was Westwinds Tokai Toki, owned by D. Youngblood, T. Reilly and D. West, Number Three was Kaido De Alicia, owned by C. Siemer. Number Four was Be My Joyful Noise, P. and L. Decelles; Number Five was Kellys Ray Gin Bull of Frerose, owned by H. and E. Kelly and F. Duane; Number Six was Hots Montana San, owned by A. and V. Grasso, and H. and J. Opel's Mill Creek Bozo.

AKITA TRACKING DOG

There was also another Tracking Dog Akita listed in the *American Kennel Gazette* in their June issue. Its name was Golden Sun's Katsuichi-Go, owned by Kathryn Kolski.

By 1983 there were many Akitas earning their titles in all categories and at last the breed was on record with the proof that they are highly motivated toward obedience training with great success.

THE DOG OBEDIENCE CLASSICS

Within the dog fancy there are, of course, opportunities for obedience achievement other than through the various systems.

In March 1976, the Gaines Dog Research Center, located in White Plains, New York, began its sponsorship of the United States Dog Obedience Classic. Founded by the Illini Obedience Association in 1975, the first Classic was held in Chicago.

Gaines' motive in the support of the regional events and the Classic was to emphasize to dog owners, both present and future, their belief that an obedience-trained dog is a better citizen and an asset to any community. Their support was to offer rosettes, trophies, and plaques, as well as prize money, for a series of regional competitions and for the Classic at the year's end. Prize money for the regional awards was almost $3,000, while the Classic prize money was in excess of $5,000. Each year the Classic is held in another area, where a local obedience club plays host to participants from all over the country.

By 1978, when the two-day Classic was held in Los Angeles at the Sports Arena, people from twenty-three states exhibited with an entry well over the 180-dog limit and with dogs going through their paces in eight rings. The top winner in this competition earns the title of Super Dog and, along with other prizes and money, takes home the sterling silver dumbbell trophy.

The Gaines Dog Obedience Classic competition is open to all breeds and owners who qualify and who enjoy the challenge of teamwork with their dogs, no matter how big or small they may be.

Captions for pages 156-157.
1. Krug's Snowfire with mini-dachshund friend, Tinka. Owned by Nanci Opel, Bearhold Kennels, Beltsville, Maryland. 2. Tractable and trainable... the Akita loves to work. Mary's Kumo Djuna De Alicia, owned by Francesca Belanger and Irwin Cohen of New York City, demonstrates how eager she is to please. Photo by James L. McGuire. 3. Kosho Ki's Haru Musume, in harness, at eight months of age. Haru is owned by Betty Hinson of Jonesboro, Arkansas. 4. "Waiting for a bite...." C.D. Crill's three-year-old male, Taisho Osama, goes along on a fishing trip. 5. A breed disqualification... the Dudley nose. 6. Marc Eisenstock's Ichi-Ban photographed at one-and-a-half years of age.

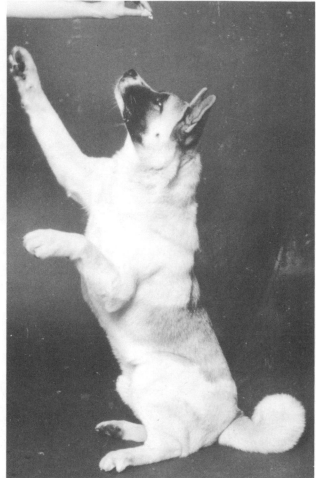

1   2

3

4　5

6

OTHER OBEDIENCE ACTIVITIES

For those interested in the obedience sport, there are many other activities connected with dog training.

There are scent dog seminars, hurdle races, World Series of Dog Obedience in Canada, and the Association of Obedience Clubs and Judges, to name just a few. The best possible way to keep informed of activities on both a national and local scale is by membership in kennel and obedience clubs—and by reading dog magazines and newspapers published by obedience experts and enthusiasts.

Front and Finish, the dog trainers' newspaper, is perhaps the leading publication. It features the Delaney System obedience results, along with many columns of wide interest on all phases of obedience. Current subscription rates may be obtained by writing to H. and S. Publications, Inc., 113 S. Arthur Avenue, Galesburg, Illinois 61401. A. J. Jarler and Robert T. Self are co-editors of this most worthy and informative publication.

UNDERSTANDING AN OBEDIENCE TRIAL

For those interested in attending a trial, it is suggested they read a booklet entitled, "How To Understand and Enjoy an Obedience Trial," available free of charge from the Ralston Purina Company, Checkerboard Square, St. Louis, Missouri 63188.

The American Kennel Club publishes the Obedience Regulations booklet and offers it free of charge when single copies are requested. A check or money order for fifteen cents per copy is required when ordering in quantities for clubs or organizations. Anyone thinking about becoming active in obedience training should read this booklet before joining an obedience club.

TO TRAIN OR NOT TO TRAIN

There are those obedience buffs who will tell you that the Akita, or any other large breed, must be obedience trained. This is very true! Any large dog needs to be kept under control at all times and the best way to establish and set this pattern is through obedience training. The high intelligence in the Akita can make training an enjoyable and rewarding experience, so why not go for it? If you are going to go for a degree, there will always be that doubt lingering in the back of your mind as to whether or not your dog will or won't perform in the ring for the test, but it will still be great fun for those of us who love a challenge.

More and more Akitas are receiving their degrees, and more and more training methods and devoted owners are succeeding where others have failed, proving that it can be done. While it is not advisable to force a dog into working toward a degree, basic training for it will pay off in general good manners if nothing else. If the natural ability is there you may wish to go on to higher "degrees" to give your dog the opportunity to display his natural desire to please his owner.

TRAINING YOUR DOG

While the American Kennel Club will gladly send along booklets and information regarding rules and regulations for competition at the shows, you must be prepared to start basic training with your dog long before you start thinking about entering obedience trials. There are few things in the world a dog would rather do than please his master; therefore, obedience training—even the learning of his name—will be a pleasure for your dog. If taught correctly, it will certainly make him a much nicer animal to live with the rest of his life.

EARLY TRAINING AT HOME

Some breeders believe in starting the training as early as two weeks of age. Repeating the puppy's name and encouraging the puppy to come when called is a good start, as long as you don't expect too much too soon. Some recommend placing a narrow ribbon around the puppy's neck to get him used to the feel of what will later be a collar and leash. The puppy can play with it and learn the pressure of the pull on his neck before he is actually expected to respond to it.

If you intend to show your puppy, there are other formalities which you can observe as early as four weeks of age that will help later on. One of the most important points is setting him up on a table in show stance while repeating "stand" and "stay" commands. If this is repeated gently several times a day, it can be handled like a game. And don't forget the lavish praise when the dog obeys!

WHEN TO START FORMAL TRAINING

Official training should not start until the puppy is about six months of age unless it shows a natural tendency toward learning very early. Most obedience trainers will not take dogs in their classes much before this age. As the puppy grows, however, you can certainly get him used to his name, to coming when called, and to the meaning of words like "no," and "come," and other basic commands. Repetition and patience are the keys to success since most puppies are not ready for a wide range of words in their rather limited attention span. If your dog is to be a show dog, it would be wise to concentrate on the "stand" and "stay" commands early in the game.

THE REWARD METHOD

The only acceptable kind of training is the kindness-and-reward method which will build a strong bond between dog and trainer. Try to establish respect and attention, not fear of punishment. Give each command, preceded by the dog's name, and make it stick. Do not move on to another command or lesson until the first one is mastered. At first, train where there are no distractions, and never when the dog is tired or right after eating. When interest wanes, quit until another session later in the day. Two or three sessions a day with a bright dog, increasing the time from, say, five minutes to fifteen minutes might be right. Each dog is different, and you must establish and set your own schedule according to your own dog's learning ability.

WHAT YOU NEED TO START TRAINING

The soft nylon show leads available at all pet stores are best for early training. Later, a choke chain may be used. Let the puppy play with the lead or even carry it around when you first put it on. Too much pressure pulling at the end of a lead is likely to get him off to a bad start.

FORMAL SCHOOL TRAINING

The time will come when your dog is ready to join obedience classes to work along with other dogs amid outside distractions.

The yellow pages of your telephone book can lead you to dog training schools or classes for this official training, or your local dog club can tell you where classes are being held at dog training schools or adult education sessions. Usually the lessons are moderately priced, and you should start making inquiries when the puppy is about four months of age so you will be ready for the start of the next classes.

If you intend to show your dog, training *yourself* along with the dog will benefit both of you.

OBEDIENCE DEGREES

Several obedience titles are recognized by the American Kennel Club. Dogs may earn these through a process of completed exercises. The Companion Dog, or C.D. degree, is divided into three classes: Novice, Open and Utility, with a total score of 200 points. After a dog has qualified with a score of at least 170 points, it has earned the right to have included the letters C.D. after its name, and is eligible to compete in Open Class competition and earn a Companion Dog Excellent degree, or C.D.X. After qualify-

Captions for pages 160-161.
1. Tobe's Empress Ginger and friend Kristy Clark at the Tobe Kennels of Bev and Tom Bonadonna in Branchville, New Jersey. A perfect example of the guardian instincts and love of children most all of our Akitas have. 2. Stephanie Johnson is defending herself from the playful puppies of the Wotan Kennels. 3. Two young ladies with two young puppies. . .these from the Akita lines of Lillian Koehler, Hatboro, Pennsylvania. 4. Stephanie Johnson shares a bed with her Akita puppy pal at the Wotan Kennels. 5. Yushosha No Atamakabu pictured at seven months of age with his charge, one-year-old Jolene Marie Clark. Parents and breeders are Tom and Judy Clark of Edmonds, Washington. The sire of Yushosha was Am. and Can. Ch. Rising Sun's Chiisai Cha Kuma out of Am. and Can. Ch. Asahi Yama No Chiisai Takara. This charming photograph was taken on Jolene's first birthday, May 31, 1983.

1

2

3 4

Two-year-old Jessica, on rehearsal for becoming a search and rescue dog for Dogs East, Inc., the non-profit organization trained to find lost persons. Bred by Virginia M. Jure, she is owned by James and Susan White. Her sire was Ch. Lijo's Grizzly ex Bru-Marc Betsy Ross.

ing in three shows for this title, it may compete for the Utility Dog title, or U.D. Also, Tracking Dog and Tracking Dog Excellent titles may be earned, the requirements for which may be obtained from the American Kennel Club.

OBEDIENCE TRIAL CHAMPIONSHIPS

The Board of Directors of the American Kennel Club approved Obedience Trial Championships titles in July 1977. Points for these championship titles are recorded only for those dogs that have earned the U.D. title. Any dog that has been awarded the title of Obedience Trial Champion may continue to compete. Dogs that complete requirements receive an Obedience Trial Championship Certificate from the American Kennel Club and are permitted the use of the letters O.T.Ch. preceding their name.

There is great satisfaction for both the owner and dog in earning those titles, and when considering such training for your dog, you would do well to recall St. Mathilde's Prayer:

O, God,
Give unto me by grace
that obedience which thou hast
given to my little dog
by nature.

Check Points for Obedience Competitors

• Do your training and have your lessons down pat before entering the show ring.

• Make sure you and your dog are ready before entering a show.

• Don't expect more than your dog is ready to give. Obedience work is progressive, not all learned in the first few lessons.

• It's okay to be nervous, but try not to let your dog know it by your over-handling or fidgeting.

• Do not punish your dog in or out of the ring; if the dog isn't working well, it is probably your fault and not his.

• Pay attention to the judge, and follow instructions exactly.

• Pay attention to your own dog, and don't talk or advise or criticize others.

• Don't forget to exercise your dog before entering the ring.

• Be a good loser; if you don't win today, you can try again another day.

• Have confidence in your dog's intelligence; his greatest desire is to please you if you have earned his respect.

• If it isn't fun for you and your dog, stay out of the ring and try another sport!

Chapter 12

The Akita as a Search and Rescue Dog

Ask any Akita owner about the breed as a search and rescue dog and he'll be quick to tell you that Saint Bernards and Bloodhounds are not the only breeds that are renowned for finding lost persons—especially now that there is an organization in Rockville, Maryland, called Dogs-East, Incorporated, that has a reputation for training paraprofessional search dogs. This non-profit corporation has a 24-hour alerting system connected with the Prince William County Fire Rescue squad that goes into action when a person is reported missing.

This Dogs-East operation serves the Mid-Atlantic region with the idea of providing quick response for search assistance in Northern Virginia, Southern Maryland, the Greater Washington area, and other nearby counties. There is no charge for this service locally, and the service is available for distant locations at which time transportation cooperation through Scott Air Force Base is required if more than four hours' travel time is involved.

When they arrive at the search site, Dogs-East personnel set up a base for their operations to work hand-in-hand with the requesting agency and field teams. Radio logs and maps documenting their search progress are kept. Handlers are all trained in radio communications and can accompany the teams as well as maintaining contact with the main base.

HOW THE DOGS WORK

An air-scenting search dog is trained to scan the air currents for the scent of the human being, trying to locate the source of the scent, at which time it indicates the "find" to its handler. The search dogs will pick up the scent on a person, dead or alive, in any given area, and not just on the ground, but in the air as well. They can search effectively for days or weeks after a track has been obliterated, or in areas that have been covered by earlier searchers. They have proven themselves especially effective where human

sight is most often limited, such as in the dark, dense brush, or wooded area, and in all kinds of weather. While humans work more effectively in daylight, the search dogs work equally well in both night and daytime.

SEARCH DOG QUALIFICATIONS

Dogs-East workers are given extensive training and evaluation before being certified as operational. Handlers must have proficiency in land navigation; radio communications, first aid and medical evacuation are three of the most important requirements. The handlers must undergo wilderness survival training and must possess a current Advanced Red Cross First Aid card or Emergency Medical Technician certificate. All operational members are versed in search strategy and are trained to act as a mission leader in directing the unit's search operations. Dog/handler teams are re-evaluated yearly to ensure proficiency.

HOW SEARCH DOGS ARE ASSIGNED

Each dog and handler is assigned a sector or division of the search area. The handlers direct their dogs downwind and traverse the sector in a manner to give the dog the best scenting covering. Handlers are skilled in terrain orientation and map the area they cover. United States Government maps are used to insure accuracy and the agency supplies these to the teams. All dog teams are fielded at the same time to provide fast and thorough initial coverage of the highest probability areas. By systematic assignments the entire search area can be covered. Dog teams work in well with all other search methods.

THEIR EXTENSIVE COVERAGE

Search dogs have been credited with finding victims of floods and other natural disasters as well as buried victims, drowning, or survivors of downed aircraft, etc., but are never used in matters of criminal nature or one that would prove hazardous to either the dog or its handler. They are not protection trained.

Subject survival can depend on the speed in which the search operation is begun, and the dogs have proven highly successful where situations require minimal manpower.

IN THE BEGINNING

As early as 1980 Dogs-East personnel had been actively engaged in S.A.R. (Search and Rescue) work and had quite a record of successful "finds." Dogs-East does not charge for their services and,

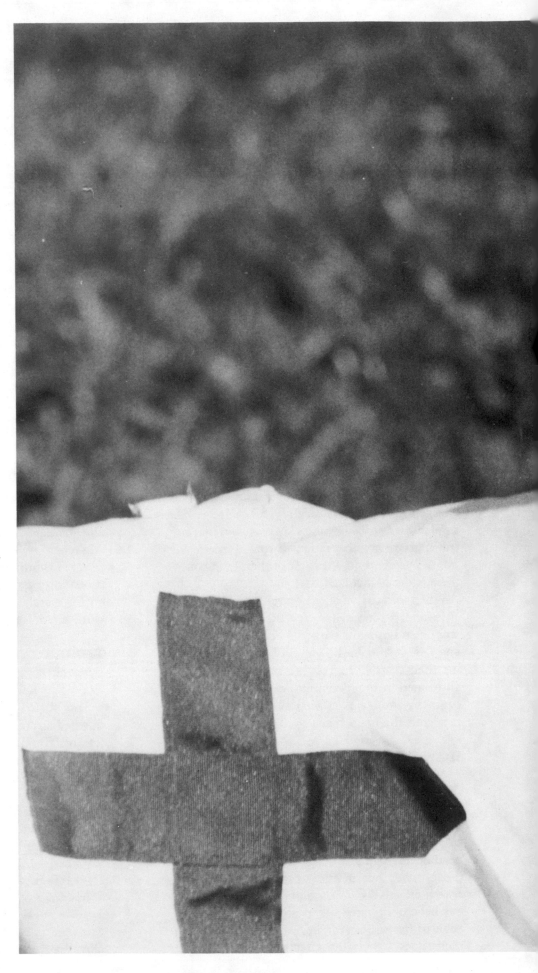

Jessica learns to carry as part of her training in search and rescue for Dogs East, Inc. Owned and trained by James and Susan White.

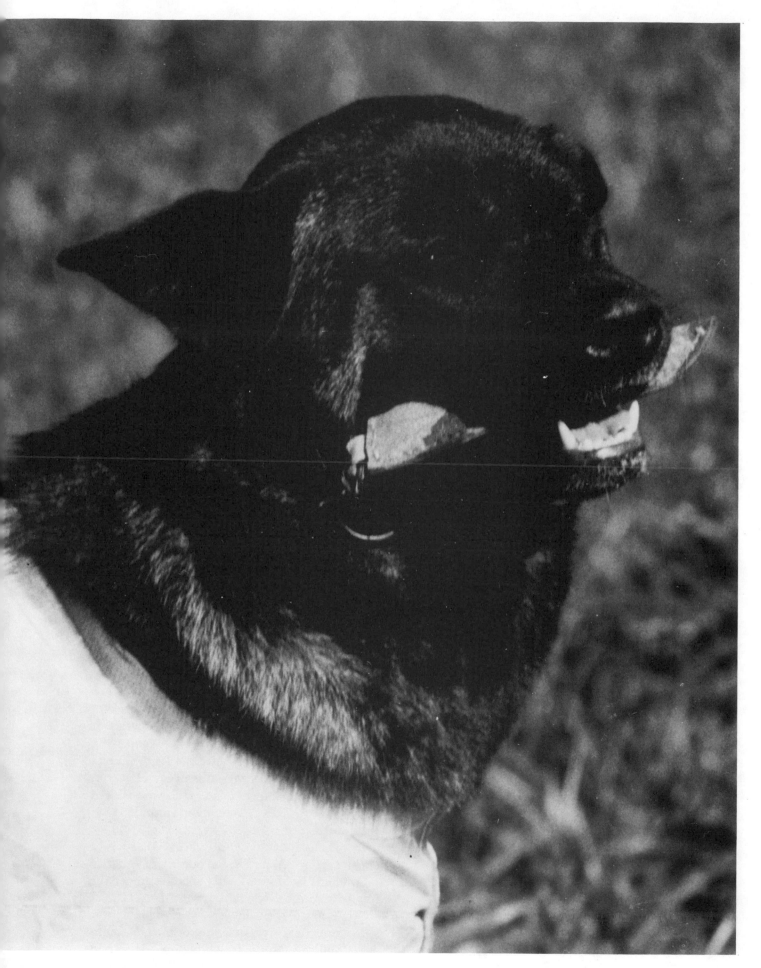

as mentioned before, call upon transportation from the Air Force; however, food, lodging, maps, and flashlight batteries after a search are all readily accepted and appreciated.

THE STORY OF JESSICA

One of the most recent search and rescue dogs we have learned about is a bitch named Jessica, owned by James M. and Susan S. White. Their two-year-old Akita will soon complete her requirements for becoming a Search and Rescue dog. Having completed certain obedience requirements and having the proper friendly disposition with people, Jessica's training is beginning to concentrate on scanning the air currents to pick up human scent. This means ignoring some very tempting human scents as well as animal scents in wooded areas where deer, rabbit and other small animals thrive.

This training to scent air currents can take several months to reach a point where the dog is considered on an operational level. Training may take as long as a year, depending on the handler's previous experience with dog training and his own personal skills and knowledge of outdoor living. It is during this time that the dog and handler build up a strong and unusual rapport that will stand them both in good stead in the field in the future.

Jessica started her training for obedience work at just three months of age and was the Whites' constant companion on canoeing trips, going shopping or even to the office with her owners. While Jessica was inclined to ignore her obedience trainer she took quite readily to the search and rescue work and is actually enthusiastic and excited while working at it. The Whites declare she acts at times in not traditional Akita style, but her natural keen sense of smell, sense of duty, physical strength and intelligence have been well evidenced in her search work.

THE SEARCH "UNIFORM"

Jessica wears a white blanket with a red cross on it while doing her work and can easily be seen and recognized in the field. Her sire was Ch. Lijo's Grizzly and she is out of Bru-Marc Betsey Ross.

THE NEWSLETTER

Dogs-East publishes a typewritten, mimeographed Newsletter which reports the activities of Dogs-East. It includes information pertaining to special training weekends in mountainous areas or along river banks to test their training and working skills. These groups head for the hills after "classroom" sessions, and after a short critique once everyone has returned to base, pot luck suppers or entertainment follows in the evenings. The next day, it's off to the hills once again for more rescue sessions.

FEEDING THE SEARCH DOG

Recently an edition of "Read This," which is the title of the so-called Newsletter, featured a fascinating supplement on Feeding the Search Dog. Needless to say, the harder and longer the dogs work the more food they need for energy and stamina. Dogs that are being fed a perfectly balanced diet need only have the amount of food increased during these times. But it must be noted that dogs will require extra B-complex vitamins, increased protein and minerals as well. They should be fed in the morning before taking off on their missions, with at least 180 calories for each 25 pounds of dog. The dog should work no longer than two hours preferably and should be fed and watered during rest periods when dry or semi-moist food can be fed. Dogs which are worked six hours should be rested at least a full hour with increased amounts of food and water. The frequent smaller amounts of food high in carbohydrates will keep the dog's energy at peak performance while working. The water improves endurance and helps burn body fat. At the end of the day the dog should drink and rest for at least a half hour before the main meal is served, to avoid bloat and gas. Needless to say, during colder weather the amount of intake must be adjusted and during hot weather shade must be provided during the rest breaks to cool body temperature.

THE AKITA RESCUE SOCIETY

In May 1976 The Akita Club of Greater Los Angeles formed a rescue operation which later became the Akita Rescue Society of America. It was incorporated as a non-profit organization, but shortly after it was formed the Akita Club of Greater Los Angeles was dissolved. However, several of the members of the club who wished to continue the Rescue operation continued with their work.

In Thousand Oaks, California, there is a chapter named Akita Rescue Society of America —Southern California. This operates under the umbrella of the National Organization.

While any Akita Club can—and, it is hoped, will—form their own rescue group, this Southern California group is willing to advise and guide them, should anyone want to start one in their area.

At the moment there seem to be more homeless Akitas in the Southern California area than anywhere else, though with the growing interest in the breed there will soon be a need for such an organization in many other parts of the country as well. In New York City particularly there is a tremendous concentration of them, with more and more showing up at the humane organizations and eventually having to be destroyed.

At the present time the group in Southern California rent kennel space from a commercial kennel. The kennel owner gives them space at half the usual fee and the dogs are in residence there until homes can be found for them. The bitches are spayed a week after being brought in, which gives them time to get used to their new quarters before undergoing surgery. The males are neutered if funds are available.

The Rescue Society has two volunteers, Kay Lee and Stephanie O'Donoghue. They live close to the kennel facilities and take turns checking on the animals, taking them to the veterinarian if need be and in general keep an eye on the operation. They also alternate giving the dogs baths and grooming them and make themselves available at least four days a week to interview and meet with prospective new owners.

These new owners must sign a contract, agreeing to provide the dog with a fenced-in yard, any medical care that might be needed, and agreeing to neuter a male if he has not been neutered already. The contract also makes it perfectly clear that the dog must be returned to the Society if it does not work out for any reason. At the time of the return the owners may either select another Akita or their money will be refunded. There is a charge of one hundred dollars for the younger dogs, but no charge for older dogs, and the cost is tax deductible.

WHERE THE DOGS COME FROM

The Rescue Society usually *purchases* the Akitas from animal shelters. The various shelters call the Society whenever an Akita is brought in and arrangements are made for the Akita to be purchased and picked up and brought into the Society rescue unit.

Anyone finding an Akita must first take it to a shelter, and after the shelter calls the Society and they buy it, the transaction becomes legal. Most of these turn-ins are a result of an owner not being able to handle a large, strong dog, and unfor-

tunately, a great number of Akitas brought into the Rescue Society must also be destroyed because they have been treated badly, as well as handled badly, and as a result have become excessively aggressive. Very old or sickly animals must also be put down, which is the saddest part of humane work.

The Rescue Society also keeps records of lost Akitas, with the hope that they can be reunited with their owners. Homes are also found for some of the Akitas through ads in the newspapers and also by word of mouth, and most of the animals are placed before they have been with the Society for a year.

1

2

3

4

5

Chapter 13

Breeding Your Akita

Let us assume the time has come for your dog to be bred, and you have decided you are in a position to enjoy producing a litter of puppies that you hope will make a contribution to the breed. The bitch you purchased is sound, her temperament is excellent and she is a most worthy representative of the breed.

You have a calendar and counted off the 10 days since the first day of red staining and have determined the 10th to 14th day, which will more than likely be the best days for the actual mating. You have additionally counted off 60 to 65 days before the puppies are likely to be born to make sure everything necessary for their arrival will be in good order by that time.

From the moment the idea of having a litter occurred to you, your thoughts should have been given to the correct selection of a proper stud. Here again, the novice would do well to seek advice on analyzing pedigrees and tracing bloodlines for the best breedings. As soon as the bitch is in season and you see color (or staining) and a swelling of the vulva, it is time to notify the owner of the stud you selected and make appointments for the breedings. There are several pertinent questions you will want to ask the stud owners after having decided upon the pedigree. The owners, naturally, will also have a few questions they wish to ask you. These questions will concern your bitch's bloodlines, health, age, how many previous litters she's had, if any, etc.

THE POWER IN PEDIGREES

Someone in the dog fancy once remarked that the definition of a show prospect puppy is one third the pedigree, one third what you see and one third what you *hope* it will be! Well, no matter how you break down your qualifying fractions, we all quite agree that good breeding is essential if you have any plans at all for a show career for your dog. Many breeders will buy on pedigree alone, counting largely on what they themselves can do with the puppy by way of feeding, conditioning, and training. Needless to say, that very important piece of paper common-ly referred to as the "pedigree" is mighty reassuring to a breeder or buyer new at the game or to one who has a breeding program in mind and is trying to establish his own bloodline.

One of the most fascinating aspects of tracing pedigrees is the way the names of the really great dogs of the past keep appearing in the pedigrees of the great dogs of today—positive proof of the strong influence of heredity and witness to a great deal of truth in the statement that great dogs frequently reproduce themselves, though not necessarily in appearance only. A pedigree represents something of value when one is dedicated to breeding better dogs.

To the novice buyer or one who is perhaps merely switching to another breed and sees only a frolicking, leggy, squirming bundle of energy in a fur coat, a pedigree can mean everything! To those of us who believe in heredity, a pedigree is more like an insurance policy—so always read it carefully and take heed.

For the even more serious breeder of today who wishes to make a further study of bloodlines in relation to his breeding program, the American Kennel Club library stud books can and should be consulted.

THE HEALTH OF THE BREEDING STOCK

Some of your first questions should concern whether the stud has already proved himself by siring a normal healthy litter. Also inquire as to whether the owners have had a sperm count made to determine just exactly how fertile or potent the stud is. Determine for yourself whether the dog has two normal testicles.

When considering your bitch for this mating, you must take into consideration a few important points that lead to a successful breeding. You and the owner of the stud will want to recall whether she has had normal heat cycles, whether there were too many runts in the litter and whether a Caesarean section was ever necessary. Has she ever had a vaginal infection? Could she take care of her puppies by herself, or was there a milk shortage? How many surviving puppies were there from the litter, and what did they grow up to be in comparison to the requirements of the breed Standard?

Don't buy a bitch that has problems in heat and has never had a live litter. Don't be afraid, however, to buy a healthy maiden bitch, since chances are, if she is healthy and from good stock, she will be a healthy producer. Don't buy a monorchid male, and certainly not a cryptorchid. If there is any doubt in your mind about his potency, get a sperm count from the veterinarian. Older dogs that have been good producers and are for sale are usually not too hard to find at good established kennels. If they are not too old and have sired quality show puppies, they can give you some excellent show stock from which to establish your own breeding lines.

WHEN TO BREED A GROWN BITCH

The best advice used to be not until her second heat. Today with our new scientific knowledge, we have become acutely aware of such things as hip dysplasia, juvenile cataracts, and other congenital diseases. The best advice now seems to be aimed at not breeding your dogs before two years of age when both the bitch and the sire have been examined by qualified veterinarians and declared—in writing—to be free and clear of these conditions.

THE DAY OF THE MATING

Now that you have decided upon the proper male and female combination to produce what you hope will be—according to the pedigrees—a fine litter of puppies, it is time to set the date. You have selected the two days (with a one day lapse in between) that you feel are best for the breeding, and you call the owner of the stud. The bitch always goes to the stud, unless, of course, there are extenuating circumstances. You set the date and the time and arrive with the bitch *and* the money.

Standard procedure is payment of a stud fee at the time of the first breeding, if there is a tie. For the stud fee, you are entitled to two breedings with ties. Contracts may be written up with specific conditions on breeding terms, of course, but this is general procedure. Often a breeder will take the pick of a litter to protect and maintain his bloodlines; this can be especially desirable if he needs an outcross for his breeding program or if he wishes to continue his own bloodlines if he sold you the bitch to start with, and this mating will continue his line-breeding program. This should all be worked out ahead of time and written and signed before the two dogs are bred. Remember that the payment of the stud fee is for the services of the stud—not for a guarantee of a litter of puppies. This is why is it so important to make sure you are using a proven stud. Bear in mind also that the American Kennel Club will not register a litter of puppies

sired by a male that is under eight months of age. In the case of an older dog, they will not register a litter sired by a dog over 12 years of age, unless there is a witness to the breeding in the form of a veterinarian or other responsible person.

Many studs over 12 years of age are still fertile and capable of producing puppies, but if you do not witness the breeding there is always the danger of a "substitute" stud being used to produce a litter. This brings up the subject of sending your bitch away to be bred if you cannot accompany her.

The disadvantages of sending a bitch away to be bred are numerous. First of all, she will not be herself in a strange place, so she'll be difficult to handle. Transportation, if she goes by air (while reasonably safe), is still a traumatic experience. There is always the danger of her being put off at the wrong airport, not being fed or watered properly, etc. Some bitches get so upset that they go out of season and the trip—which may prove expensive, especially on top of a substantial stud fee—will have been for nothing.

If at all possible, accompany your bitch so that the experience is as comfortable for her as it can be. In other words, make sure before setting this kind of schedule for a breeding that there is no stud in the area that might be as good for her as the one that is far away. Don't sacrifice the proper breeding for convenience, since bloodlines are so important, but put the safety of the bitch above all else. There is always a risk in traveling, since dogs are considered cargo on a plane.

Captions for pages 172-173.
1. A little parental discipline...Ch. O'BJ Kye Kye-Go of E Oka teaches 11-week-old Yukkis Fire 'N Ice of E Oka some manners. Owned by Linda Henson and Peggy Brereton, E Oka Kennels, Peoria Heights, Illinois. 2. "Checking it out...." Father and son owned by Lil Lewis, Annandale, Virginia. 3. Ch. Tsuyoi Inu's Toshi of Toshiro, owned and bred by Barbara Cox of Placerville, California, with his son, Toyo-no of Toshire at eight weeks of age. 4. Ch. Dragon Head's Emperor Kaito wins Best of Breed while daughter Ch. Sparkle Like Kaito wins Best of Opposite Sex. Owned by Ruth and Wayne Zimmerman of Wilmington, Delaware. 5. Eight-month-old male, Obi-San's "The Duke," and two-year-old female, Kawai Hime De Alicia, owned by Mr. and Mrs. Robert Sinko of Elgin, Illinois. Photographed in 1983. 6. One of Lillian O'Shea Koehler's brood bitches from the early 1970s.

1   2

172   3

4

5 6

HOW MUCH DOES THE STUD FEE COST?

The stud fee will vary considerably—the better the bloodlines, the more winning the dog does at shows, the higher the fee. Stud service from a top winning dog could run up to $500.00. Here again, there may be exceptions. Some breeders will take part cash and then, say, third pick of the litter. The fee can be arranged by a private contract rather than the traditional procedure we have described.

Here again, it is wise to get the details of the payment of the stud fee in writing to avoid trouble.

THE ACTUAL MATING

It is always advisable to muzzle the bitch. A terrified bitch may fear-bite the stud, or even one of the people involved, and the wild or maiden bitch may snap or attack the stud to the point where he may become discouraged and lose interest in the breeding. Muzzling can be done with a lady's stocking tied around the muzzle with a half knot, crossed under the chin and knotted at the back of the neck. There is enough "give" in the stocking for her to breathe or salivate freely and yet not open her jaws far enough to bite. Place her in front of her owner, who holds onto her collar and talks to her and calms her as much as possible.

If the male will not mount on his own initiative, it may be necessary for the owner to assist in lifting him onto the bitch, perhaps even in guiding him to the proper place. Usually, the tie is accomplished once the male gets the idea. The owner should remain close at hand, however, to make sure the tie is not broken before an adequate breeding has been completed. After a while the stud may get bored, and try to break away. This could prove injurious. It may be necessary to hold him in place until the tie is broken.

We must stress at this point that while some bitches carry on physically, and vocally, during the tie, there is no way the bitch can be hurt. However, a stud can be seriously or even permanently damaged by a bad breeding. Therefore, the owner of the bitch must be reminded that she must not be alarmed by any commotion. All concentration should be devoted to the stud and a successful and properly executed service.

Many people believe that breeding dogs is simply a matter of placing two dogs, a male and a female, in close proximity, and letting nature take its course. While often this is true, you can-

not count on it. Sometimes it is hard work, and in the case of valuable stock it is essential to supervise to be sure of the safety factor, especially if one or both of the dogs are inexperienced. If the owners are also inexperienced, it may not take place at all.

ARTIFICIAL INSEMINATION

Breeding by means of artificial insemination is usually unsuccessful, unless under a veterinarian's supervision, and can lead to an infection for the bitch and discomfort for the dog. The American Kennel Club requires a veterinarian's certificate to register puppies from such a breeding. Although the practice has been used for over two decades, it now offers new promise, since research has been conducted to make it a more feasible procedure for the future.

Great dogs may eventually look forward to reproducing themselves years after they have left this earth. There now exists a frozen semen concept that has been tested and found successful. The study, headed by Dr. Stephen W.J. Seager, M.V.B., an instructor at the University of Oregon Medical School, has the financial support of the American Kennel Club, indicating that organization's interest in the work. The study is being monitored by the Morris Animal Foundation of Denver, Colorado.

Dr. Seager announced in 1970 that he had been able to preserve dog semen and to produce litters with the stored semen. The possibilities of selective world-wide breedings by this method are exciting. Imagine simply mailing a vial of semen to the bitch! The perfection of line-breeding by storing semen without the threat of death interrupting the breeding program is exciting also.

As it stands today, the technique for artificial insemination requires the depositing of semen (taken directly from the dog) into the bitch's vagina, past the cervix and into the uterus by syringe. The correct temperature of the semen is vital, and there is no guarantee of success. The storage method, if successfully adopted, will present a new era in the field of purebred dogs.

THE GESTATION PERIOD

Once the breeding has taken place successfully, the seemingly endless waiting period of about 63 days begins. For the first 10 days after the breeding, you do absolutely nothing for the bitch—just spin dreams about the delights you will share

PERPETUAL WHELPING CHART

Bred—Jan. 1 2 3 4 5 6 7 8 9 10 11 12 13 14 15 16 17 18 19 20 21 22 23 24 25 26 27   28 29 30 31
Due—March 5 6 7 8 9 10 11 12 13 14 15 16 17 18 19 20 21 22 23 24 25 26 27 28 29 30 31 April 1 2 3 4

Bred—Feb. 1 2 3 4 5 6 7 8 9 10 11 12 13 14 15 16 17 18 19 20 21 22 23 24 25 26   27 28
Due—April 5 6 7 8 9 10 11 12 13 14 15 16 17 18 19 20 21 22 23 24 25 26 27 28 29 30 May 1 2

Bred—Mar. 1 2 3 4 5 6 7 8 9 10 11 12 13 14 15 16 17 18 19 20 21 22 23 24 25 26 27 28 29   30 31
Due—May 3 4 5 6 7 8 9 10 11 12 13 14 15 16 17 18 19 20 21 22 23 24 25 26 27 28 29 30 31 June 1 2

Bred—Apr. 1 2 3 4 5 6 7 8 9 10 11 12 13 14 15. 16 17 18 19 20 21 22 23 24 25 26 27 28   29 30
Due—June 3 4 5 6 7 8 9 10 11 12 13 14 15 16 17 18 19 20 21 22 23 24 25 26 27 28 29 30 July 1 2

Bred—May 1 2 3 4 5 6 7 8 9 10 11 12 13 14 15 16 17 18 19 20 21 22 23 24 25 26 27 28 29   30 31
Due—July 3 4 5 6 7 8 9 10 11 12 13 14 15 16 17 18 19 20 21 22 23 24 25 26 27 28 29 30 31 August 1 2

Bred—June 1 2 3 4 5 6 7 8 9 10 11 12 13 14 15 16 17 18 19 20 21 22 23 24 25 26 27 28 29   30
Due—August 3 4 5 6 7 8 9 10 11 12 13 14 15 16 17 18 19 20 21 22 23 24 25 26 27 28 29 30 31 Sept. 1

Bred—July 1 2 3 4 5 6 7 8 9 10 11 12 13 14 15 16 17 18 19 20 21 22 23 24 25 26 27 28 29   30 31
Due—September 2 3 4 5 6 7 8 9 10 11 12 13 14 15 16 17 18 19 20 21 22 23 24 25 26 27 28 29 30 Oct. 1 2

Bred—Aug. 1 2 3 4 5 6 7 8 9 10 11 12 13 14 15 16 17 18 19 20 21 22 23 24 25 26 27 28 29   30 31
Due—October 3 4 5 6 7 8 9 10 11 12 13 14 15 16 17 18 19 20 21 22 23 24 25 26 27 28 29 30 31 Nov. 1 2

Bred—Sept. 1 2 3 4 5 6 7 8 9 10 11 12 13 14 15 16 17 18 19 20 21 22 23 24 25 26 27 28   29 30
Due—November 3 4 5 6 7 8 9 10 11 12 13 14 15 16 17 18 19 20 21 22 23 24 25 26 27 28 29 30 Dec. 1 2

Bred—Oct. 1 2 3 4 5 6 7 8 9 10 11 12 13 14 15 16 17 18 19 20 21 22 23 24 25 26 27 28 29   30 31
Due—December 3 4 5 6 7 8 9 10 11 12 13 14 15 16 17 18 19 20 21 22 23 24 25 26 27 28 29 30 31 Jan. 1 2

Bred—Nov. 1 2 3 4 5 6 7 8 9 10 11 12 13 14 15 16 17 18 19 20 21 22 23 24 25 26 27 28 29   30
Due—January 3 4 5 6 7 8 9 10 11 12 13 14 15 16 17 18 19 20 21 22 23 24 25 26 27 28 29 30 31 Feb. 1

Bred—Dec. 1 2 3 4 5 6 7 8 9 10 11 12 13 14 15 16 17 18 19 20 21 22 23 24 25 26 27   28 29 30 31
Due—February 2 3 4 5 6 7 8 9 10 11 12 13 14 15 16 17 18 19 20 21 22 23 24 25 26 27 28 March 1 2 3 4

with the family when the puppies arrive.

Around the 10th day it is time to begin supplementing the diet of the bitch with vitamins and calcium. We strongly recommend that you take her to your veterinarian for a list of the proper or perhaps necessary supplements and the correct amounts of each for your particular bitch. Guesses, which may lead to excesses or insufficiencies, can ruin a litter. For the price of a visit to your veterinarian, you will be confident that you are feeding properly.

The bitch should be free of worms, of course, and if there is any doubt in your mind, she should be wormed now, before the third week of pregnancy. Your veterinarian will advise you on the necessity of this and proper dosage as well.

PROBING FOR PUPPIES

Far too many breeders are overanxious about whether the breeding "took" and are inclined to feel for puppies or persuade a veterinarian to radiograph or X-ray their bitches to confirm it. Unless there is reason to doubt the normalcy of a pregnancy, this is risky. Certainly 63 days is not too long to wait, and why risk endangering the litter by probing with your inexperienced hands? Few bitches give no evidence of being in whelp, and there is no need to prove it for yourself by trying to count puppies.

ALERTING YOUR VETERINARIAN

At least a week before the puppies are due, you should telephone your veterinarian and notify him that you expect the litter and give him the date. This way he can make sure that there will be someone available to help, should there be any problems during the whelping. Most veterinarians today have answering services and alternative vets on call when they are not available themselves. Some veterinarians suggest that you call them when the bitch starts labor so that they may further plan their time, should they be needed. Discuss this matter with your veterinarian when you first take the bitch to him for her diet instructions, etc., and establish the method that will best fit in with his schedule.

DO YOU NEED A VETERINARIAN IN ATTENDANCE?

Even if this is your first litter, I would advise that you go through the experience of whelping without panicking and calling desperately for the veterinarian. Most animal births are accomplished without complications, and you should call for assistance only if you run into trouble.

When having her puppies, your bitch will appreciate as little interference and as few strangers around as possible. A quiet place, with her nest, a single familiar face, and her own instincts are all that is necessary for nature to take its course. An audience of curious children squealing and questioning, other family pets nosing around, or strange adults should be avoided. Many a bitch that has been distracted in

175

Top, left. Nap time at Lillian Koehler's Akita "headquarters" in Hatboro, Pennsylvania. **Top, right.** Akitas love the snow . . .Meadow Lakes Michado Hime and Mo-Bounce's Hsing Hsing enjoying themselves in their backyard in Denver. Owned by Joe and Pat Castronova. **Bottom, left.** Three-month-old Tamarlane's Tojo with a friend. The sire was Ch. Akita Tani's Yojimbo ex Tamarlane's Sam'l. Bred by Dr. Sophia Kaluzniacki, Green Valley, Arizona. **Bottom, right.** Nine-week-old Akita owned by Robert and Virginia Santoli of Islip, New York. Bred in Canada by S. Langan, this puppy is officially registered as Langan's Bearcat.

Am. and Can. Ch. Asahi Yama No Chiisai Takara is pictured winning under judge Dale McMackin at a recent show. Owners are Tom and Judy Clark of Edmonds, Washington. Whelped in 1980, "Kara" was sired by Am. and Can. Ch. Kin Hozan's Toklat, C.D., R.O.M., out of Altochi's Yuki Tori. She was Best of Opposite Sex at the 1981 National Specialty.

Ch. Okii Yubi's Dragon House Ko-Go, a top producer owned by Bill and B. J. Andrews of Asheville, North Carolina.

The top-winning Akita for 1979 was Ch. Tamarlane's Silver Star, co-owned by Dean and Bonnie Herrmann, and handled for them by Rusty Short. Star was the first top-winning bitch in the breed and paved the way for others of her sex when the breed was recognized.

Left: Yojo Kuma of Linmin, a dam of Champions, with her latest brood. Owned by the Great River Akita Kennels in Islip Terrace, New York. **Below:** Micha and her fifteen-day-old puppies, photographed in 1983. Bred and owned by Seawood Akitas, Alyce and Kelle Clinton, Lakebay, Washington.

A concerned mother watches over her brood of ten puppies at the LeHi Kennels of Joel and Jeanette Ward in Wescosville, Pennsylvania. The litter was sired by Ch. Groat River's Galloping Gourmet out of Wicca's Diamonds R Forever and was whelped August 1983.

Like a little teddy bear is this five-week-old Akita puppy named Tiki, owned by Bob and Nadene Fontano and Robert Player.

Tiger's Eye Butkus catches a glimpse of himself. The breeder was Janet Voss, Hoffman Estates, Illinois.

Four-week-old Swedish Akita male puppy, Okiiyama.

Pinto Piko at five weeks of age, bred and owned by Alyce and Kelle Clinton, Lakebay, Washington. The sire was Ch. Akita Tani's Daimyo, R.O.M., out of Golden Sun Soawood Wa Wa L'Wilac.

Left: Future champions Tobe's Blazer and Tobe's Renegade are pictured at seven weeks of age. Bred and owned by Tobe Kennels. Notice Renegade's correct earset even at this very early age. This beautiful photograph was taken by the late Alton Anderson. **Below:** Seven-week-old Akita puppies in their outdoor kennel run at the LeHi Kennels in Pennsylvania. The sire was Ch. Great River's Galloping Gourmet and the dam was Wicca's Diamonds R Forever. The sire, "Acorn," is owned by Robert Player and Bob and Nadene Fontano.

Right: Two Norwegian-born puppies, the male Riko-Dai-ich-Kotei and the female Shishi-Joo. **Below:** Four-week-old Wotan puppies are making friends while relaxing in their exercise pen.

Left: An eight-week-old Akita puppy owned by Marc L. Eisenstock of Worcester, Massachusetts.
Below: Ch. Storm Trooper O'B.J. is pictured at fifteen weeks of age. Trooper later went on to win the 1982 Sweepstakes at the National Specialty show as Best Junior Puppy. Owned by Mark and Sandy Jauch.

Right: Buckwheat at five weeks of age. Bred and owned by Seawood Akitas, Lakebay, Washington. Bred by Alyce and Kelle Clinton, and photographed by Kelle.
Below: Ten-week-old Tiffany, bred at the Ginsan Kennels of Robert and Virginia Santoli of Islip, New York, photographed in 1981.

Left: Four-week-old puppies bred by Janet Voss. **Below:** Joseph and Pat Castronova and some of their Akitas posed for this marvelous "family portrait" at their home in Denver, Colorado.

Two winners. Photographed in 1981, eight-year-old Leslie Spiering and her two-month-old Akita puppy, Polyanna's Kirschen, winning Best of Breed at the Bushy Run Kennel Club's Match Show. The sire was Ch. Krug's Red Kadillac ex Ch. Polyanna's Shady Lady.

Tundra at just five weeks of age, bred and owned by Snowcrest Akitas, Marvin and Barbara Hoffman of Mt. Sinai, New York.

Top. Two adorable puppies, just four weeks old, owned and bred by Janet Voss. The sire was Ch. O'BJ Zack the Spotted Bear out of Ch. Tiger's Eye Storm Warning. **Bottom.** Stephanie Johnson hugs one of Peggy Casselberry's Akita puppies.

Caption for pages 194-195.
A 5½-week-old litter sired by Nanchao's Samurai No Chenko out of Ch. Kosho Kis Shusu Kisu, C.D. Owned and bred by Betty Hinson, Jonesboro, Arkansas.

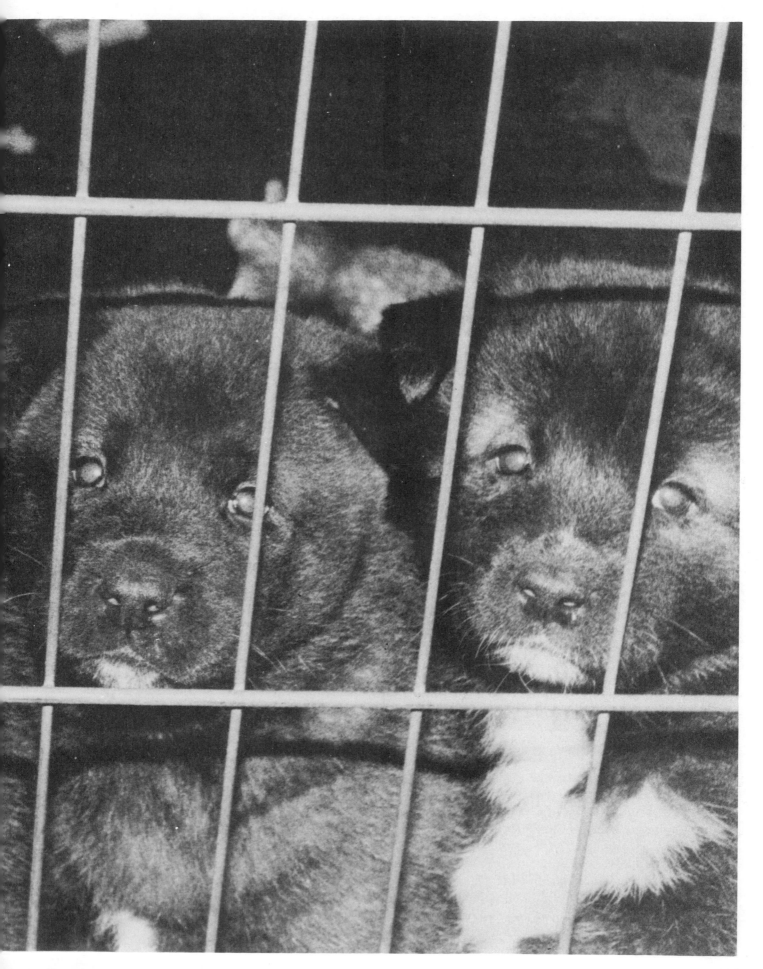

this way has been known to devour her young. This can be the horrible result of intrusion into the bitch's privacy. There are other ways of teaching children the miracle of birth, and there will be plenty of time later for the whole family to enjoy the puppies. Let them be born under proper and considerate circumstances.

LABOR

Some litters—many first litters—do not run the full term of 63 days. So, at least a week before the puppies are actually due, and at the time you alert your veterinarian as to their expected arrival, start observing the bitch for signs of the commencement of labor. This will manifest itself in the form of ripples running down the sides of her body, that will come as a revelation to her as well. It is most noticeable when she is lying on her side—and she will be sleeping a great deal as the arrival date comes closer. If she is sitting or walking about, she will perhaps sit down quickly or squat peculiarly. As the ripples become more frequent, birth time is drawing near, and you will be wise not to leave her. Usually within 24 hours before whelping she will stop eating, and as much as a week before she will begin digging a nest. The bitch should be given something resembling a whelping box with layers of newspaper (black and white only) to make her nest. She will dig more and more as birth approaches, and this is the time to begin making your promise to stop interfering unless your help is specifically required. Some bitches whimper and others are silent, but whimpering does not necessarily indicate trouble.

THE ARRIVAL OF THE PUPPIES

The sudden gush of green fluid from the bitch indicates that the water or fluid surrounding the puppies has "broken" and they are about to start down the canal and come into the world. When the water breaks, birth of the first puppy is imminent. The first puppies are usually born within minutes to a half hour of each other, but a couple of hours between the later ones is not uncommon. If you notice the bitch straining constantly without producing a puppy, or if a puppy remains partially in and partially out for too long, it is cause for concern. Breech births (puppies born feet first instead of head first) can often cause delay or hold things up, and this is often a problem that requires veterinarian assistance.

FEEDING THE BITCH BETWEEN BIRTHS

Usually the bitch will not be interested in food for about 24 hours before the arrival of the puppies, and perhaps as long as two or three days after their arrival. The placenta that she cleans up after each puppy is high in food value and will be more than ample to sustain her. This is nature's way of allowing the mother to feed herself and her babies without having to leave the nest and hunt for food during the first crucial days. In the wild the mother always cleans up all traces of birth in the wild so as not to attract other animals to her newborn babies.

However, there are those of us who believe in making food available should the mother feel the need to restore her strength during or after delivery—especially if she whelps a large litter. Raw chopped meat, beef bouillon, and milk are all acceptable and may be placed near the whelping box during the first two or three days. After that, the mother will begin to put the babies on a sort of schedule. She will leave the whelping box at frequent intervals, take longer exercise periods and begin to take interest in other things. This is where the fun begins for you. Now the babies are no longer soggy little pinkish blobs. They begin to crawl around and squeal and hum and grow before your very eyes!

It is at this time, if all has gone normally, that the family can be introduced gradually and great praise and affection given to the mother.

BREECH BIRTHS

Puppies normally are delivered head first; however, some are presented feet first or in other abnormal positions, and this is referred to as a "breech birth." Assistance is often necessary to get the puppy out of the canal, and great care must be taken not to injure the puppy or the dam.

Aid can be given by grasping the puppy with a piece of turkish toweling and pulling gently during the dam's contractions. Be careful not to squeeze the puppy too hard; merely try to ease it out by moving it gently back and forth. Because even this much delay in delivery may mean the puppy is drowning, do not wait for the bitch to remove the sac. Do it yourself by tearing the sac open to expose the face and head. Then cut the cord anywhere from one-half to three-quarters of an inch away from the navel. If the cord bleeds excessively, pinch the end of it with your fingers and count five. Repeat if necessary. Then pry open the mouth with your finger and hold the puppy upside down for a moment to drain any fluids from the lungs. Next, rub the puppy briskly with turkish or paper toweling. You should get it wriggling and whimpering by this time.

If the litter is large, this assistance will help conserve the strength of the bitch and will probably be welcomed by her. However, it is best to allow her to take care of at least the first few herself to preserve the natural instinct and to provide the nutritive values obtained by her consumption of one or more of the afterbirths as nature intended.

DRY BIRTHS

Occasionally the sac will break before the delivery of a puppy and will be expelled while the puppy remains inside, thereby depriving the dam of the necessary lubrication to expel the puppy normally. Inserting vaseline or mineral oil via your finger will help the puppy pass down the birth canal. This is why it is essential that you be present during the whelping—so that you can count puppies and afterbirths and determine when and if assistance is needed.

THE TWENTY-FOUR HOUR CHECKUP

It is smart to have a veterinarian check the mother and her puppies within 24 hours after the last puppy is born. The veterinarian can check the puppies for cleft palates or umbilical hernia and may wish to give the dam—particularly if she is a show dog—an injection of Pituitin to make sure of the expulsion of all afterbirths and to tighten up the uterus. This can prevent a sagging belly after the puppies are weaned and the bitch is being readied for the show ring.

FALSE PREGNANCY

The disappointment of a false pregnancy is almost as bad for the owner as it is for the bitch. She goes through the gestation period with all the symptoms—swollen stomach, increased appetite, swollen nipples—even makes a nest when the time comes. You may even take an oath that you noticed the ripples on her body from the labor pains. Then, just as suddenly as you made up your mind that she was definitely going to have puppies, you will know that she definitely is not! She may walk around carrying a toy as if it were a puppy for a few days, but she will soon be back to normal and acting just as if nothing happened—and nothing did!

CAESAREAN SECTION

Should the whelping reach the point where there is complication, such as the bitch's not being capable of whelping the puppies herself, the "moment of truth" is upon you and a Caesarean section may be necessary. The bitch may be too small or too immature to expel the puppies herself, her cervix may fail to dilate enough to allow the young to come down the birth canal, there may be torsion of the uterus, a dead or monster puppy, a sideways puppy blocking the canal, or perhaps toxemia. A Caesarean section will be the only solution. No matter what the cause, get the bitch to the veterinarian immediately to insure your chances of saving the mother and/or the puppies.

The Caesarean section operation (the name derived from the idea that Julius Caesar was delivered by this method) involves the removal of the unborn young from the uterus of the dam by surgical incision into the walls through the abdomen. The operation is performed when it has been determined that for some reason the puppies cannot be delivered normally. While modern surgical methods have made the operation itself reasonably safe, with the dam being perfectly capable of nursing the puppies shortly after the completion of the surgery, the chief danger lies in the ability to spark life into the puppies immediately upon their removal from the womb. If the mother dies, the time element is even more important in saving the young, since the oxygen supply ceases upon the death of the dam, and the difference between life and death is measured in seconds.

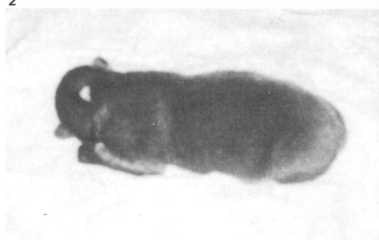

1

2

3   4

5

6

After surgery, when the bitch is home in her whelping box with the babies, she will probably nurse the young without distress. You must be sure that the sutures are kept clean and that no redness or swelling or ooze appears in the wound. Healing will take place naturally, and no salves or ointments should be applied unless prescribed by the veterinarian, for fear the puppies will get it into their systems. If there is any doubt, check the bitch for fever, restlessness (other than the natural concern for her young), or a lack of appetite, but do not anticipate trouble.

EPISIOTOMY

Even though most dogs are generally easy whelpers, any number of reasons might occur to cause the bitch to have a difficult birth. Before automatically resorting to Caesarean section, many veterinarians are now trying the technique known as episiotomy.

Used rather frequently in human deliveries, episiotomy (pronouced E-PEASE-E-OTT-O-ME) is the cutting of the membrane between the rear opening of the vagina back almost to the opening of the anus. After delivery it is stitched together, and barring complications, heals easily, presenting no problem in future births.

SOCIALIZING YOUR PUPPY

The need for puppies to get out among other animals and people cannot be stressed enough. Kennel-reared dogs are subject to all sorts of idiosyncrasies and seldom make good house dogs or normal members of the world around them when they grow up.

The crucial age that determines the personality and general behavior patterns that will predominate during the rest of the dog's life are formed between the ages of three and 10 weeks. This is particularly true during the 21st and 28th day. It is essential that the puppy be socialized during this time by bringing him into family life as much as possible. Walking on floor surfaces, indoor and outdoor, should be experienced; handling by all members of the family and visitors is important; preliminary grooming gets him used to a lifelong necessity; light training, such as setting him up on tables and cleaning teeth and ears and cutting nails, etc., has to be started early if he is to become a show dog. The puppy should be exposed to car riding, shopping tours, a leash around its neck, children —your own and others—and in all possible ways relationships with humans.

It is up to the breeder, of course, to protect the puppy from harm or injury during this initiation into the outside world. The benefits reaped from proper attention will pay off in the long run with a well-behaved, well-adjusted grown dog capable of becoming an integral part of a happy family.

REARING THE FAMILY

Needless to say, even with a small litter there will be certain considerations that must be adhered to in order to insure successful rearing of the puppies. For instance, the diet for the mother should be appropriately increased as the puppies grow and take more and more nourishment from her. During the first few days of rest while the bitch just looks over her puppies and regains her strength, she should be left pretty much alone. It is during these first days that she begins to put the puppies on a feeding schedule and feels safe enough about them to leave the whelping box long enough to take a little extended exercise.

It is cruel, however, to try to keep the mother away from the puppies any longer than she wants to be because you feel she is being too attentive or to give the neighbors a chance to peek in at the puppies. The mother should not have to worry about harm coming to her puppies for the first few weeks. The veterinary checkup will be enough of an experience for her to have to endure until she is more like herself once again.

EVALUATING THE LITTER

A show puppy prospect should be outgoing, (probably the first one to fall out of the whelping box!) and all efforts should be made to socialize the puppy that appears to be the most shy. Once the puppies are about three weeks old, they can and should be handled a great deal by friends and members of the family.

During the third week they begin to try to walk instead of crawl, but they are unsteady on their feet. Tails are used for balancing, and they begin to make sounds.

The crucial period in a puppy's life occurs when the puppy is from 21 to 28 days old, so all the time you can devote to them at this time will reap rewards later on in life. This is the age when several other important steps must be taken in a puppy's life. Weaning should start if it hasn't already, and it is the time to check for worms. Do not worm unnecessarily. A veterinarian should advise on worming and appropriate dosage and he can also discuss with you at this time the schedule for serum or vaccination, which will depend on the size of the puppies as well as their age.

Exercise and grooming should be started at this time, with special care and consideration given to the diet. You will find that the dam will help you wean the puppies, leaving them alone more and more as she notices that they are eating well on their own. Begin by leaving them with her during the night for comfort and warmth; eventually when she shows less interest, keep them separated entirely.

By the time the fifth week arrives, you will already be in love with every member of the litter and desperately searching for reasons to keep them all. They recognize you—which really gets to you!—and they box and chew on each other and try to eat your finger and a million other captivating antics that are special with puppies. Their stomachs seem to be bottomless pits, and their weight will rise. At eight to 10 weeks, the puppies will be weaned and ready to go.

SPAYING AND CASTRATING

A wise old philosopher once said, "Timing in life is everything!" No statement could apply more readily to the age-old question that every dog owner is faced with sooner or later . . . to spay or not to spay.

For the one-bitch pet owner, spaying is the most logical answer, for it solves many problems. The pet is usually not of top breeding quality, and therefore there is no great loss to the bloodline; it takes the pressure off the family if the dog runs free with children, and it certainly eliminates the problem of repeated litters of unwanted puppies or a backyard full of eager males twice a year.

But for the owner or breeder, the extra time and protection that must be afforded a purebred quality bitch can be most worthwhile—even if it is only until a single litter is produced after the first heat. It is then not too late to spay; the progeny can perpetuate the bloodline, the bitch will have been fulfilled—though it is merely an old wives' tale that bitches should have at least one litter to be "normal"—and she may then be retired to her deserved role as family pet once again.

With spaying, the problem of staining and unusual behavior around the house is eliminated, as is the necessity of having to keep her in "pants" or administering pills, sprays, or shots . . . which most veterinarians do not approve of anyway.

In the case of males, castration is seldom contemplated, which to me is highly regrettable. The owner of the male dog merely overlooks the dog's ability to populate an entire neighborhood, since they do not have the responsibility of rearing and disposing of the puppies. When you take into consideration all the many females the male dog can impregnate, it is almost more essential that the males rather than the females be taken out of circulation. The male dog will still be inclined to roam but will be less frantic about leaving the grounds, and you will find that a lot of the *wanderlust* has left him.

STERILIZING FOR HEALTH

When considering the problem of spaying or castrating, the first consideration after the population explosion should actually be the health of the dog or bitch. Males are frequently subject to urinary diseases, and sometimes castration is a help. Your veterinarian can best advise you on this problem. Another aspect to consider is the kennel dog that is no longer being used at stud. It is unfair to keep him in a kennel with females in heat when there is no chance for him to be used. There are other more personal considerations for both kennel and one-dog owners, but when making the decision remember that it is final. You can always spay or castrate, but once the deed is done there is no return.

Captions for pages 202-203.
1. Magnificent head study of Ch. Okii Yubi's Sachmo of Makoto, #1 Akita sire and #1 Working Group sire of all time. He produced 100 champions, and was owned by B. J. and Bill Andrews of Asheville, North Carolina. 2. A double-header for the Tobe Kennels. . .Best of Breed to Ch. Tobe's Obi-Wan Kenobi, C.D., a Top Producer, and Best of Opposite Sex to Ch. Tobe's Tuff Stuff, at this 1980 Staten Island Kennel Club show. 3. Ch. O'B.J. Nikki No Nikki, a Top Producer, owned by B. J. Andrews of Asheville, North Carolina. 4. Tamara Hall's water color portrait of Ch. Akita Tani's Daimyo, R.O.M. Dog and portrait owned by Ellen Martinelli.

2

3   4

203

A bevy of beauties at the Seawood Kennels in Lakebay, Washington. Owned and bred by Alyce and Kelle Clinton, the sire was Ch. Akita Tani's Daimyo, R.O.M., ex Golden Sun Seawood WaWa L'Wilac.

TOP PRODUCERS FOR 1982

By 1982 the final standings of the Top Producing Sires and Dams in the breed was indeed an impressive list. Published in the July-August issue of *The Akita Review,* many of the top dogs in the country were also listed as the Top Producers for the breed.

Heading the list was Ch. Okii Yubi's Sachmo of Makoto, R.O.M., with sixteen champions to his credit. Five of these were out of one bitch, Ch. O'BJ Nikki No Nikki, R.O.M.

In second place with nine champions was Ch. Hot's I Have Arrived, R.O.M., with seven of the nine being out of Ch. Kita Hoshi Kuma of Windrift, R.O.M. All of this says a lot for these dams as well, ranking them Number One and Number Two on the dam's side of the final standings.

In third place were four studs, each of which produced five champions. They were Ch. Akita Tani's Daimyo, R.O.M., Ch. Jakura's Pharfossa

Michael, R.O.M., Ch. Sakusaku's Steamboat Willie, and Ch. Windrift's Teddy Bear, R.O.M.

Champion Minkee's Arcturus Mekahn, Ch. Okami's Tiberius of Salt Bush, and Ch. Tobe's Obi Wan Kenobi all produced three champions each.

On the distaff side, Ch. Kita Hoshi Kuma of Windrift, R.O.M., was Number One with seven champions; Ch. O'BJ Nikko No Nikki, R.O.M., was second with five champions; Ch. Okami's Kori of Krug was third with three champions; Ch. Okii Yubi's Dragonhouse Ko-Go, R.O.M., was in a tie with Showman's Lotus Flower, who also whelped three champions.

The list of others that produced two or a single champion was long and impressive and their owners and breeders are to be complimented on the results. As years go by we can hope these statistics continue to be compiled as both a tribute and a record for quality breedings.

Chapter 14

Feeding and Nutrition

FEEDING PUPPIES

There are many diets today for young puppies, including all sorts of products on the market for feeding the newborn, for supplementing the feeding of the young, and for adding "this or that" to diets, depending on what is lacking in the way of a complete diet.

When weaning puppies it is necessary to put them on four meals a day, even while you are tapering off with the mother's milk. Feeding at six in the morning, noontime, six in the evening and midnight is about the best schedule since it fits in with most human eating plans. Meals for the puppies can be prepared immediately before or after your own meals without too much of a change in your own schedule.

6 A.M.

Two meat and two milk meals serve best and should be served alternately, of course. Assuming the 6 A.M. feeding is a milk meal, the contents should be as follows: goat's milk is the very best milk to feed puppies, but is expensive and usually available only at drug stores, unless you live in farm country where it could be readily available fresh and less expensive. If goat's milk is not available, use evaporated milk (which can be changed to powdered milk later on) diluted two parts evaporated milk and one part water, along with raw egg yolk, honey, or Karo syrup, sprinkled with high-protein baby cereal and some wheat germ. As the puppies mature, cottage cheese may be added or, at one of the two milk meals, it can be substituted for the cereal.

NOONTIME

A puppy chow that has been soaked in warm water or beef broth according to the time specified on the wrapper should be mixed with raw or simmered chopped meat in equal proportions with vitamin powder added.

6 P.M.

Repeat the milk meal—perhaps varying the type of cereal from wheat to oats, corn, or rice.

MIDNIGHT

Repeat the meat meal. If raw meat was fed at noon, the evening meal might be simmered.

Please note that specific proportions on this suggested diet are not given; however, it's safe to say that the most important ingredients are the milk and cereal, and the meat and puppy chow that forms the basis of the diet. Your veterinarian can advise on the portion sizes if there is any doubt in your mind as to how much to use.

If you notice that the puppies are cleaning their plates, you are perhaps not feeding enough to keep up with their rate of growth. Increase the amount at the next feeding. Observe them closely; puppies should each "have their fill," because growth is very rapid at this age. If they have not satisfied themselves, increase the amount so that they do not have to fight for the last morsel. They will not overeat if they know there is enough food available. Instinct will usually let them eat to suit their normal capacity.

If there is any doubt in your mind as to any ingredient you are feeding, ask yourself, "Would I give it to my own baby?" If the answer is no, then don't give it to your puppies. At this age, the comparison between puppies and human babies can be a good guide.

If there is any doubt in your mind, I repeat: ask your veterinarian to be sure.

Captions for pages 206-207.
1. Ch. Conan the Conqueror, son of Ch. Okii Yubi Sachmo of Makoto and owned by the Byrds of Bakersfield, California. 2. Ch. Dragon Head's White Wings, youngest Akita bitch in breed history to finish for her championship, though pictured here at 7 years of age. Owned by Ruth and Wayne Zimmerman of Wilmington, Delaware. 3. A trio of five-week-old puppies out of Ch. Kinouk's Show-Down, owned by Chandra Sargent of Sun Valley, California. 4. Ounce of Bounce, owned by Joe and Pat Castronova of Denver, Colorado, photographed in 1982. The sire was Ch. Kia Hozan's Mogami ex Meadow Lake's Michado Hime. 5. One of the Seawood Kennels' Akitas with F. M. Clinton at their Lakebay, Washington, kennel. Photo by Kelle Clinton. 6. Ch. Great River's Hoshi of Ginsan, bred by Robert Player. "Star" is pictured here at eleven months of age with owner Ginnie Santoli. 7. An eight-week-old Akita puppy named Red Witch and belonging to Bill and B. J. Andrews of Asheville, North Carolina.

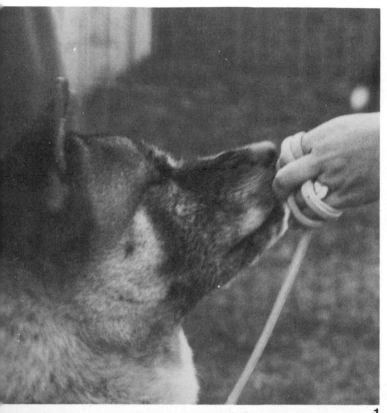

4

5

6

7

Many puppies will regurgitate their food, perhaps a couple of times, before they manage to retain it. If they do bring up their food, allow them to eat it again, rather than clean it away. Sometimes additional saliva is necessary for them to digest it, and you do not want them to skip a meal just because it is an unpleasant sight for you to observe.

This same regurgitation process holds true sometimes with the bitch, who will bring up her own food for her puppies every now and then. This is a natural instinct on her part that stems from the days when dogs were giving birth in the wild. The only food the mother could provide at weaning time was too rough and indigestible for her puppies; therefore, she took it upon herself to predigest the food until it could be taken and retained by her young. Bitches today will sometimes resort to this, especially bitches that love having litters and have a strong maternal instinct. Some dams will help you wean their litters and even give up feeding entirely once they see you are taking over.

WEANING THE PUPPIES

When weaning the puppies, the mother is kept away from the little ones for longer and longer periods of time. This is done over a period of several days. At first she is separated from the puppies for several hours, then all day, leaving her with them only at night for comfort and warmth. This gradual separation aids in helping the mother's milk to dry up gradually, and she suffers less distress after feeding a litter.

If the mother continues to carry a great deal of milk with no signs of its tapering off, consult your veterinarian before she gets too uncomfortable. She may cut the puppies off from her supply of milk too abruptly if she is uncomfortable, before they should be completely on their own.

There are many opinions on the proper age to start weaning puppies. If you plan to start selling them between six and eight weeks, weaning should begin between two and three weeks of age. (Here again, each bitch will pose a different situation.) The size and weight of the litter should help determine the time, and your veterinarian will have an opinion as he determines the burden the bitch is carrying by the size of the litter and her general condition. If she is being pulled down by feeding a large litter, he may suggest that you start at two weeks. If she is glorying in her motherhood without any apparent taxing of her strength, he may suggest

three to four weeks. You and he will be the best judges. But remember, there is no substitute that is as perfect as mother's milk—and the longer the puppies benefit from it, the better. Other food yes, but mother's milk first and foremost for the healthiest puppies.

FEEDING THE ADULT DOG

The puppies' schedule of four meals a day should drop to three by six months and then to two by nine months; by the time the dog reaches one year of age, it is eating one meal a day.

The time when you feed the dog each day can be a matter of the dog's preference or your convenience, so long as once in every 24 hours the dog receives a meal that provides it with a complete, balanced diet. In addition, of course, fresh clean water should be available at all times.

There are many brands of dry food, kibbles, and biscuits on the market that are all of good quality. There are also many varieties of canned dog food that are of good quality and provde a balanced diet for your dog. But, for those breeders and exhibitors who show their dogs, additional care is given to providing a few "extras" that enhance the good health and good appearance of show dogs.

A good meal or kibble mixed with water or beef broth and raw meat is perhaps the best ration to provide. In cold weather many breeders add suet or corn oil (or even olive or cooking oil) to the mixture and others make use of the bacon fat after breakfast by pouring it over the dog's food.

Salting a dog's food in the summer helps replace the salt he "pants away" in the heat. Many breeders sprinkle the food with garlic powder to sweeten the dog's breath and prevent gas, especially in breeds that gulp or wolf their food and swallow a lot of air. I prefer garlic powder; the salt is too weak and the clove is too strong.

There are those, of course, who cook very elaborately for their dogs, which is not necessary if a good meal and meat mixture is provided. Many prefer to add vegetables, rice, tomatoes, etc., in with everything else they feed. As long as the extras do not throw the nutritional balance off, there is little harm, but no one thing should be fed to excess. Occasionally liver is given as a treat at home. Fish, which most veterinarians no longer recommend even for cats, is fed to puppies, but should not be given in excess of once a week. Always remember that no one food should be given as a total diet. Balance is most important; a 100 per cent meat diet can kill a dog.

THE ALL-MEAT DIET CONTROVERSY

In March of 1971 the National Research Council investigated a great stir in the dog fancy about the all-meat dog-feeding controversy. It was established that meat and meat by-products constitute a complete balanced diet for dogs only when it is further fortified.

Therefore, a good dog chow or meal mixed with meat provides the perfect combination for a dog's diet. While the dry food is a complete diet in itself, the fresh meat additionally satisfies the dog's anatomically and physiologically meat-oriented appetite. While dogs are actually carnivores, it must be remembered that when they were feeding themselves in the wild they ate almost the entire animal they captured, including its stomach contents. This provided some of the vitamins and minerals we must now add to the diet.

In the United States the standard for diets that claim to be "complete and balanced" is set by the Subcommittee on Canine Nutrition of the National Research Council (NRC) of the National Academy of Sciences. This is the official agency for establishing the nutritional requirements of dog foods. Most foods sold for dogs and cats meet these requirements and manufacturers are proud to say so on their labels, so look for this when you buy. Pet food labels must be approved by the Association of American Feed Control Officials (AAFCO) Pet Foods Committee. Both the Food and Drug Administration and the Federal Trade Commission of the AAFCO define the word "balanced" when referring to dog food as follows:

"Balanced is a term which may be applied to pet food having all known required nutrients in a proper amount and proportion based upon the recommendations of a recognized authority (The National Research Council is one) in the field of animal nutrition, for a given set of physiological animal requirements."

With this much care given to your dog's diet, there can be little reason for not having happy well-fed dogs in proper weight and proportions for the show ring.

OBESITY

As we mentioned before, there are many "perfect" diets for your dogs on the market today. When fed in proper proportions, they should keep your dogs in "full bloom." However, there are those owners who, more often than not, indulge their own appetites and are inclined to overfeed their dogs as well. A study in Great Britain in the early 1970's found that a major percentage of obese people also had obese dogs. The entire family was overfed and all suffered from the same condition.

Obesity in dogs is a direct result of the animal's being fed more food that he can properly "burn up" over a period of time, so it is stored as fat or fatty tissue in the body. Pet dogs are more inclined to become obese than show dogs or working dogs, but obesity also is a factor to be considered with the older dog since his exercise is curtailed.

A lack of "tuck up" on a dog, or not being able to feel the ribs, or great folds of fat that hang from the underside of the dog can all be considered as obesity. Genetic factors may enter into the picture, but usually the owner is at fault.

The life span of the obese dog is decreased on several counts. Excess weight puts undue stress on the heart as well as on the joints. The dog becomes a poor anesthetic risk and has less resistance to viral or bacterial infections. Treatment is seldom easy or completely effective, so emphasis should be placed on not letting your dog get FAT in the first place!

Captions for pages 210-211.
1. Ninety-eight pound lap dog! Ch. Kin Hozan's Mogami is pictured with his Aunt Marty in July 1983. 2. Krug's Yamato Damashi, owned by Janet Voss of Hoffman Estates, Illinois. 3. Helping with the Christmas tree. . .Joe Castronova gets some questionable assistance from one of his Akitas at their Denver residence. 4. Am. and Can. Ch. Tobe's Black Bronco, owned by Elaine Andiorio of Bernardsville, New Jersey. 5. Ch. Akita Tani's Yojimbo of Tamarlane with friend Mike. The sire was Akita Tani's Kuro Chikara, R.O.M., ex Akita Tani's Kibo San. Owned by Dr. Sophia Kaluznlacki of Green Valley, Arizona.

1 2

3 4

ORPHANED PUPPIES

The ideal solution to feeding orphaned puppies is to be able to put them with another nursing dam who will take them on as her own. If this is not possible within your own kennel, or a kennel that you know of, it is up to you to care for and feed the puppies. Survival is possible but requires a great deal of time and effort on your part.

Your substitue formula must be precisely prepared, always served heated to body temperature, and refrigerated when not being fed. Esbilac, a vacuum-packed powder, with complete feeding instructions on the can, is excellent and about as close to mother's milk as you can get. If you can't get Esbilac, or until you do get Esbilac, there are two alternative formulas that you might use.

Mix one part boiled water with five parts of evaporated milk and add one teaspoonful of dicalcium phosphate per quart of formula. Dicalcium phosphate can be secured at any drug store. If they have it in tablet form only, you can powder the tablets with the back part of a tablespoon. The other formula for newborn puppies is a combination of eight ounces of homogenized milk mixed well with two egg yolks.

You will need baby bottles with three-hole nipples. Sometimes doll bottles can be used for the newborn puppies, which should be fed at six-hour intervals. If they are consuming sufficient amounts, their stomachs should look full, or slightly enlarged, though never distended. The amount of formula to be fed is proportionate to the size, age, growth, and weight of the puppy, and is indicated on the can of Esbilac, or consult the advice of your veterinarian. Many breeders like to keep a baby scale nearby to check the weight of the puppies to be sure they are thriving on the formula.

At two to three weeks you can start adding Pablum or some other high protein baby cereal to the formula. Also, baby beef can be licked from your finger at this age, or added to the formula. At four weeks the surviving puppies should be taken off the diet of Esbilac and put on a more substantial diet, such as wet puppy meal or chopped beef; however, Esbilac powder can still be mixed in with the food for additional nutrition. The baby foods of pureed meats in jars make for a smooth changeover also, and can be blended into the diet.

HOW TO FEED THE NEWBORN PUPPIES

When the puppy is a newborn, remember that it is vitally important to keep the feeding procedure as close to the natural mother's routine as possible. The newborn puppy should be held in your lap in your hand in an almost upright position with the bottle at an angle to allow the entire nipple area to be full of the formula. Do not hold the bottle upright so the puppy's head has to reach straight up toward the ceiling. Do not let the puppy nurse too quickly or take in too much air and possibly get the colic. Once in awhile take the bottle away and let him rest a moment and swallow several times. Before feeding, test the nipple to see that the fluid does not come out too quickly, or by the same token, too slowly so that the puppy gets tired of feeding before he has had enough to eat.

When the puppy is a little older, you can place him on his stomach on a towel to eat, and even allow him to hold on to the bottle or to "come and get it" on his own. Most puppies enjoy eating and this will be a good indication of how strong an appetite he has and his ability to consume the contents of the bottle.

It will be necessary to "burp" the puppy. Place a towel on your shoulder and hold the puppy on your shoulder as if it were a human baby, patting and rubbing it gently. This will also encourage the puppy to defecate. At this time, you should observe for diarrhea or other intestinal disorders. The puppy should eliminate after each feeding with occasional eliminations between times as well. If the puppies do not eliminate on their own after each meal, massage their stomachs and under their tails gently until they do.

You must keep the puppies clean. Under no circumstances should fecal matter be allowed to collect on their skin or fur.

All this—plus your determination and perseverance—might save an entire litter of puppies that would otherwise have died without their real mother.

GASTRIC TORSION

Gastric torsion, or bloat, sometimes referred to as "twisted stomach," has become more and more prevalent. Many dogs that in the past had been thought to die of blockage of the stomach or intestines because they had swallowed toys or other foreign objects are now suspected of having been the victims of gastric torsion and the bloat that followed.

Though life can be saved by immediate surgery to untwist the organ, the rate of fatality is high. Symptoms of gastric torsion are unusual restlessness, excessive salivation, attempts to vomit, rapid respiration, pain, and the eventual bloating of the abdominal region.

The cause of gastric torsion can be attributed to overeating, excess gas formation in the stomach, poor function of the stomach or intestine, or general lack of exercise. As the food ferments in the stomach, gases form which may twist the stomach in a clockwise direction so that the gas is unable to escape. Surgery, where the stomach is untwisted counter-clockwise, is the safest and most successful way to correct the situation.

To avoid the threat of gastric torsion, it is wise to keep your dog well exercised to be sure the body is functioning normally. Make sure that food and water are available for the dog at all times, thereby reducing the tendency to overeat. With self-service dry feeding, where the dog is able to eat intermittently during the day, there is not the urge to "stuff" at one time.

If you notice any of the symptoms of gastric torsion, call your veterinarian immediately. Death can result within a matter of hours!

SUGAR—YES OR NO?

One of the latest controversies on the feeding of dogs is whether or not to add sugar to their diets.

Sugar is a carbohydrate, and there is no denying that dogs need carbohydrates in their diets for complete balance, but many people maintain that there are sufficient carbohydrates in the chows that we feed to constitute a balanced diet. Enzymes found in a dog's stomach digest carbohydrates, and a dietary imbalance would occur if a certain amount of carbohydrates were not included in the various grains fed to dogs. This by no means indicates that candy should be included as a form of carbohydrate—not that there is a danger of cavities if dogs are fed candy, but there can be other ill effects. If no sugar (i.e. carbohydrates) is fed, protein is utilized for energy, when in reality the protein in the body should be used for other essential body building and maintaining body tissue.

So . . . while an occasional treat is not harmful, too much *can* be harmful. This is another good reason for carefully reading the labels on all foods you feed your dog.

K-9 CANDY

In 1983 it was reported in the October issue of the *DVM Newsmagazine* that there were indications that theobromine, a caffeine-related stimulant found in chocolate, can cause incontinence, seizures, and even death in dogs.

In truth, most all forms of "human candy" prove to be somewhat harmful to dogs. Sweets and plain sugar in any form is highly questionable. The same applies to alcoholic beverages. It is not "cute" to give your dog a cocktail while you are enjoying your own. Alcoholic drinks can produce sneezing fits or other symptoms, including fatal allergy attacks. If candy is a "key" word in your house, make sure the candy you give your dog is clearly marked, DOG candy.

Captions for pages 214-215.
1. Ch. Dragon Head's Emperor Kaito, Group-winning Akita on the list of Top Ten Akitas for 1982 and 1983. Bred by Melissa Kell, he is owned by Ruth Zimmerman of Wilmington, Delaware. 2. Ch. Kinouk's Show-Down, #3 Akita in the United States in 1982. The sire was Ch. Okii Yubi Sachmo of Makoto. Co-owned by Chandra Sargent and Joan Harper Young. 3. Sparkle Like Kaito at eleven months of age poses in her backyard in Wilmington, Delaware. Owned by Ruth and Wayne Zimmerman. 4. Am. and Can. Ch. Rising Sun's Chiisai Cha Kuma was photographed here winning at a show at four years old. Kuma was sired by Am. and Can. Ch. Kin Hozan's Toklat, C.D., R.O.M., out of Oshio's Tango Bay's Musume. He was one of the Top Ten Akitas in the U.S. in 1979 and 1980 according to the Akita Journal System. He was also #3 Akita in Canada in 1980 and 1981 according to *Dogs in Canada*. Always owner-handled by Judy and Tom Clark of Edmonds, Washington. 5. Bounce and puppy, Ounce of Bounce, relaxing in the backyard after attending the Fort Collins Match Show. Owned by Joe and Pat Castronova of Denver. 6. Ch. Matsukaze's Holly-Go Litely wins the Working Group at a 1982 show. Holly was bred by Gus D. Bell and is handled by Rusty Cunningham Short for owner Bea Hunt of Kin Hozan Akitas. Holly is a multiple Best in Show winner. 7. Ch. Hozam of Matsukaze, owned by Gus D. Bell. He is pictured here in 1977 with handler Rusty Cunningham Short at a California show.

1

2 3

4

5

PARK SHORE
KENNEL CLUB
JULY 17 1982

WORKING
GROUP

BOOTH
PHOTO

WORKING GROUP

6

7

WHY DOGS CHEW

Puppies need something with resistance to chew on while their teeth and jaws are developing: for cutting the puppy teeth, to induce growth of the permanent teeth under the puppy teeth, to assist in getting rid of the puppy teeth at the proper time, to help the permanent teeth through the gums, to assure normal jaw development and to settle permanent teeth solidly in the jaws.

The adult dog's desire to chew stems from the instinct for toothcleaning effect, gum massage and jaw exercise—plus the need of an outlet for periodic doggie tensions.

Dental caries as it affects the teeth of humans is virtually unknown in dogs—but tartar accumulates on the teeth of dogs, particularly at the gum line, more rapidly than on the teeth of humans. These accumulations, if not removed, bring irritation and then erode the tooth enamel and ultimately destroy the teeth at the roots. Most chewing by adult dogs is an effort to do something about this problem for themselves.

Tooth and jaw development will normally continue until your dog is more than a year old—but sometimes much longer, depending upon the breed, chewing exercise, the rate at which calcium can be utilized and many other factors, known and unknown, which affect the development of individual dogs. Diseases, like distemper for example, may sometimes arrest development of the teeth and jaws, which may resume months, or even years, later.

This is why dogs, especially puppies and young dogs, will often destroy valuable property when their chewing instinct is not diverted from their owner's possessions, particularly during the widely varying critical period for young dogs.

Saving your possessions from destruction—assuring proper development of teeth and jaws—providing for "interim" toothcleaning and gum massage—and channeling tension into a non-destructive outlet— are, therefore, all dependent upon your dog having something suitable for chewing readily available when his instinct tells him to chew. If your purposes and those of your dog are to be accomplished, what you provide for chewing must be appealing to him and have the necessary functional qualities; and above all, be safe for him.

It is very important that dogs not be permitted to chew on anything they can break, or indigestible things from which they can bite sizeable chunks. Sharp pieces from bones which can be broken when they fall to the ground may pierce the intestine wall and can kill. Indigestible things which can be bitten off in chunks, such as toys made of rubber or cheap plastic, may cause an intestinal stoppage if not regurgitated—and can cause painful death unless surgery is performed immediately.

Sturdy natural bones, such as four to eight inch lengths of round shin bones from mature beef—either the kind you can get from your butcher or one of the variety available commercially in pet stores—may serve your dog's teething needs, if his mouth is large enough to handle them effectively, but constant chewing on hard bones wears down a dog's teeth. Natural bones are very abrasive and should be used sparingly.

You may be tempted to give your puppy a smaller bone and he may not be able to break it when you do—but puppies grow rapidly and the power of their jaws constantly increases until they are full grown. This means that a growing dog may break one of the smaller bones as it grows, swallow the pieces and die painfully before you realize what is wrong.

Many think of their dog's teeth in terms of the teeth of the wild carnivore or those of the dogs of antiquity. The teeth of the wild carnivorous animals and the teeth found in the fossils of the dog-like creatures of antiquity had far thicker and stronger enamel than those of our contemporary dogs. Nature provides over the centuries only that which the animal needs to survive and procreate—and dogs have been domesticated now for many thousands of years.

All hard natural bones are highly abrasive. If your dog is an avid chewer, natural bones may wear away his teeth prematurely; hence, they then should be taken away from your dog when the teething purposes have been served. The badly worn, and usually painful, teeth of many mature dogs can be traced to excessive chewing on natural bones.

Contrary to popular belief, knuckle bones which can be chewed up and swallowed by the dogs provide little, if any, useable calcium or other nourishment. They do, however, disturb the digestion of most dogs and cause them to vomit the nourishing food they need.

Rawhide products sometimes swell in the throat or cause constipation, but are less dangerous than rubber or plastic toys. Nylabone® is the best and the safest and certainly longer-lasting than the others. Especially when there are bone fractions added. Dogs cannot break them or bite off chunks; therefore, they

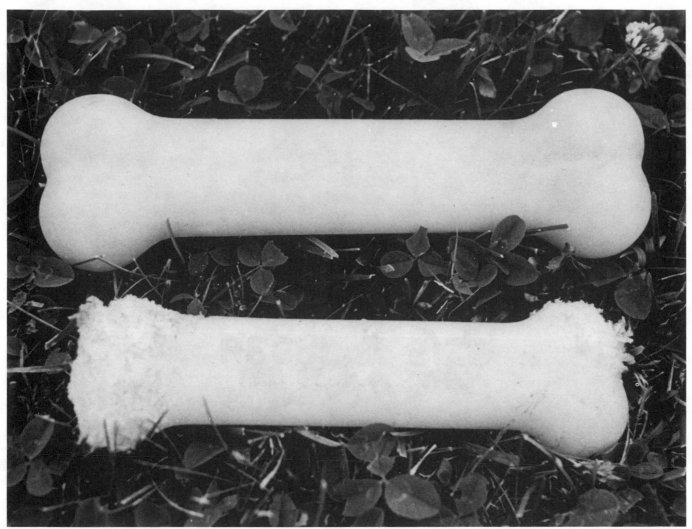

Nylabones® are safe and durable chewing products for all dogs, and Akitas are no exception. Ask your local pet shop or your veterinarian about them.

are also economical. Hard chewing on them raises little bristle-like projections on the surface of the nylon to provide effective interim tooth cleaning and gum massage. The little projections are raked off and swallowed in the form of thin shavings that break down in the stomach fluids and pass through the dog without ill effects.

The toughness provides the strong chewing resistance needed for important jaw exercise and effective help for the teething functions and yet is unabrasive. The nylon also does not support the growth of microorganisms, can be washed in soap and water, or sterilized, comes in various sizes and shapes and is relatively inexpensive.

Captions for pages 218-219.
1. Marc Eisenstock's year-old Ichi-Ban, protector and companion at his home in Worcester, Massachusetts. 2. One of the largest Akitas in Northern California. . .28-inch, 6-year-old Ch. Kuma Ryoshi, (1969-1981). This 125 pound, personality-plus Akita was a crowd favorite at the San Francisco Cherry Blossom annual parade in which he participated for nine years. This all-white beauty was owned by Shogun Akitas. 3. Ch. Mill Creek Bozo Jo, C.D., at the Bearhold Kennels in Beltsville, Maryland. 4. Versatility is the name of the game with the Akita. Ch. Mill Creek Bozo Jo, C.D., loves pulling a cart. Owned by Howard and Judith Opel, Beltsville, Maryland. 5. An eleven-week-old Akita puppy owned by Tom and Judy Clark of Edmonds, Washington, pictured at their Yushosha Akitas Kennel. 6. White King Go, or Tomodachi, with Lillian (O'Shea) Koehler several years ago. 7. The first Am., Can. and Bda. Ch. Kenjiko Royal Tenji, R.O.M., pictured winning the 1982 Akita Club of America National Specialty show over an entry of 194 Akitas. Pictured are judge John Patterson, owner Frederick O. Duane, handler John Fabian, and Akita Club of America president Jim Sailer.

217

1　2

3　4

5   6

7

Chapter 15

Your Dog, Your Veterinarian and You

The purpose of this chapter is to explain why you should never attempt to be your own veterinarian. Quite the contrary, we urge emphatically that you establish good liaison with a reputable veterinarian who will help you maintain happy, healthy dogs. Our purpose is to bring you up-to-date on the discoveries made in modern canine medicine and to help you work with your veterinarian by applying these new developments to your own animals.

We have provided here "thumbnail" histories of many of the most common types of diseases your dog is apt to come in contact with during his lifetime. We feel that if you know a little something about the diseases and how to recognize their symptoms, your chances of catching them in the preliminary stages will help you and your veterinarian effect a cure before a serious condition develops.

Today's dog owner is a realistic, intelligent person who learns more and more about his dog —inside and out—so that he can care for and enjoy the animal to the fullest. He uses technical terms for parts of the anatomy, has a fleeting knowledge of the miracles of surgery, and is fully prepared to administer clinical care for his animals at home. This chapter is designed for study and/or reference and we hope you will use it to full advantage.

We repeat, we do *not* advocate your playing "doctor." This includes administering medication without veterinary supervision, or even doing your own inoculations. General knowledge of diseases, their symptoms, and side effects will assist you in diagnosing diseases for your veterinarian. He does not expect you to be an expert, but will appreciate your efforts in getting a sick dog to him before it is too late and he cannot save its life.

ASPIRIN: A DANGER

There is a common joke about doctors telling their patients, when they telephone with a complaint, to take an aspirin, go to bed and let him know how things are in the morning. Unfortunately, that is exactly the way it turns out with a lot of dog owners who think aspirins are cure-alls and give them to their dogs indiscriminately. They finally call the veterinarian when the dog has an unfavorable reaction.

Aspirins are not panaceas for everything—certainly not for every dog. In an experiment, fatalities in cats treated with aspirin in one laboratory alone numbered 10 out of 13 within a two-week period. Dogs' tolerance was somewhat better, as to actual fatalities, but there was considerable evidence of ulceration on the stomach linings in varying degrees when necropsy was performed.

Aspirin has been held in the past to be almost as effective for dogs as for people when given for many of the everyday aches and pains. The fact remains, however, that medication of any kind should be administered only after veterinary consultation and a specific dosage suitable to the condition is recommended.

While aspirin is chiefly effective in reducing fever, relieving minor pains, and cutting down on inflammation, the acid has been proven harmful to the stomach when given in strong doses. Only your veterinarian is qualified to determine what the dosage is or whether it should be administered to your particular dog at all.

WHAT THE THERMOMETER CAN TELL YOU

You will notice in reading this chapter dealing with the diseases of dogs that practically everything a dog might contract in the way of sickness has basically the same set of symptoms: loss of appetite, diarrhea, dull eyes, dull coat, warm and/or runny nose and FEVER!

Therefore, it is most advisable to have a thermometer on hand for checking temperature. There are several inexpensive metal rectal-type thermometers that are accurate and safer than the glass variety that can be broken. This may happen either by dropping it or perhaps by its breaking off in the dog because of improper insertion or an aggravated condition with the dog that makes him violently resist the insertion of the thermometer.

Whatever type you use, it should first be sterilized with alcohol and then lubricated with Vaseline to make the insertion as easy as possible.

The normal temperature for a dog is 101.5 degrees Fahrenheit, as compared to the human 98.6 degrees. Excitement as well as illness can cause this to vary a degree or two, but any sudden or extensive rise in body temperature must be considered as cause for alarm. Your first indication will be that your dog feels unduly "warm" and this is the time to take the temperature, *not* when the dog becomes very ill or manifests additional serious symptoms. With a thermometer on hand, you can check temperature quickly and perhaps prevent some illnesses from becoming serious.

COPROPHAGY

Perhaps the most unpleasant of all phases of dog breeding is to come up with a dog that takes to eating stool. This practice, which is referred to politely as coprophagy, is one of the unsolved mysteries in the dog world. There simply is no confirmed explanation as to why some dogs do it.

However, there are several logical theories, all or any of which may be the cause. Some people cite nutritional deficiencies; others say that dogs that are inclined to gulp their food (which passes through them not entirely digested) find it still partially palatable. There is another theory that the preservatives used in some meat are responsible for an appealing odor that remains through the digestive process. Then again, poor quality meat can be so tough and unchewable that dogs swallow it whole and it passes through them in large undigested chunks.

There are others who believe the habit is strictly psychological, the result of a nervous condition or insecurity. Others believe the dog cleans up after itself because it is afraid of being punished as it was when it made a mistake on the carpet as a puppy. Some people claim boredom is the reason, or even spite. Others will tell you a dog does not want its personal odor on the premises for fear of attracting other hostile animals to itself or its home.

The most logical of all explanations and the one veterinarians are inclined to accept is that it is a deficiency of dietary enzymes. Too much dry food can be bad and many veterinarians suggest trying meat tenderizers, monosodium glutamate, or garlic powder, all of which give the stool a bad odor and discourage the dog. Yeast or certain vitamins or a complete change of diet are even more often suggested. By the time you try each of the above you will probably discover that the dog has outgrown the habit anyway. However, the condition cannot be ignored if you are to enjoy your dog to the fullest.

There is no set length of time that the problem persists, and the only real cure is to walk the dog on leash, morning and night and after every meal. In other words, set up a definite eating and exercising schedule before coprophagy is an established pattern.

MASTURBATION

A source of embarrassment to many dog owners, masturbation can be eliminated with a minimum of training.

The dog that is constantly breeding anything and everything, including the leg of the piano or perhaps the leg of your favorite guest, can be broken of the habit by stopping its cause.

The over-sexed dog—if truly that is what he is —which will never be used for breeding can be castrated. The kennel stud dog can be broken of the habit by removing any furniture from his quarters or keeping him on leash and on verbal command when he is around people or in the house where he might be tempted to breed pillows, people, etc.

Captions for pages 222-223.
1. Tobe's Abrakadabra, pictured at seven months old winning Best in Match at a recent Akita Club of Long Island Show. Bred and owned by the Tobe Kennels in Branchville, New Jersey. 2. Ch. Tobe's Peking Jumbo, C.D., #1 Akita in 1980 and the Best of Breed winner at the 1981 Westminster Kennel Club show. Jumbo is also a multiple Group winner. 3. Ch. Tobe's Princess Leia Organa, C.D., winning the Sweepstakes at just seven months of age. Bred and owned by Bev and Tom Bonadonna, Tobe Kennels, Branchville, New Jersey. 4. Ch. Tobe's Sno-Storm Ram Charger is pictured winning under judge Joe Tacker at this 1981 dog show. Bred by Tobe Kennels and owned by M. M. Rotkewski. 5. The impressive Ch. Tobe's Lucan V. Stedway, pictured winning on the way to his championship. Bred and owned by the Tobe Kennels. 6. Ch. Lijo's Spirit of Tobe, R.O.M., the foundation of the Tobe Kennels of Bev and Tom Bonadonna. She is the dam of eight champions, including two of the Top Ten Akitas for 1979. 7. Kristy Clark and Tobe's Empress Ginger. 8. Tobe's Hurry Sundown, bred and owned by the Tobe Kennels, Branchville, New Jersey. Brute is eleven months old in this photo.

1 2

3 4

5 6

7 8

Hormone imbalance may be another cause and your veterinarian may advise injections. Exercise can be of tremendous help. Keeping the dog's mind occupied by physical play when he is around people will also help relieve the situation.

Females might indulge in sexual abnormalities like masturbation during their heat cycle, or, again, because of a hormone imbalance. But if they behave this way because of a more serious problem, a hysterectomy may be indicated.

A sharp "no!" command when you can anticipate the act, or a sharp "no!" when caught in the act will deter most dogs if you are consistent in your correction. Hitting or other physical abuse will only confuse a dog.

RABIES

The greatest fear in the dog fancy today is still the great fear it has always been—rabies.

What has always held true about this dreadful disease still holds true today. The only way rabies can be contracted is through the saliva of a rabid dog entering the bloodstream of another animal or person. There is, of course, the Pasteur treatment for rabies which is very effective.

It should be administered immediately if there is any question of exposure. There was of late the incident of a little boy who survived being bitten by a rabid bat. Even more than dogs being found to be rabid, we now know that the biggest carriers are bats, skunks, foxes, rabbits, and other warmblooded animals that pass it from one to another since they do not have the benefit of inoculation. Dogs that run free should be inoculated for protection against these animals. For city or house dogs that never leave their owner's side, it may not be as necessary.

For many years, Great Britain (because it is an island and because of the country's strictly enforced six-month quarantine) was entirely free of rabies. But in 1969 a British officer brought back his dog from foreign duty and the dog was found to have the disease soon after being released from quarantine. There was a great uproar about it, with Britain killing off wild and domestic animals in a great scare campaign, but the quarantine is once again down to six months and things seem to have returned to a normal, sensible attitude.

Health departments in rural towns usually provide rabies inoculations free of charge. If your dog is outdoors a great deal, or exposed to other animals that are, you might wish to call the town hall and get information on the program in your area. One cannot be too cautious about this dread disease. While the number of cases diminishes each year, there are still thousands being reported and there is still the constant threat of an outbreak where animals roam free. Never forget, there is no cure.

Rabies is caused by a neurotropic virus which can be found in the saliva, brain, and sometimes the blood of the afflicted warmblooded animal. The incubation period is usually two weeks or as long as six months, which means you can be exposed to it without any visible symptoms. As we have said, while there is still no known cure, it can be controlled.

You can help effect this control by reporting animal bites and by educating the public on the dangers, symptoms, and prevention of it, so that we may reduce the fatalities.

There are two kinds of rabies; one form is called "furious" and the other is referred to as "dumb." The mad dog goes through several stages of the disease. His disposition and behavior change radically and suddenly; he becomes irritable and vicious. The eating habits alter, and he rejects food for things like stones and sticks; he becomes exhausted and drools saliva out of his mouth constantly. He may hide in corners, look glassy eyed and suspicious, bite at the air as he races around snarling and attacking with his tongue hanging out. At this point paralysis sets in, starting at the throat so that he can no longer drink water though he desires it desperately; hence, the term hydrophobia is given. He begins to stagger and eventually convulse, and death is imminent.

In "dumb" rabies paralysis is swift; the dog seeks dark, sheltered places and is abnormally quiet. Paralysis starts with the jaws, spreads down the body, and death is quick. Contact by humans or other animals with the drool from either of these types of rabies on open skin can produce the fatal disease, so extreme haste and proper diagnosis is essential. In other words, you do not have to be bitten by a rabid dog to have the virus enter your system. An open wound or cut that comes in touch with the saliva is all that is needed.

The incubation and degree of infection can vary. You usually contract the disease faster if the wound is near the head, since the virus travels to the brain through the spinal cord. The deeper the wound, the more saliva is injected into the body, and the more serious the infection. So, if bitten by a dog under any circumstances—

or any warmblooded animal for that matter—immediately wash out the wound with soap and water, bleed it profusely, and see your doctor as soon as possible.

Also, be sure to keep track of the animal that bit, if at all possible. When rabies is suspected, the public health officer will need to send the animal's head away to be analyzed. If it is found to be rabies free, you will not need to undergo treatment. Otherwise, your doctor may advise that you have the Pasteur treatment, which is extremely painful. It is rather simple, however, to have the veterinarian examine a dog for rabies without having the dog sent away for positive diagnosis of the disease. A ten-day quarantine is usually all that is necessary for everyone's peace of mind.

Rabies is no respecter of age, sex, or geographical location. It is found all over the world from North Pole to South Pole, and has nothing to do with the old wives' tale of dogs going mad in the hot summer months. True, there is an increase in reported cases during summer, but only because that is the time of the year for animals to roam free in good weather and during the mating season when the battle of the sexes is taking place. Inoculation and a keen eye for symptoms and bites on our dogs and other pets will help control the disease until the cure is found.

VACCINATIONS

If you are to raise a puppy, or a litter of puppies, successfully, you must adhere to a realistic and strict schedule of vaccinations. Many puppyhood diseases can be fatal—all of them are debilitating. According to the latest statistics, 98 per cent of all puppies are being inoculated after 12 weeks of age against the dread distemper, hepatitis, and leptospirosis and manage to escape these horrible infections. Orphaned puppies should be vaccinated every two weeks until the age of 12 weeks. Distemper and hepatitis live-virus vaccines should be used, since orphaned puppies are not protected with the colostrum normally supplied to them through the mother's milk. Puppies weaned at six to seven weeks should also be inoculated repeatedly because they will no longer be receiving mother's milk. While not all will receive protection from the serum at this early age, it should be given and they should be vaccinated once again at both nine and 12 weeks of age.

Leptospirosis vaccination should be given at four months of age with thought given to

booster shots if the disease is known in the area, or in the case of show dogs which are exposed on a regular basis to many dogs from far and wide. While animal boosters are in order for distemper and hepatitis, every two or three years is sufficient for leptospirosis, unless there is an outbreak in your immediate area. The one exception should be the pregnant bitch, since there is reason to believe that inoculation might cause damage to the fetus.

Strict observance of such a vaccination schedule will not only keep your dog free of these debilitating diseases, but will prevent an epidemic in your kennel, or in your locality, or to the dogs that are competing at the shows.

SNAKEBITE

As field trials and hunts and the like become more and more popular with dog enthusiasts, the incident of snakebite becomes more of a likelihood. Dogs that are kept outdoors in runs or dogs that work the fields and roam on large estates are also likely victims.

Most veterinarians carry snakebite serum, and snakebite kits are sold to dog owners for just such a purpose. To catch a snakebite in time might mean the difference between life and death, and whether your area is populated with snakes or not, it behooves you to know what to do in case it happens to you or your dog.

Captions for pages 226-227.
1. Wotan's Ami Akagane Hana winning the Breed and on to Group Second at the 1983 Lorain County Kennel Club show. Owned by Peggy Casselberry, Wotan Kennels, North Canton, Ohio. 2. Three, 3½-month-old look-alikes! Wotan Kennels puppies named Ami Akagane Hana, Dust Devil, and Royal Soga Hime. 3. Six-month-old Toranaga's Sama of Wotan, one of the breeding representatives at the Wotan Kennels. 4. Wotan's Royal Soga Hime, a Mr. Man grandson, pictured at 3½ months of age. The sire was Ch. Bo Echols Ambec Minke ex River View's Perfect Ten. Bred and owned by the Wotan Kennels. 5. Ch. Hot's Okamaku, owned by Victor Rivera, M.D., and photographed at Purchase, New York in 1982 by John Rivera. The sire was Ch. Windrifts' Huggy Bear, C.D., ex Hot's Tomba Jean of Hachiuco. 6. Annette Rivera with her pal "Kuma," registered as Boshi Akai Hachimitsu, owned and photographed by John A. Rivera of Yonkers, New York. The sire was Ch. Windrift's Huggy Bear, C.D., ex Hot's Sarene Sharene of Yuko. 7. John Rivera's 1981 photograph of his Emperor Genghis Banzai I on Hunter Mountain, New York. The sire was Ch. Bar-K's MacGreggor ex Jamar's Alco.

1 2

3 4

5 6

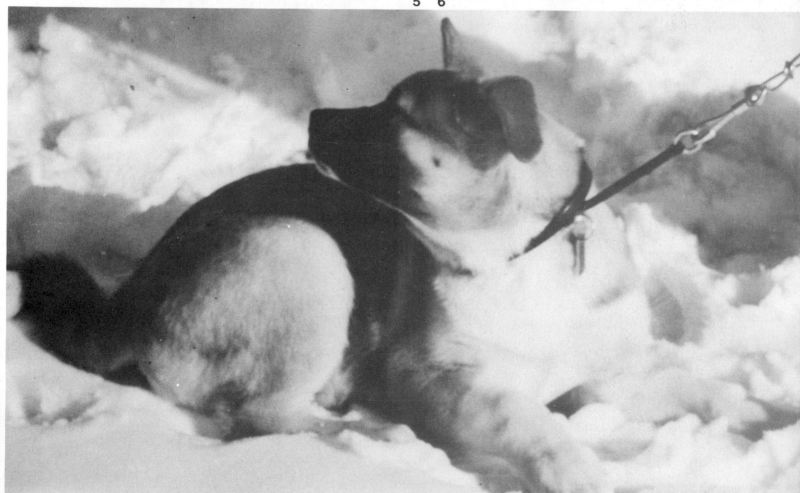

7

Your primary concern should be to get to a doctor or veterinarian immediately. The victim should be kept as quiet as possible (excitement or activity spreads the venom through the body more quickly) and if possible the wound should be bled enough to clean it out before applying a tourniquet, if the bite is severe.

First of all, it must be determined if the bite is from a poisonous or non-poisonous snake. If the bite carries two horseshoe-shaped pinpoints of a double row of teeth, the bite can be assumed to be non-poisonous. If the bite leaves two punctures or holes—the result of the two fangs carrying venom—the bite is very definitely poisonous and time is of the essence.

Recently, physicians have come up with an added help in the case of snakebite. A first aid treatment referred to as "hypothermia," which is the application of ice to the wound to lower body temperature to a point where the venom spreads less quickly, minimizes swelling, helps prevent infection, and has some influence on numbing the pain. If ice is not readily available, the bite may be soaked in ice-cold water. But even more urgent is the need to get the victim to a hospital or a veterinarian for additional treatment.

EMERGENCIES

No matter how well you run your kennel or keep an eye on an individual dog, there will almost invariably be some emergency at some time that will require quick treatment until you get the animal to the veterinarian. The first and most important thing to remember is to keep calm! You will think more clearly and your animal will need to know he can depend on you to take care of him. However, he will be frightened and you must beware of fear biting. Therefore, do not shower him with kisses and endearments at this time, no matter how sympathetic you feel. Comfort him reassuringly, but keep your wits about you. Before getting him to the veterinarian try to alleviate the pain and the shock.

If you can take even a minor step in this direction it will be a help toward the final cure. Listed here are a few of the emergencies that might occur and what you can do AFTER you have called the vet and told him you are coming.

BURNS

If you have been so foolish as to not turn your pot handles toward the back of the stove—for your children's sake as well as your dog's—and the dog is burned by the contents of a pot that has been knocked off its burner, apply ice or ice-cold water and treat for shock. Electrical or chemical burns are treated the same, but with an acid or alkali burn, use, respectively, a bicarbonate of soda and a vinegar solution. Check the advisability of covering the burn when you call the veterinarian.

DROWNING

Most animals love the water but sometimes get in "over their heads." Should your dog take in too much water, hold him upside down and open his mouth so that water can empty from the lungs, then apply artificial respiration or mouth-to-mouth resuscitation. With a large dog, hang the head over a step or off the end of a table while you hoist the rear end in the air by the back feet. Then treat for shock by covering him with a blanket.

FITS AND CONVULSIONS

Prevent the dog from thrashing about and injuring himself, cover with a blanket, and hold down until you can get him to the veterinarian.

FROSTBITE

There is no excuse for an animal getting frostbite if you are "on your toes" and care for the animal; however, should frostbite set in, thaw out the affected area slowly by massaging with a circular motion and stimulation. Use Vaseline to help keep the skin from peeling off and/or drying out.

HEART ATTACK

Be sure the animal keeps breathing by applying artificial respiration. A mild stimulant may be used, and give him plenty of air. Treat for shock as well, and get him to the veterinarian quickly.

SHOCK

Shock is a state of circulatory collapse that can be induced by a severe accident, loss of blood, heart failure, or any injury to the nervous system. Until you can get the dog to the veterinarian, keep him warm by covering him with a blanket. Try to keep the dog quiet until the appropriate medication can be prescribed. Relapse is not uncommon, so the dog must be observed carefully for several days after initial shock.

SUFFOCATION

Administer artificial respiration and treat for shock with plenty of air.

SUN STROKE

Cooling the dog off immediately is essential. Ice packs, submersion in ice water, and plenty of cool air are needed.

WOUNDS

Open wounds or cuts that produce bleeding must be treated with hydrogen peroxide, and tourniquets should be used if bleeding is excessive. Also, shock treatment must be given, and the animal must be kept warm.

THE FIRST AID KIT

It would be sheer folly to try to operate a kennel or to keep a dog without providing for certain emergencies that are bound to crop up when there are active dogs around. Just as you would provide a first aid kit for people, you should also provide a first aid kit for the animals on the premises.

The first aid kit should contain the following items:

medicated powder

jar of Vaseline

cotton swabs

bandage—1" gauze

adhesive tape

Band-Aids

cotton gauze or cotton balls

boric acid powder

A trip to your veterinarian is always safest, but there are certain preliminaries for cuts and bruises of a minor nature that you can care for yourself.

Cuts, for instance, should be washed out and medicated powder or Vaseline applied with a bandage. The lighter the bandage the better so that the most air possible can reach the wound. Q-tips can be used for removing debris from the eyes, after which a mild solution of boric acid wash can be applied. As for sores, use dry powder on wet sores, and Vaseline on dry sores. Use cotton for washing out wounds and drying them.

A particular caution must be given here on bandaging. Make sure that the bandage is not too tight to hamper the dog's circulation. Also, make sure the bandage is applied correctly so that the dog does not bite at it trying to remove it. A great deal of damage can be done to a wound by a dog tearing at a bandage to get it off.

If you notice the dog is starting to bite at it, do it over or put something on the bandage that smells and tastes bad to him. Make sure, however, that the solution does not soak through the bandage and enter the wound. Sometimes, if it is a leg wound, a sock or stocking slipped on the dog's leg will cover the bandage edges and will also keep it clean.

HOW NOT TO POISON YOUR DOG

Ever since the appearance of Rachel Carson's book *Silent Spring*, people have been asking, "Just how dangerous are chemicals?" In the animal fancy where disinfectants, room deodorants, parasitic sprays, solutions, and aerosols are so widely used, the question has taken on even more meaning. Veterinarians are beginning to ask, "What kind of disinfectant do you use?" "Have you any fruit trees that have been sprayed recently?" When animals are brought in to their offices in a toxic condition, or for unexplained death, or when entire litters of puppies die mysteriously, there is good reason to ask such questions.

The popular practice of protecting animals against parasites has given way to their being exposed to an alarming number of commercial products, some of which are dangerous to their very lives. Even flea collars can be dangerous, especially if they get wet or somehow touch the genital regions or eyes. While some products are much more poisonous than others, great care must be taken that they be applied in proportion to the size of the dog and the area to be covered. Many a dog has been taken to the vet with an

Captions for pages 230-231.
1. Kisu's The Block Buster and Ch. Kisu's Musume No Ikioi, owned by Betty Hinson of Jonesboro, Arkansas. 2. Betty Hinson's "Atosha" goes Winners Bitch at six months of age. 3. The Japanese type Akita. Kita Kaze with Betty Hinson's son, Derek. Kaze is four months old in this picture. 4. Going at it. . .Ch. Tamarlane's Capella and nephew Kum Yama's Tugger having a good romp. Owned by Akitas of Tamarlane, Green Valley, Arizona. 5. Ch. Tamarlane's Black Mariah, an example of the desired true velvet black pigmentation on a quality representative of the breed. Bred and owned by Sophia Kaluzniacki. 6. Ch. Tamarlane's Kenju Akuma, litter brother to Ch. Tamarlane's Silver Star, top winning Akita in the United States in 1979. The sire was Ch. Akita Tani's Daimyo, R.O.M., ex Ch. Frerose's Sarah Lei, R.O.M. Bred and owned by Dr. Sophia Kaluzniacki, Akitas of Tamarlane. 7. The top winning Akita Bitch for 1983 is Ch. Tamarlane's Capella. Owned by Carolyn Rennie and Dr. Sophia Kaluzniacki, she is another example of the Sarah-Daimyo cross that has produced 11 champions to date with 5 more pointed.

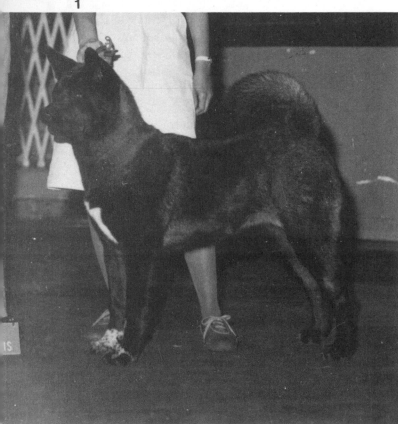

1

2 3

4 5

6 7

unusual skin problem that was a direct result of having been bathed with a detergent rather than a proper shampoo. Certain products that are safe for dogs can be fatal for cats. Extreme care must be taken to read all ingredients and instructions carefully before using the products on any animal.

The same caution must be given to outdoor chemicals. Dog owners must question the use of fertilizers on their lawns. Lime, for instance, can be harmful to a dog's feet. The unleashed dog that covers the neighborhood on his daily rounds is open to all sorts of tree and lawn sprays and insecticides that may prove harmful to him, if not as a poison, then as a producer of an allergy.

There are numerous products found around the house that can be lethal, such as rat poison, boric acid, hand soap, detergents, car anti-freeze, and insecticides. These are all available in the house or garage and can be tipped over easily and consumed. Many puppy fatalities are reported as a result of puppies eating mothballs. All poisons should be placed on high shelves out of the reach of *both* children and animals.

Perhaps the most readily available of all household poisons are plants. Household plants are almost all poisonous, even if taken in small quantities. Some of the most dangerous are the elephant ear, the narcissus bulb, any kind of ivy leaves, burning bush leaves, the jimson weed, the dumb cane weed, mock orange fruit, castor beans, Scottish broom seeds, the root or seed of the plant called "four o'clock," cyclamen, pimpernel, lily of the valley, the stem of the sweet pea, rhododendrons of any kind, spider lily bulbs, bayonet root, foxglove leaves, tulip bulbs, monkshood roots, azalea, wisteria, poinsettia leaves, mistletoe, hemlock, locoweed, and arrowglove. In all, there are over 500 poisonous plants in the United States. Peach, elderberry, and cherry trees can cause cyanide poisoning if the bark is consumed. Rhubarb leaves, either raw or cooked, can cause death or violent convulsions. Check out your closets, fields, and grounds around your home, and especially the dog runs, to see what should be eliminated to remove the danger to your dogs.

SYMPTOMS OF POISONING

Be on the lookout for vomiting, hard or labored breathing, whimpering, stomach cramps, and trembling as a prelude to convulsions. Any delay in a visit to your veterinarian can mean death. Take along the bottle or package or a sample of the plant you suspect to be the cause to help the veterinarian determine the correct antidote.

The most common type of poisoning, which accounts for nearly one-fourth of all animal victims, is staphylococcic—infected food. Salmonella ranks third. These can be avoided by serving fresh food and not letting it lie around in hot weather.

There are also many insect poisonings caused by animals eating cockroaches, spiders, flies, butterflies, etc. Toads and some frogs give off a fluid that can make a dog foam at the mouth— and even kill him—if he bites just a little too hard!

Some misguided dog owners think it is "cute" to let their dogs enjoy a cocktail with them before dinner. There can be serious effects resulting from encouraging a dog to drink— sneezing fits, injuries as a result of intoxication, and heart stoppage are just a few. Whiskey for medicinal purposes, or beer for brood bitches should be administered only on the advice of your veterinarian.

There have been cases of severe damage and death when dogs have emptied ash trays and eaten cigarettes, resulting in nicotine poisoning. Leaving a dog alone all day in a house where there are cigarettes available on a coffee table is asking for trouble. Needless to say, the same applies to marijuana. The narcotic addict who takes his dog along with him on "a trip" does not deserve to have a dog. All the ghastly side effects are as possible for the dog as for the addict, and for a person to submit an animal to this indignity is indeed despicable. Don't think it doesn't happen. Unfortunately, in all our major cities the practice is becoming more and more a problem for the veterinarian.

Be on the alert and remember that in the case of any type of poisoning, the best treatment is prevention.

THE CURSE OF ALLERGY

The heartbreak of a child being forced to give up a beloved pet because he is suddenly found to be allergic to it is a sad but true story. Many families claim to be unable to have dogs at all; others seem to be able only to enjoy them on a restricted basis. Many children know animals only through occasional visits to a friend's house or the zoo.

While modern veterinary science has produced some brilliant allergists, the field is still working on a solution for those who suffer from exposure to their pets. There is no permanent cure as yet.

Over the last quarter of a century there have been many attempts at a permanent cure, but none has proven successful because the treatment was needed too frequently, or was too expensive to maintain over extended periods of time.

However, we find that most people who are allergic to their animals are also allergic to a variety of other things as well. By eliminating the other irritants, and by taking medication given for the control of allergies in general, many are able to keep pets on a restricted basis. This may necessitate the dog's living outside the house, being groomed at a professional grooming parlor instead of by the owner, or merely being kept out of the bedroom at night. A discussion of this "balance" factor with your medical and veterinary doctors may give new hope to those willing to try.

A paper presented by Mathilde M. Gould, M.D., a New York allergist, before the American Academy of Allergists in the 1960's and reported in the September-October 1964 issue of the *National Humane Review* magazine, offered new hope to those who are allergic by a method referred to as hyposensitization. You may wish to write to the magazine and request the article for discussion of your individual problem.

Surely, since the sixties there have been additional advances in the field of allergy since so many people—and animals—are affected in so many ways.

ALLERGIES IN DOGS

It used to be that you recognized an allergy in your dog when he scratched out his coat and developed a large patch of raw skin or sneezed himself almost to death on certain occasions. A trip to the veterinarian involved endless discussion as to why it might be and an almost equally endless "hit and miss" cure of various salves and lotions with the hope that one of them would work. Many times the condition would correct itself.

However, during the 1970's through preliminary findings at the University of Pennsylvania Veterinary School there evolved a diagnosis for allergie that eliminated the need for skin sensitivity tests. It is called RAST, and is a radioallergosobant test performed with a blood serum sample. It is not even necessary in all cases for the veterinarian to see the dog.

A cellulose disc laced with a suspected allergen is placed in the serum, and if the dog is allergic to that particular allergen the serum will contain a specific antibody that adheres to the allergen on the disc. The disc is placed in a radioactively "labeled" antiserum that is attracted to that particular antibody. The antiserum binds with the antibody and can be detected with a radiation counter.

Furthermore, the scientists at the University of Pennsylvania also found that the RAST test has shown to be a more accurate diagnostic tool than skin testing because it measures the degree, and not merely the presence, of allergic reactions.

DO ALL DOGS CHEW?

Chewing is the best possible method of cutting teeth and exercising gums. Every puppy goes through this teething process, and it can be destructive if the puppy uses shoes or table corners or rugs instead of the proper item for the best possible results. All dogs should have a Nylabone available for chewing, not only to teethe on but also for inducing growth of the permanent teeth, to assure normal jaw development, and to settle the permanent teeth solidly in the jaws. Chewing on a Nylabone also has a cleaning effect and serves as a "massage" for the gums, keeping down the formation of tartar that erodes tooth enamel.

1

When you see a puppy pick up an object to chew, immediately remove it from his mouth with a sharp "No!" and replace the object with a Nylabone. Puppies take anything and everything into their mouths so they should be provided with several Nylabones to prevent damage to the household. This same Nylabone eliminates the need for the kind of "bone" which may chip your dog's mouth or stomach or intestinal walls. Cooked bones, soft enough to be powdered and added to the food, are also permissible if you have the patience to prepare them, but Nylabone serves all the purposes of bones for chewing that your dog may require, so why take a chance on meat bones?

Electrical cords and wires of any kind present a special danger that must be eliminated during puppyhood, and glass dishes that can be broken and played with are also hazardous.

The answer to the question about whether all dogs chew is an emphatic *yes*, and the answer if even more emphatic in the case of puppies.

SOME REASONS FOR CHEWING

Chewing can also be a form of frustration or nervousness. Dogs sometimes chew for spite, if owners leave them alone too long or too often. Bitches will sometimes chew if their puppies are taken away from them too soon; insecure puppies often chew thinking they're nursing. Puppies that chew wool, blankets, carpet corners, or certain other types of materials may have a nutritional deficiency or something lacking in their diet. Sometimes a puppy will crave the starch that might be left in material after washing. Perhaps the articles have been near something that tastes good and they have retained the odor of food.

The act of chewing has no connection with particular breeds or ages, any more than there is a logical reason for dogs to dig holes outdoors or dig on wooden floors indoors.

So we repeat, it is up to you to be on guard at all times until the need—or habit—passes.

HIP DYSPLASIA

Hip dysplasia, or HD, is one of the most widely discussed of all animal afflictions, since it has appeared in varying degrees in just about every breed of dog. True, the larger breeds seem most susceptible, but it has hit the small breeds and is beginning to be recognized in cats as well.

While HD in man has been recorded as far back as 370 B.C., HD in dogs was more than

likely referred to as rheumatism until veterinary research came into the picture. In 1935 Dr. Otto Schales, at Angell Memorial Hospital in Boston, wrote a paper on hip dysplasia and classified the four degrees of dysplasia of the hip joints as follows:

Grade 1—slight (poor fit between ball socket)
Grade 2—moderate (moderate but obvious shallowness of the socket)
Grade 3—severe (socket quite flat)
Grade 4—very severe (complete displacement of head of femur at early age)

HD is an incurable, hereditary, though not congenital disease of the hip sockets. It is transmitted as a dominant trait with irregular manifestations. Puppies appear normal at birth but the constant wearing away of the socket means the animal moves more and more on muscle, thereby presenting a lameness, a difficulty in getting up, and severe pain in advanced cases.

The degree of severity can be determined around six months of age, but its presence can be noticed from two months of age. The problem is determined by X-ray, and if pain is present it can be relieved temporarily by medication. Exercise should be avoided since motion encourages the wearing away of the bone surfaces.

Dogs with HD should not be shown or bred, if quality in the breed is to be maintained. It is essential to check a pedigree for dogs known to be dysplastic before breeding, since this disease can be dormant for many generations.

ELBOW DYSPLASIA

The same condition can also affect the elbow joints and is known as elbow dysplasia. This also causes lameness, and dogs so affected should not be used for breeding.

THE UNITED STATES REGISTRY

In the United States we have a central Hip Dysplasia Foundation, known as the OFA (Orthopedic Foundation for Animals). This HD control registry was formed in 1966. X-rays are sent for expert evaluation by qualified radiologists.

All you need do for complete information on getting an X-ray for your dog is to write to the Orthopedic Foundation for Animals at 817 Virginia Ave., Columbia, MO. 65201, and request their dysplasia packet. There is no charge for this kit. It contains an envelope large enough to hold your X-ray film (which you will have taken by your own veterinarian), and a drawing showing how to position the dog properly for

X-rays. There is also an application card for proper identification of the dog. Then, hopefully, your dog will be certified "normal." You will be given a registry number which you can put on his pedigree, use in your advertising, and rest assured that your breeding program is in good order.

All X-rays should be sent to the address above. Any other information you might wish to have may be requested from Mrs. Robert Bower, OFA, Route 1, Constantine, Mo. 49042.

We cannot urge strongly enough the importance of doing this. While it involves time and effort, the reward in the long run will more than pay for your trouble. To see the heartbreak of parents and children when their beloved dog has to be put to sleep because of severe hip dysplasia as the result of bad breeding is a sad experience. Don't let this happen to you or to those who will purchase your puppies!

Additionally, we should mention that there is a method of palpation to determine the extent of affliction. This can be painful if the animal is not properly prepared for the examination. There have also been attempts to replace the animal's femur and socket. This is not only expensive, but the percentage of success is small.

For those who refuse to put their dog down, there is a new surgical technique that can relieve pain but in no way constitutes a cure. This technique involves the severing of the pectinius muscle which for some unknown reason brings relief from pain over a period of many months—even up to two years. Two veterinary colleges in the United States are performing this operation at the present time. However, the owner must also give permission to "de-sex" the dogs at the time of the muscle severance. This is a safety measure to help stamp out hip dysplasia, since obviously the condition itself remains and can be passed on through generations.

HD PROGRAM IN GREAT BRITAIN

The British Veterinary Association (BVA) has made an attempt to control the spread of HD by appointing a panel of members of their profession who have made a special study of the disease to read X-rays. Dogs over one year of age may be X-rayed and certified as free. Forms are completed in triplicate to verify the tests. One copy remains with the panel, one copy is for the owner's veterinarian, and one for the owner. A record is also sent to the British Kennel Club for those wishing to check on a particular dog for breeding purposes.

GERIATRICS

If you originally purchased good healthy stock and cared for your dog throughout his life, there is no reason why you cannot expect your dog to live to a ripe old age. With research and the remarkable foods produced for dogs, especially in this past decade or so, his chances of longevity have increased considerably. If you have cared for him well, your dog will be a sheer delight in his old age, just as he was while in his prime.

We can assume you have fed him properly if he is not too fat. Have you ever noticed how fat people usually have fat dogs because they indulge their dog's appetite as they do their own? If there has been no great illness, then you will find that very little additional care and attention are needed to keep him well. Exercise is still essential, as is proper food, booster shots, and tender loving care.

Captions for pages 238-239.
1. Ch. Tamarlane's Kuma Yama Khan winning his first Working Group, owner-handled by Dean Herrmann. The Kuma Yama Kennels are in Whitewood, South Dakota. 2. Ch. Tamarlane's Kuma Yama Khan winning the Breed at a 1983 dog show under judge Charles Mulock. Owned by Bonnie and Dean Herrmann, Kuma Yama Kennels, Whitewood, South Dakota. 3. Ch. Kuma Yama's Ima Star, winning under judge Janet Wilcox at a recent show. Owned by Bonnie Herrmann of Whitewood, South Dakota. 4. Playing coy...Kuma Yama's Kazan, owned and bred by Bonnie and Dean Herrmann. 5. Ch. Kuma Yama's Smokin Joe, the first of many champions produced by Bonnie and Dean Herrmann at their Kuma Yama Kennels. 6. Kuma Yama's Kobe is pictured at eight months of age going Winners Dog for a 3-point major at this 1981 show. The sire was Tamarlane's Brigadoon ex Ch. Kuma Yama's Gold Star. 7. Ch. Bear Buttes Apache Dancer is pictured winning at a 1983 show under judge Robert Ligon. This Black Bart daughter is owned by Bonnie and Dean Herrmann, Kuma Yama Kennels.

FOURTH IN GROUP
FARGO - MOORHEAD K.C.
JUNE 5, 1983
OLSON PHOTO

1

BEST OF
BREED
KLAMATH
DOG FANCIERS
SEPTEMBER 1983

2   3

4

5

6

7

239

Even if a heart condition develops, there is still no reason to believe your dog cannot live to an old age. A diet may be necessary, along with medication and limited exercise, to keep the condition under control. In the case of deafness, or partial blindness, additional care must be taken to protect the dog, but neither infirmity will in any way shorten his life. Prolonged exposure to temperature variances; overeating; excessive exercise; lack of sleep; or being housed with younger, more active dogs may take an unnecessary toll on the dog's energies and induce serious trouble. Good judgment, periodic veterinary checkups, and individual attention will keep your dog with you for many added years.

When discussing geriatrics, the question of when a dog becomes old or aged usually is asked. We have all heard the old saying that one year of a dog's life is equal to seven years in a human. This theory is strictly a matter of opinion, and must remain so, since so many outside factors enter into how quickly each individual dog "ages." Recently, a new chart was devised that is more realistically equivalent:

DOG	MAN
6 months	10 years
1 year	15 years
2 years	24 years
3 years	28 years
4 years	32 years
5 years	36 years
6 years	40 years
7 years	44 years
8 years	48 years
9 years	52 years
10 years	56 years
15 years	76 years
21 years	100 years

It must be remembered that such things as serious illnesses, poor food and housing, general neglect, and poor beginnings as puppies will take their toll of a dog's general health and age him more quickly than a dog that has led a normal, healthy life. Let your veterinarian help you determine an age bracket for your dog in his later years.

While good care should prolong your dog's life, there are several "old age" disorders to watch for no matter how well he may be doing. The tendency toward obesity is the most common, but constipation is another. Aging teeth and a slowing down of the digestive processes may hinder digestion and cause constipation, just as any major change in diet can bring on diarrhea. There is also the possibility of loss or impairment of hearing or eyesight which will also tend to make the dog wary and distrustful. Other behavioral changes may result as well, such as crankiness, loss of patience, and lack of interest; these are the most obvious changes. Other ailments may manifest themselves in the form of rheumatism, arthritis, tumors and warts, heart disease, kidney infections, male prostatism, and female disorders. Of course, all these require a veterinarian's checking the degree of seriousness and proper treatment.

DOG INSURANCE

Much has been said for and against canine insurance, and much more will be said before this kind of protection for a dog becomes universal and/or practical. There has been talk of establishing a Blue Cross-type plan similar to the one now existing for humans. However, the best insurance for your dog is YOU! Nothing compensates for tender, loving care. Like the insurance policies for humans, there will be a lot of fine print in the contracts revealing that the dog is not covered after all. These limited conditions usually make the acquisition of dog insurance expensive and virtually worthless.

Blanket coverage policies for kennels or establishments that board or groom dogs can be an advantage, especially in transporting dogs to and from their premises. For the one-dog owner, however, whose dog is a constant companion, the cost for limited coverage is not necessary.

THE HIGH COST OF BURIAL

Pet cemeteries are mushrooming across the nation. Here, as with humans, the sky can be the limit for those who wish to bury their pets ceremoniously. The costs of plots and satin-lined caskets, grave stones, flowers, etc., run the gamut of prices to match the emotions and means of the owner.

IN THE EVENT OF YOUR DEATH

This is a morbid thought perhaps, but ask yourself the question, "If death were to strike at this moment, what would become of my dogs?"

Perhaps you are fortunate enough to have a relative, child, spouse, or friend who would take over immediately, if only on a temporary basis. Perhaps you have already left instructions in your last will and testament for your pet's housing, as well as a stipend for its care.

Provide definite instructions before a disaster

occurs and your dogs are carted off to the pound to be destroyed, or stolen by commercially inclined neighbors with "resale" in mind. It is a simple thing to instruct your lawyer about your wishes in the event of sickness or death. Leave instructions as to feeding, etc., posted on your kennel room or kitchen bulletin board, or wherever your kennel records are kept. Also, tell several people what you are doing and why. If you prefer to keep such instructions private, merely place them in sealed envelopes in a known place with directions that they are to be opened only in the event of your death. Eliminate the danger of your animals suffering in the event of an emergency that prevents your personal care of them.

KEEPING RECORDS

Whether you have one dog or a kennel full of them, it is wise to keep written records. It takes only a few moments to record dates of inoculations, trips to the vet, tests for worms, etc. It can avoid confusion or mistakes or having your dog not covered with immunization if too much time elapses between shots because you have to guess at the date of the last shot.

Make the effort to keep all dates in writing rather than trying to commit them to memory. A rabies injection date can be a problem if you have to recall that "Fido had the shot the day Aunt Mary got back from her trip abroad, and, let's see, I guess that was around the end of June."

In an emergency, these records may prove their value if your veterinarian cannot be reached and you have to call on another, or if you move and have no case history on your dog for the new veterinarian.

Friendly enemies? Just friends at the Bearhold Kennels in Maryland.

Captions for pages 242-243.
1. Ch. Reiun Me No Shori is winning under judge Connie Bosold at a 1973 show. Owned by Mary Keen of Marlborough, Connecticut. 2. Ch. Echol's Daughter of Dai. 3. Ch. Matsu-Kaze's Mifune of Echols takes the Breed at a 1974 show. Owned by Mary Keen of Marlborough, Connecticut. 4. Ch. Va-Guas Kao Kuro Kuma, owned by P. Musil at a 1978 show.

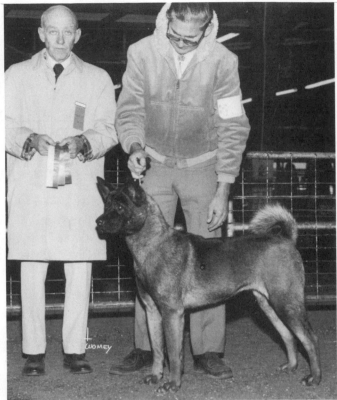

1 2

Petrulis

Chapter 16

The Blight of Parasites

Anyone who has ever spent hours peering intently at their dog's warm, pink stomach waiting for a flea to appear will readily understand why I call this chapter the "blight of parasites." It is that dreaded onslaught of the pesky flea that heralds the subsequent arrival of worms.

If you have seen even one flea scoot across that vulnerable expanse of skin, you can be sure there are more lurking on other areas of your dog. They seldom travel alone. So, it is now an established fact that *la puce*, as the French refer to the flea, has set up housekeeping on your dog! It is going to demand a great deal of your time before you manage to evict them—probably just temporarily at that—no matter which species your dog is harboring.

Fleas are not always choosy about their host, but chances are your dog has what is commonly known as *Ctenocephalides canis*, the dog flea. If you are a lover of cats also, your dog might even be playing host to a few *Ctenocephalides felis*, the cat flea, or vice versa. The only thing you can be really sure of is that your dog is supporting an entire community of them, all hungry and sexually oriented, and you are going to have to be persistent in your campaign to get rid of them.

One of the chief reasons fleas are so difficult to catch is that what they lack in beauty and eyesight (they are blind at birth, throughout infancy, and see very poorly if at all during adulthood), they make up for in their fantastic ability to jump and scurry about.

While this remarkable ability to jump—some claim 150 times the length of their bodies—stands them in good stead with circus entrepreneurs and has given them claim to fame as chariot pullers and acrobats in side show attractions, the dog owner can be reduced to tears at the very thought of the onset of fleas.

Modern research has provided a panacea in the form of flea sprays, dips, collars, and tags which can be successful to varying degrees. However, there are those who still swear by the good old-fashioned methods of removing them by hand, which can be a challenge to your sanity as well as your dexterity.

Since the fleas' conformation (they are built like envelopes, long and flat), with their spiny skeletal system on the outside of their bodies, is specifically provided for slithering through forests of hair, they are given a distinct advantage to start with. Two antennae on the head select the best spot for digging and then two mandibles penetrate the skin and hit a blood vessel. It is also at this moment that the flea brings into play his spiny contours to prop himself against surrounding hairs to avoid being scratched off as he puts the bite on your dog. A small projecting tube is then lowered into the hole to draw out blood and another tube pumps saliva into the wound; this prevents the blood from clotting and allows the flea to drink freely. Simultaneously, your dog jumps into the air and gets one of those back legs into action, scratching endlessly and in vain, and ruining some coat at the same time!

If you should be so lucky as to catch an itinerant flea as it mistakenly shortcuts across your dog's stomach, the best hunting grounds in the world are actually in the deep fur all along the dog's back from neck to tail. However, the flea, like every other creature on earth, must have water, so several times during its residency it will make its way to the moister areas of your dog's anatomy such as the corners of the mouth, the eyes, or the genital parts. This is when the flea collars and tags are useful. Their fumes prevent fleas from passing the neck to get to the head of your dog.

Your dog can usually support several generations of fleas, if it doesn't scratch itself to death or go out of its mind with the itching in the interim. The propagation of the flea is insured by the strong mating instinct and the well-judged decision of the female flea as to the best time to deposit her eggs. She has the rare capacity to store semen until the time is right to lay the eggs after some previous brief encounter with a passing member of the opposite sex.

When that time comes for her to lay, she does so without so much as a backward glance and moves on. The dog shakes the eggs off during a normal day's wandering, and they remain on the ground until hatched and the baby fleas are ready to jump back onto a passing dog. If any of the eggs have remained on the original dog, chances are that in scratching an adult flea, he will help the baby fleas emerge from their shells.

Larval fleas are small and resemble slender maggots; they begin their lives eating their own egg shells until the dog comes along and offers them a return to the world of adult fleas, whose excrement provides the predigested blood pellets they must have to thrive. They cannot survive on fresh blood, nor are they capable at this tender age of digging for it themselves.

After a couple of weeks of this freeloading, the baby flea makes his own cocoon and becomes a pupa. This stage lasts long enough for the larval flea to grow legs, mandibles, and sharp spines and to flatten out and in general become identifiable as the commonly known and obnoxious *Ctenocephalides canis*. The process can take several weeks or several months, depending on weather conditions, heat, moisture, etc., but generally three weeks is all that is required to enable the flea to start gnawing your dog in its own right.

And so the life-cycle of the flea is renewed and begun again. If you don't have plans to stem the tide, you will certainly see a population explosion that will make the human one resemble an endangered species. Getting rid of fleas can be accomplished by the aforementioned spraying of the dog, or the flea collars and tags, but air, sunshine and a good shaking out of beds, bedding, carpets, cushions, etc., certainly must be undertaken to get rid of the eggs or larvae lying around the premises.

Should you be lucky enough to get hold of a flea, you must squeeze it to death (which isn't likely) or break it in two with a sharp, strong fingernail (which also isn't likely) or you must release it *underwater* in the toilet bowl and flush immediately. This prospect is only slightly more likely.

There are those dog owners, however, who are much more philosophical about the flea, since, like the cockroach, it has been around since the beginning of the world. For instance, that old-time philosopher, David Harum, has been much quoted with his remark, "A reasonable amount of fleas is good for a dog. They keep him from broodin' on bein' a dog." We would rather agree with John Donne who in his *Devotions* reveals that, "The flea, though he kill none, he does all the harm he can." This is especially true if your dog is a show dog! If the scratching doesn't ruin the coat, the inevitable infestation of parasites left by the fleas will!

We readily see that dogs can be afflicted by both internal and external parasites. The external parasites are known as the aforementioned fleas, plus ticks and lice; while all of these are bothersome, they can be treated. However, the internal parasites, or worms of various kinds, are usually well-entrenched before discovery and more substantial means of ridding the dog of them completely are required.

INTERNAL PARASITES

The most common worms are the round worms. These, like many other worms, are carried and spread by the flea and go through a cycle within the dog host. They are excreted in egg or larval form and passed on to other dogs in this manner.

Worm medicine should be prescribed by a veterinarian, and dogs should be checked for worms at least twice a year—or every three months if there is a known epidemic in your area— and during the summer months when fleas are plentiful.

Major types of worms are hookworms, whipworms, tapeworms (the only non-round worms in this list), ascarids (the "typical" round worms), heartworms, kidney and lung worms. Each can be peculiar to a part of the country or may be carried by a dog from one area to another. Kidney and lung worms are fortunately

Captions for pages 246-247.
1. Ch. Toshi, owned by Barbara J. Cox of Placerville, California. 2. Ch. Jamel Tomadachi Eni Meanie, whelped in 1976, owned by Jackie and Mel Towbin. The sire was Ch. Va-Guas Jamel The Mean Machine ex Ch. Fallonway Chiisai No Ureshi. 3. Emperor Genghis Banzai I and his mistress Annette Rivera, photographed by John Rivera while on a walk in the woods in the fall of 1980. Banzai and Annette are "owned" by John and Nancy Rivera of Yonkers, New York. 4. Eleven-month-old Ch. Great River's Tsuki-Ko of Ginsan, bred by Robert Player and co-owned by Robert and Virginia Santoli of Islip, New York. 5. Twelve-year-old Jiro-Maru-No-Toyohashi, owned by Dr. and Mrs. Roger G. Gerry of Roslyn, New York. This photograph pictures "Sugi" in 1978, two years before his death at the age of fourteen.

1 2

3 4

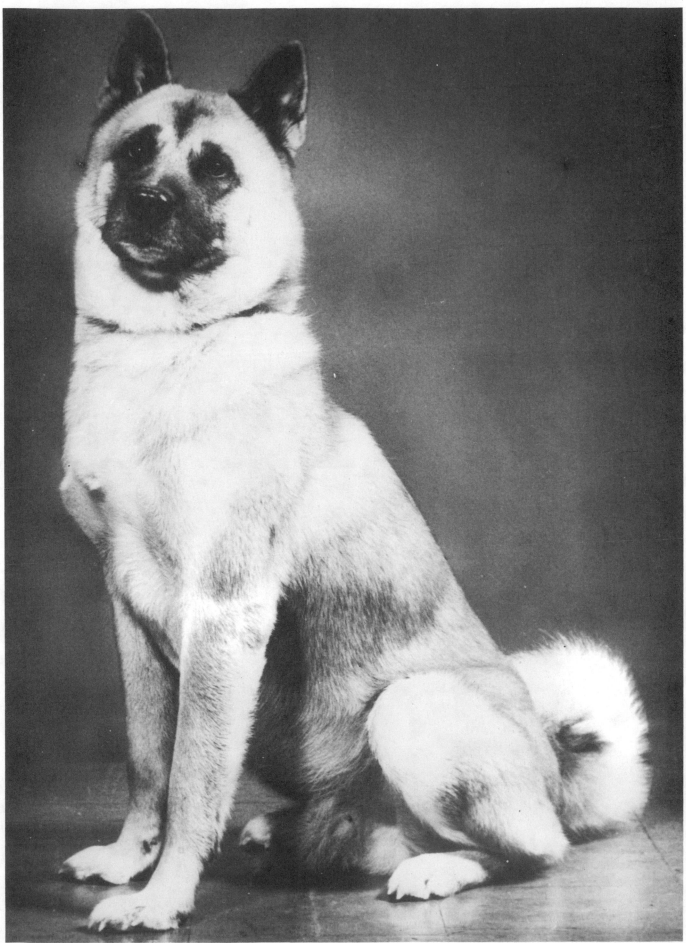

John and Nancy Rivera's "JJ" at the 1982 Greenwich Kennel Club show with handler Gale Schwartz. Photograph by John Rivera.

quite rare; the others are not. Some symptoms for worms are vomiting intermittently, eating grass, lack of pep, bloated stomach, rubbing the tail along the ground, loss of weight, dull coat, anemia and pale gums, eye discharge, or unexplained nervousness and irritability. A dog with worms will usually eat twice as much as he normally would.

Never worm a sick dog or a pregnant bitch after the first two weeks she has been bred, and never worm a constipated dog . . . it will retain the strong medicine within the body for too long a time.

HOW TO TEST FOR WORMS

Worms can kill your dog if the infestation is severe enough. Even light infestations of worms can debilitate a dog to the point where he is more susceptible to other serious diseases that can kill, if the worms do not.

Today's medication for worming is relatively safe and mild, and worming is no longer the traumatic experience for either the dog or owner that it used to be. Great care must be given, however, to the proper administration of the drugs. Correct dosage is a "must" and clean quarters are essential to rid your kennel of these parasites. It is almost impossible to find an animal that is completely free of parasites, so we must consider worming as a necessary evil.

However mild today's medicines may be, it is inadvisable to worm a dog unnecessarily. There are simple tests to determine the presence of worms and this chapter is designed to help you learn how to administer these tests yourself. Veterinarians charge a nominal fee for this service, if it is not part of their regular office visit examination. It is a simple matter to prepare fecal slides that you can read yourself on a periodic basis. Over the years it will save you much time and money, especially if you have more than one dog or a large kennel.

All that is needed by way of equipment is a microscope with 100X power. These can be purchased in the toy department of a department or regular toy store for a few dollars. The basic, least expensive sets come with the necessary glass slides and attachments.

After the dog has defecated, take an applicator stick, a toothpick with a flat end, or even an old-fashioned wooden matchstick and gouge off a piece of the stool about the size of a small pea. Have one of the glass slides ready with a large drop of water on it. Mix the two together until

you have a cloudy film over a large area of the slide. This smear should be covered with another slide or a cover slip—though it is possible to obtain readings with just the one open slide. Place your slide under the microscope and prepare to focus in on it. To read the slide you will find that your eye should follow a certain pattern. Start at the top and read from left to right, then right back to the left and then left over to the right side once again until you have looked at every portion of the slide from the top left to the bottom right side.

Make sure that your smear is not too thick or watery or the reading will be too dark and confused to make proper identification. If you decide you would rather not make your own fecal examinations, but would prefer to have the veterinarian do it, the proper way to present a segment of the stool for him to examine is as follows:

After the dog has defecated, a portion of the stool, say a square inch from different sections of it, should be placed in a glass jar or plastic container and labeled with the dog's name and address of the owner. If the sample cannot be examined within three or four hours after passage, it should be refrigerated.

Captions for pages 250-251.
1. Father-son winning combination under judge B. Wyler. Best of Breed win to the first Am. Can. and Bda. Ch. Kenji Ko Royal Tenji, R.O.M., with handler Dick Yates. Jo-Jo's son, Am. and Can. Ch. Frerose's Emperor Kenji is with handler Diane Murphy. Owned by Frederick Duane, Frerose Kennels, Shohola, Pennsylvania. 2. Lola of Frerose is pictured winning on the way to her championship under Judge Larry Goldworm. Diane Murphy handled for owner Frederick Duane. 3. Ch. Chishon Omori of Frerose, handled by Kay Martin for owner Frederick O. Duane. 4. Krug's Chocho-San of Zen, pictured winning under the late judge Len Carey at a 1982 show. Lisa Tschoke handled for owner Virginia Zwolinski of Hicksville, New York. "Candy" won a three-point major as Best of Winners and went on to Best of Breed over five Specials. Candy's sire was Ch. Krug's Red Kaddillac, top Akita male for 1981, out of Ch. Okami's Kori of Krug. 5. Krug's Kori No Akiko, bred by Bettye Krug and Eloise Seward and owned by Patricia Berglund. Akiko is pictured winning at the 1983 Catonsville Kennel Club show. The sire was Ch. Krug's Aka Shogun Okami Go ex Hanna of Chiko. 6. Ch. Krug's Hi Jo Zen is pictured here winning at a 1980 show on the way to his championship. "Bruiser" was handled by Lisa Tschoke to this win under judge J. J. Berry, Jr., for owners Ed and Virginia Zwolinski of Hicksville, New York. The sire was Ch. Krug's Yoshinari ex Ch. Krug's Hi Jo. 7. Asagao's Kumo No Kita, C.D., bred by Constance and Thomas Ditmore and owned by Patricia and Robert Berglund, of Hampstead, Maryland.

1

2   3

BEST OF WINNERS
BROOKHAVEN K.C.
OCTOBER 1, 1982
W. BUSHMAN PHOTO

WINNERS
ATONSVILLE
KENNEL CLUB
1983
ASHBEY

4 **5**

BEST OF WINNERS
DEVON
DOG SHOW ASSOC INC
KLEIN   OCT 1980

WINNERS
SHEER PHOTO

6 **7**

Chapter 17

Pursuing a Career in Dogs

One of the biggest joys for those of us who love dogs is to see someone we know or someone in our family grow up in the fancy and go on to enjoy the sport of dogs in later life. Many dog lovers, in addition to leaving codicils in their wills, are providing in other ways for veterinary scholarships for deserving youngsters who wish to make their association with dogs their profession.

Unfortunately, many children who have this earnest desire are not always able to afford the expense of an education that will take them through veterinary school, and they are not eligible for scholarships. In the 1960's during my tenure as editor of *Popular Dogs* magazine, I am happy to say I had something to do with the publicizing of college courses whereby those who could not go all the way to a veterinary degree could earn an Animal Science degree and thus still serve the fancy in a significant way. The Animal Science courses cost less than half of what it would take to become a veterinarian, and those achieving these titles have become a tremendous assistance to the veterinarian.

We all have experienced the more and more crowded waiting rooms at the veterinary offices, and are aware of the demands on the doctor's time, not just for office hours but for his research, consultation, surgery, etc. The tremendous increase in the number of dogs and cats and other domestic animals, both in cities and the suburbs, has resulted in an almost overwhelming consumption of veterinarians' time.

Until recently most veterinary assistance was made up of kennel men or women who were restricted to services more properly classified as office maintenance rather than actual veterinary aid. Needless to say, their part in the operation of a veterinary office is both essential and appreciated, as are the endless details and volumes of paperwork capably handled by office secretaries and receptionists.

With exactly this additional service in mind, many colleges are now conducting two-year courses in animal science for the training of such para-professionals, thereby opening a new field for animal technologists. The time saved by the assistance of these trained technicians, who now relieve the veterinarians of the more mechanical chores and allow them additional time for diagnosing and general servicing of their clients, will be beneficial to all involved.

"Delhi Tech," the State University Agricultural and Technical College at Delhi, New York, was one of the first to offer the required courses for this degree. Now, many other institutions of learning are offering comparable courses at the college level. Entry requirements are usually that each applicant must be a graduate of an approved high school or have taken the State University admissions examination. In addition, each applicant for the Animal Science Technology program must have some previous credits in mathematics and science, with chemistry an important part of the science background.

The program at Delhi was a new educational venture dedicated to the training of competent technicians for employment in the biochemical field and has been generously supported by a five-year grant, designated as a "Pilot Development Program in Animal Science." This grant provided both personal and scientific equipment with obvious good results when it was done originally pursuant to a contract with the United States Department of Health, Education, and Welfare. Delhi is a unit of the State University of New York and is accredited by the Middle States Association of Colleges and Secondary Schools. The campus provides offices, laboratories, and animal quarters and is equipped with modern instruments to train technicians in laboratory animal care, physiology, pathology, microbiology, anesthesia, X-ray, and germ-free techniques. Sizable animal colonies are maintained in air-conditioned quarters: animals housed include mice, rats, hamsters, guinea pigs, gerbils and rabbits, as well as dogs and cats.

First-year students are given such courses as livestock production, dairy food science, general, organic and biological chemistry, mammalian anatomy, histology and physiology, pathogenic microbiology, and quantitative and instrumental analysis, to name a few. Second year students matriculate in general pathology, animal parasitology, animal care and anesthesia, introductory psychology, animal breeding, animal nutrition, hematology and urinalysis, radiology, genetics, food sanitation and meat inspection, histological techniques, animal laboratory practices, and axenic techniques. These, of course, may be supplemented by electives that prepare the student for contact with the public in the administration of these duties. Such recommended electives include public speaking, botany, animal reproduction, and other related subjects.

In addition to Delhi, one of the first to offer this program was the State University of Maine. Part of their program offered some practical training for the students at the Animal Medical Center in New York City. Often after this initial "in the field" experience, the students could perform professionally immediately upon entering a veterinarian's employ as personnel to do laboratory tests, X-rays, blood work, fecal examinations, and general animal care. After the courses at college, they were equipped to perform all of the following procedures as para-professionals:

* Recording of vital information relative to a case. This would include such information as the client's name, address, telephone number, and other facts pertinent to the visit. The case history would include the breed, age of animal, its sex, temperature, etc.
* Preparation of the animal for surgery.
* Preparation of equipment and medicaments to be used in surgery.
* Preparation of medicaments for dispensing to clients on prescription of the attending veterinarian.
* Administration and application of certain medicines.
* Administration of colonic irrigations.
* Application or changing of wound dressings.
* Cleaning of kennels, exercise runs, and kitchen utensils.
* Preparation of food and the feeding of patients.
* Explanation to clients on the handling and restraint of their pets, including needs for exercise, house training, and elementary obedience training.
* First-aid treatment for hemorrhage, including the proper use of tourniquets.
* Preservation of blood, urine, and pathologic material for the purpose of laboratory examination.
* General care and supervision of the hospital or clinic patients to insure their comfort. Nail trimming and grooming of patients.

Credits are necessary, of course, to qualify for this program. Many courses of study include biology, zoology, anatomy, genetics, and animal diseases, and along with the abovementioned courses the fields of client and public relations are touched upon as well as a general study of the veterinary medical profession.

By the mid-seventies there were a reported 30,000 veterinarians practicing in the United States. It is estimated that within the following decade more than twice that number will be needed to take proper care of the domestic animal population in this country. While veterinarians are graduated from 22 accredited veterinary colleges in this country and Canada, recent figures released by the Veterinary Medical Society inform us that only one out of every seven applicants is admitted to these colleges. It becomes more and more obvious that the para-professional person will be needed to back up the doctor.

Students having the desire and qualifications to become veterinarians, however, may suffer financial restrictions that preclude their education and licensing as full-fledged veterinarians. The Animal Science Technologist with an Associate degree in Applied Science may very well become the answer as a profession in an area close to their actual desire.

Captions for pages 254-255.
1. Ch. O'BJ's Wild Alaska of Northland, multiple Group-Placing bitch that finished at 10 months of age. Owner-handled to this win by Loren Egland of Rochester, Minnesota, at the 1983 Mason City Kennel Club show. The sire was Ch. Okii Yubi Sachmo of Makoto ex Ch. Katagi No Ayame Go. 2. Ch. O'B.J. Silver Chalice of Tomoko pictured winning Best of Breed at 3 years of age. Tomo was a champion at 9 months of age. Owned by Marvin and Elaine Nussbaum of Greenbelt, Maryland. 3. Ch. O'B.J. Char-Ko at seven months of age winning Best of Breed at the 1981 Hendersonville Kennel Club Show under judge Thomas Cately. Owned by Bill and B. J. Andrews of Asheville, North Carolina. 4. Ch. O'BJ Kye-Kye-Go of E Oka, pictured at 10 weeks of age and already into mischief. Owned by Linda Henson and Peggy Brereton of Peoria Heights, Illinois. 5. Am. and Can. Ch. Windrift's Fujiko-Chan, handled by Barbara Shanks for owners David and Barbara Shanks and Pat Mucher. 6. The #1 Bitch in 1983 and winner of Best of Opposite Sex at the 1983 Akita Club of America National Specialty show was Ch. O'BJ Kye-Kye-Go of E Oka. She is pictured here winning a Group at the 1983 Illinois Valley Kennel Club show. Owned by E Oka Kennels. 7. Ch. Bar-BJ's Honcho of Windrift, owned by Pat Mucher, was whelped in 1978 and bred by Barbara and B. J. Hampton of Las Vegas, Nevada. 8. Ch. Bar-BJ's Brown Bomber, bred and owned by Barbara and B. J. Hampton. He is pictured winning Best of Breed over Specials from the classes on the way to his championship under judge Don Bradley.

1

2

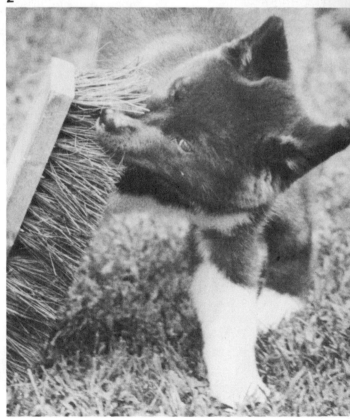

3

4

5 6

7 8

255

Their assistance in the pharmaceutical field, where drug concerns deal with laboratory animals, covers another wide area for trained assistants. The career opportunities are varied and reach into job opportunities in medical centers, research institutions, and government health agencies; at present, the demand for graduates far exceeds the current supply of trained personnel.

As to financial remuneration, beginning yearly salaries are relatively low and estimated costs of basic college expenses relatively high but the latter include tuition, room and board, college fees, essential textbooks, and limited personal expenses. These personal expenses, of course, will vary with individual students, as well as their other expenses, though the costs are about half of those involved in becoming a full-fledged veterinarian.

High school graduates with a sincere affection and regard for animals and a desire to work with veterinarians and perform such clinical duties as mentioned above will find they fit in especially well.

Those interested in pursuing a career of this nature might obtain the most current list of accredited colleges and universities offering these programs by consulting the American Veterinary Medical College, 600 S. Michigan Avenue, Chicago, Illinois 60605.

As the popularity of this profession increased, additional attention was given to the list of services, and the degrees to which one could aspire was expanded. There are para-professionals with Associate of Science degrees, and some colleges and universities have extended the courses to four years duration which lead to Bachelor of Science degrees.

At the University of Minnesota Technical College, a two year course offers a degree of Associate in Applied Science after the successful completion of 108 credit hours. This Animal Health Technology course prepares the students for future careers in the following fields:

* Laboratory Animal Technician (Junior)
* Experimental Animal Technician
* Clinical Laboratory Animal Assistant
* Laboratory Animal Assistant in Radiology
* Laboratory Animal Research Assistant
* Small Animal Technician (General)
* Small Animal Veterinarian's Assistant
* Small Animal Veterinarian's Receptionist
* Animal Hospital Technician

* Zoo Technician
* Large Animal Technician (General)
* Large Animal Veterinarian's Receptionist
* Large Animal Clinic Assistant

CANINE COLLEGE IN JAPAN

The Japanese love dogs. Recent statistics report that there is one dog for every thirteen people, adding up to about 8,000,000 dogs on those small islands. True, some Orientals eat dog meat, but most cherish their dogs as pets, guards, and companions. There is a large dog-loving population in the Land of the Rising Sun.

In 1967 Ryouju Yamazaki, a Japanese career counselor, saw the need for a school to train young Japanese women in the art of caring for animals.

Over the years this unique school has had an acknowledged influence on Japanese culture concerning human-animal relationships, and the 400 or more young women engaged in the two-year course are well versed in the grooming, training, and biological research work involved in their career. After graduation these young women will be capable of serving as professional licensed technicians for veterinarians.

The extensive course offered includes canine psychology, veterinary science, public health, judging, ethics, physics, biology, chemistry, business administration, and law. It also touches on specialized training in counseling for the loss of beloved pets, care, therapy, and the like. A specially interesting course is that of health promotion for disturbed children. Forty-five technicians serve on the faculty. Many more highly technical courses are provided in the college curriculum. President Yamazaki is president of the International Dog Education Association, and their health promotion services are comparable to those offered by the University of Pennsylvania and University of Minnesota.

PART TIME KENNEL WORK

Youngsters who do not wish to go on to become veterinarians or animal technicians can get valuable experience and extra money by working part-time after school and on weekends, or full-time during summer vacations, in a veterinarian's office. The exposure to animals and office procedure will be time well spent.

Kennel help is also an area that is wide open for retired men and women. They are able to help out in many areas where they can learn and stay active, and most of the work allows them to set their own pace. The understanding and patience that age and experience brings is also beneficial to the animals they will deal with; for their part, these people find great reward in their contribution to animals and will be keeping active in the business world as well.

PROFESSIONAL HANDLING

For those who wish to participate in the sport of dogs and whose interests or abilities do not center around the clinical aspects of the fancy, there is yet another avenue of involvement.

For those who excel in the show ring, who enjoy being in the limelight and putting their dogs through their paces, a career in professional handling may be the answer. Handling may include a weekend of showing a few dogs for special clients, or it may be a full-time career that can also include boarding, training, conditioning, breeding, and showing dogs for several clients.

Depending on how deep your interest is, the issue can be solved by a lot of preliminary consideration before it becomes necessary to make a decision. The first move would be to have a long, serious talk with a successful professional handler to learn the pros and cons of such a profession. Watching handlers in action from ringside as they perform their duties can be revealing.

Professional handling is not all glamour in the show ring. There is plenty of "dirty work" behind the scenes 24 hours of every day. You must have the necessary ability and patience for this work, as well as the ability and patience to deal with the CLIENTS—the dog owners who value their animals above almost anything else and would expect a great deal from you in the way of care and handling.

DOG TRAINING

Like the professional handler, the professional dog trainer has a most responsible job. You need not only to be thoroughly familiar with the correct and successful methods of training a dog but must also have the ability to communicate with dogs.

Training schools are quite the vogue nowadays, with all of them claiming success. Careful investigation should be made before enrolling a dog, and even more careful investigation should be made of their methods and of their actual successes before becoming associated with them.

DOG JUDGING

There are also those whose professions, age, or health prevent them from owning, breeding, or showing dogs, and who turn to judging at dog shows after their active years in the show ring are no longer possible. Breeder-judges make a valuable contribution to the fancy by judging in accordance with their years of experience in the fancy, and the assignments are enjoyable. Judging requires experience and a good eye for dogs.

GROOMING PARLORS

If you do not wish the 24-hour a day job that is required by a professional handler or professional trainer, but still love working with and caring for dogs, there is always the very profitable grooming business. Poodles started the ball rolling for the swanky, plush grooming establishments that sprang up all over the major cities, many of which seem to be doing very well. Here again, handling dogs and the public well is necessary for a successful operation, in addition to skill in the actual grooming of dogs of all breeds.

While shops flourish in the cities, some of the suburban areas are now featuring mobile units which by appointment will visit your home with a completely equipped shop on wheels and will groom your dog right in your own driveway.

Captions for pages 258-259.
1. This 1974 champion is Kufuku-No's Kaminari O-Sama, owned by Mary Keen of Marlborough, Connecticut, and handled for her to this win under judge John Stanek by Nancy Stuck. 2. An early champion, Ch. Matsu-Kaze's Kuro Kitsune, owned by Mary Keen. 3. Ch. Echols Honesty Best Policy, handled by Mary Keen at this 1981 show. 4. Ch. Costa Brava's A Touch of Class, owned by James Sailer, and pictured on her way to championship at a 1977 show. 5. Ch. Echols Sunset Warrior, owned and handled by Mary Echols Keen of Marlborough, Connecticut. The Warrior is pictured here winning at a 1981 show on the way to his championship. 6. Ch. Echols Haiiro Kitsune, with Mary Keen handling at this 1978 show. 7. Winning Best of Winners io Echols Charlemagne of Haiku on the way to his championship. Owned by Mary Keen.

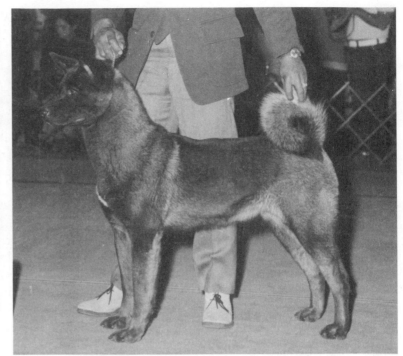

1   2

3   4

258

5

6　7

Glossary

Achilles heel. The major tendon attaching the muscles of the calf from the thigh to the hock.

AKC. The American Kennel Club. Address: 51 Madison Avenue, New York, NY 10010.

Albino. Pigment deficiency, usually a congenital fault.

Almond eye. The shape of the eye opening, rather than the eye itself, which slants upwards at the outer edge, hence giving it an almond shape.

American Kennel Club. Registering body for canine world in the United States. Headquarters for the stud book, dog registrations, and federation of kennel clubs. It also creates and enforces rules and regulations governing dog shows.

Angulation. The angles formed by the meeting of the bones.

Anus. Anterior opening found under the tail for purposes of alimentary canal elimination.

Apple-head. An irregular roundness of topskull. A domed skull.

Apron. On long-coated dogs, the longer hair that frills outward from the neck and chest.

Balanced. A symmetrical, correctly proportioned animal; one having correct balance of one part in regard to another.

Barrel. Rounded rib section; thorax, chest.

Bat ear. An erect ear, broad at base, rounded or semi-circular at top, with opening directly in front.

Beard. Profuse whisker growth.

Beauty spot. Usually roundish colored hair on a blaze of another color. Found mostly between the ears.

Beefy. Overdevelopment or overweight in a dog, particularly hindquarters.

Bitch. The female dog.

Blaze. A type of marking; white stripe running up the center of the face between the eyes.

Blocky. Square head.

Bloom. Dogs in top condition are said to be "in full bloom."

Blue merle. A color designation. Blue and gray mixed with black; marbled-like appearance.

Bossy. Overdevelopment of the shoulder muscles.

Brace. Two dogs (a matched pair) that move in unison.

Breeching. Tan-colored hair on inside of the thighs.

Brindle. Even mixture of black hairs with brown, tan, or gray.

Brisket. The forepart of the body below the chest.

Broken color. A color broken by white or another color.

Broken-haired. A wiry coat.

Broken-up face. Receding nose together with deep stop, wrinkle, and undershot jaw.

Brood bitch. A female used for breeding.

Brush. A bushy tail.

Burr. Inside part of the ear which is visible to the eye.

Butterfly nose. Parti-colored nose or entirely flesh color.

Button ear. The edge of the ear which folds to cover the opening of the ear.

C.A.C.I.B. Award made in European countries to international champion dogs.

Canine. Animals of the Canidae family which includes not only dogs, but foxes, wolves, and jackals.

Canines. The four large teeth in the front of the mouth often referred to as fangs.

Castrate. To surgically remove the testicles on the male dog.

Cat-foot. Round, tight, high-arched feet said to resemble those of a cat.

Character. The general appearance or expression said to be typical of the breed.

Cheeky. Fat cheeks or protruding cheeks.

Chest. Forepart of the body between the shoulder blades and above the brisket.

China eye. A clear blue wall-eye.

Chiseled. A clean-cut head, especially when chiseled out below the eye.

Chops. Jowls or pendulous lips.

Clip. Method of trimming coats according to an individual breed standard.

Cloddy. Thick set or plodding dog.

Close-coupled. A dog short in loins; comparatively short from withers to hipbones.

Cobby. Short-bodied; compact.

Collar. Usually a white marking, resembling a collar, around the neck.

Condition. General appearance of a dog showing good health, grooming, and good care.

Conformation. The form and structure of the bone or framework of the dog in comparison with requirements of the breed.

Corky. Active and alert dog.

Couple. Two dogs.

Coupling. Leash or collar-ring for a brace of dogs.

Couplings. Body between the withers and the hipbones.

Cowhocked. When the hocks turn toward each other and sometimes touch.

Crank tail. Tail carried down.

Crest. Arched portion of the back of the neck.

Cropping. Cutting or trimming of the ear leather to get ears to stand erect.

Crossbred. A dog whose sire and dam are of two different breeds.

Croup. The back part of the back above the hind legs. Area from hips to tail.

Crown. The highest part of the head; the topskull.

Cryptorchid. Male dog with neither testicle visible.

Culotte. The long hair on the back of the thighs.

Cushion. Fullness of upper lips.

Dappled. Mottled marking of different colors with none predominating.

Deadgrass. Dull tan color.

Dentition. Arrangement of the teeth.

Dewclaws. Extra claws, or functionless digits on the inside of the front and/or rear legs.

Dewlap. Loose, pendulous skin under the throat.

Dish-faced. When nasal bone is so formed that nose is higher at the end than in the middle or at the stop.

Disqualification. A dog that has a fault making it ineligible to compete in dog show competitions.

Distemper teeth. Discolored or pitted teeth as a result of having had distemper.

Dock. To shorten the tail by cutting.

Dog. A male dog, though used freely to indicate either sex.

Domed. Evenly rounded in topskull; not flat but curved upward.

Down-faced. When nasal bone inclines toward the tip of the nose.

Down in pastern. Weak or faulty pastern joints; a let-down foot.

Drop ear. The leather pendant which is longer than the leather of the button ear.

Dry neck. Taut skin.

Dudley nose. Flesh-colored or light brown pigmentation in the nose.

Elbow. The joint between the upper arm and the forearm.

Elbows out. Turning out or off the body and not held close to the sides.

Ewe neck. Curvature of the top of neck.

Expression. Color, size, and placement of the eyes which give the typical expression associated with a breed.

Faking. Changing the appearance of a dog by artificial means to make it more closely resemble the standard. Using chalk to whiten white fur, etc.

Fall. Hair which hangs over the face.

Feathering. Longer hair fringe on ears, legs, tail, or body.

Feet east and west. Toes turned out.

Femur. The large heavy bone of the thigh.

Fiddle front. Forelegs out at elbows, pasterns close, and feet turned out.

Flag. A long-haired tail.

Flank. The side of the body between the last rib and the hip.

Captions for pages 262-263.
1. Birthday party for Royal Yoko Hime and Ch. Tsuyoi Inu's Toshi. Yoko celebrates her first birthday and Toshi his second with a birthday cake of chopped liver "iced" with cottage cheese. The party-giver was Barbara Cox of Placerville, California. 2. Toyo has a tug of war with a Cocker Spaniel friend. Owned by Barbara Cox. 3. Waiting at poolside for summer to return! Black Bronco and friend at Tobe Kennels, Branchville, New Jersey. 4. Tamarlane's Unsinkable Molly, owned by famous singer Linda Ronstadt, and bred by Sophia Kaluzniacki, D.V.M., Green Valley, Arizona. The sire was Ch. Akita Tani's Nishiki Ryu ex Ch. Tamarlane's Akita Tani Ursula. 5. Ch. Kin Hozan's Mogami winning under judge John Stanek with handler Janne Tuck. Owned by Pat Castronova of Denver, Colorado. 6. Ruth Zimmerman and seven-month-old The Candy Man of Northwood at their home in Wilmington, Delaware.

1

2

3 4

5 6

Flare. A blaze that widens as it approaches the topskull.

Flashy. Term used to describe outstanding color-pattern of dog.

Flat bone. When girth of the leg bones is correctly elliptical rather than round.

Flat sided. Ribs insufficiently rounded as they meet the breastbone.

Flews. Upper lips, particularly at inner corners.

Forearm. Bone of the foreleg between the elbow and the pastern.

Foreface. Front part of the head; before the eyes; muzzle.

Fringes. Same as feathering.

Frogface. Usually overshot jaw where nose is extended by the receding jaw.

Front. Forepart of the body as viewed head-on.

Furrow. Slight indentation or median line down center of the skull to the top.

Gay tail. Tail carried above the topline.

Gestation. The period during which a bitch carries her young; normally 63 days.

Goose rump. Too steep or too sloping a croup.

Grizzle. Bluish-gray color.

Guard hairs. The longer, stiffer hairs that protrude through the undercoat.

Hare foot. A narrow foot.

Harlequin. A color pattern; patched or pied coloration, predominantly black and white.

Haw. A third eyelid or membrane at the inside corner of the eye.

Height. Vertical measurement from the withers to the ground or from shoulders to the ground.

Hock. The tarsus bones of the hind leg that form the joint between the second thigh and the metatarsals.

Hocks well let down. When the distance from hock to ground is close to the ground.

Hound. Dog commonly used for hunting by scent.

Hound-marked. Three-color dogs; white, tan, and black, predominating color mentioned first.

Hucklebones. The top of the hipbones.

Humerus. The bone of the upper arm.

Inbreeding. The mating of closely related dogs of the same breed, usually brother to sister.

Incisors. The cutting teeth found between the fangs in the front of the mouth.

Isabella. Fawn or light bay color.

Kink tail. A tail which is abruptly bent, appearing to be broken.

Knuckling over. An insecurely knit pastern joint often causing irregular motion while dog is standing still.

Layback. Well placed shoulders; also, receding nose accompanied by an undershot jaw.

Leather. The flap of the ear.

Level bite. The front or incisor teeth of the upper and lower jaws meeting exactly.

Line breeding. The mating of dogs of the same breed related to a common ancestor; controlled inbreeding, usually grandmother to grandson, or grandfather to granddaughter.

Lippy. Lips that do not meet perfectly.

Loaded shoulders. When shoulder blades are out of alignment due to overweight or overdevelopment on this particular part of the body.

Loin. The region of the body on either side of the vertebral column between the last ribs and the hindquarters.

Lower thigh. Same as second thigh.

Lumber. Excess fat on a dog.

Lumbering. Awkward gait on a dog.

Mane. Profuse hair on the upper portion of the neck.

Mantle. Dark-shaded portion of the coat or shoulders, back, and sides.

Mask. Shading on the foreface.

Median line. Same as furrow.

Molera. Abnormal ossification of the skull.

Molars. Rear teeth used for actual chewing.

Mongrel. Puppy or dog whose parents are of different breeds.

Monorchid. A male dog with only one testicle apparent.

Muzzle. The head in front of the eyes; includes nose, nostril, and jaws, as well as foreface.

Muzzle band. White markings on the muzzle.

Nictitating eyelid. The thin membrane at the inside corner of the eye which is drawn across the eyeball. Sometimes referred to as the third eyelid.

Nose. Scenting ability.

Occipital protuberance. The raised occiput itself.

Occiput. The upper crest or point at the top of the skull.

Occlusion. The meeting or bringing together of the upper and lower teeth.

Olfactory. Pertaining to the sense of smell.

Otter tail. A tail that is thick at the base, with hair parted on under side.

Out at shoulder. Shoulder blades set in such a manner that the joints are too wide, hence jut out from the body.

Outcrossing. The mating of unrelated individuals of the same breed.

Overhang. A very pronounced eyebrow.

Overshot. The front incisor teeth on top overlap the front teeth of the lower jaw. Also called pig jaw.

Pack. Several hounds kept together in one kennel.

Paddling. Moving with the forefeet wide, to encourage a body roll motion.

Pads. The undersides, or soles, of the feet.

Parti-color. Variegated in patches of two or more colors.

Pastern. The collection of bones forming the joint between the radius and ulna, and the metacarpals.

Peak. Same as occiput.

Penciling. Black lines dividing the colored hair on the toes.

Pied. Comparatively large patches of two or more colors. Also called parti-colored or piebald.

Pig jaw. Jaw with overshot bite.

Pigeon breast. A protruding breastbone.

Pile. The soft hair in the undercoat.

Pincer bite. A bite where the incisor teeth meet exactly.

Plume. A feathered tail which is carried over the back.

Points. Color on face, ears, legs, and tail in contrast to the rest of the body color.

Pompon. Rounded tuft of hair left on the end of the tail after clipping.

Prick ear. Carried erect and pointed at tip.

Puppy. Dog under one year of age.

Quality. Refinement; fineness.

Quarters. Hind legs as a pair.

Racy. Tall; of comparatively slight build.

Rat tail. The root thick and covered with soft curls—tip devoid of hair or giving the appearance of having been clipped.

Ring tail. Carried up and around and almost in a circle.

Ringer. A substitute for close resemblance.

Roach back. Convex or upward curvature of back; poor topline.

Roan. A mixture of colored hairs with white hairs. Blue roan, orange roan, etc.

Roman nose. A nose whose bridge has a convex line from forehead to nose tip; ram's nose.

Rose ear. Drop ear which folds over and back, revealing the burr.

Rounding. Cutting or trimming the ends of the ear leather.

Ruff. The longer hair growth around the neck.

Sable. A lacing of black hair in or over a lighter ground color.

Saddle. A marking over the back, like a saddle.

Scapula. The shoulder blade.

Scissors bite. A bite in which the upper teeth just barely overlap the lower teeth.

Screw tail. Naturally short tail twisted in spiral fashion.

Self color. One color with lighter shadings.

Semiprick ears. Carried erect with just the tips folding forward.

Septum. The line extending vertically between the nostrils.

Shelly. A narrow body that lacks the necessary size required by the breed standard.

Sickle tail. Carried out and up in a semicircle.

Slab sides. Insufficient spring of ribs.

Sloping shoulder. The shoulder blade which is set obliquely or "laid back."

Snipey. A pointed nose.

Snowshoe foot. Slightly webbed between the toes.

Soundness. The general good health and appearance of a dog.

Spayed. A female whose ovaries have been removed surgically.

Specialty club. An organization that sponsors and promotes an individual breed.

Specialty show. A dog show devoted to the promotion of a single breed.

Spectacles. Shading or dark markings around the eyes or from eyes to ears.

Splashed. Irregularly patched; color on white, or vice versa.

Captions for pages 266-267.
1. This six-year-old male, Toka, was turned in to the Akita Rescue Society with his papers by his owner. His breeder refused to take him back, claiming to "have too many dogs already!" 2. Three-year-old Sato, turned in to the Rescue Society by her owner who moved to an apartment where they did not accept pets. Placed once and returned for attacking another dog, she was replaced in a home without other animals. 3. Sweetie, a three-year-old Akita bitch found wandering the streets and taken to the Akita Rescue Society shelter in Los Angeles. 4. Shogun, four years old, was turned into a shelter for biting a child who climbed over a fence into his yard. Rescued by the Society, he was later placed in a home without children and is now an adored pet. 5. "Time out..." Ten-week-old Jade and her Beagle friend take time out for a nap at the Wotan Kennels in North Canton, Ohio. 6. Two-year-old Kuma, a male Akita turned into the Los Angeles Akita Rescue Society of America and later placed in another home.

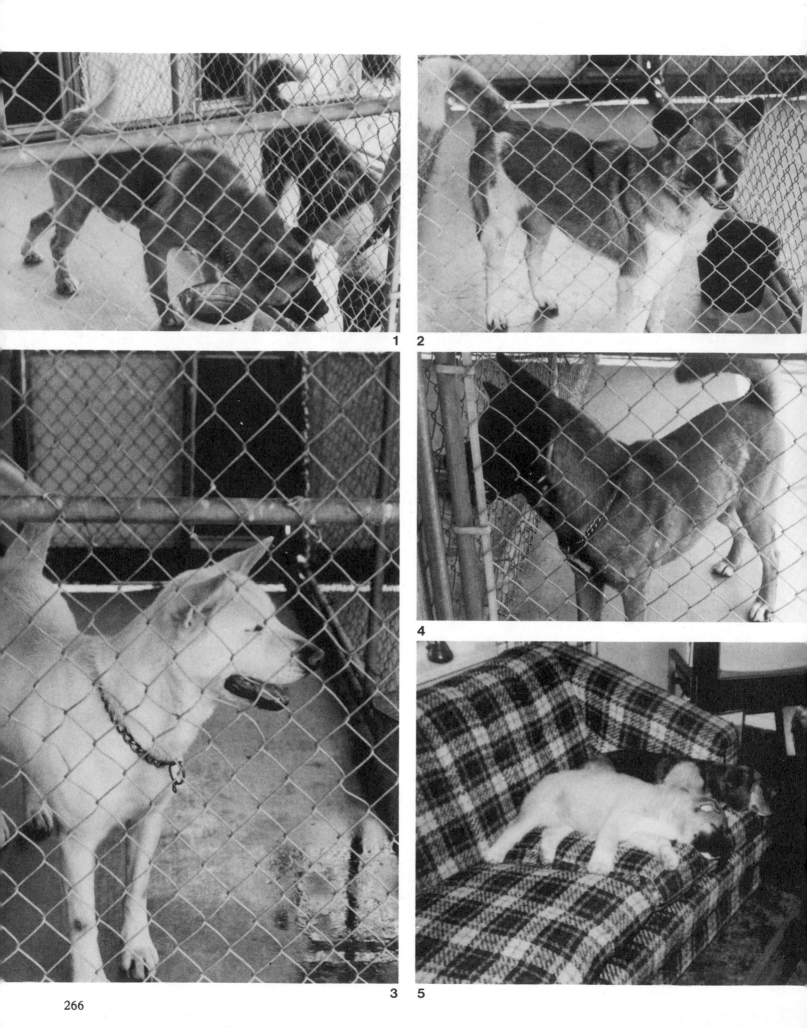

1 2

4

3 5

Splay foot. A flat or open-toed foot.

Spread. The width between the front legs.

Spring of ribs. The degree of rib roundness.

Squirrel tail. Carried up and curving slightly forward.

Stance. Manner of standing.

Staring coat. Dry harsh hair; sometimes curling at the tips.

Station. Comparative height of a dog from the ground—either high or low.

Stern. Tail (or rudder) of a sporting dog or hound.

Sternum. Breastbone.

Stifle. Joint of hind leg between thigh and second thigh; sometimes called the ham.

Stilted. Choppy, up-and-down gait of straight-hocked dog.

Stop. The step-up from nose to skull between the eyes.

Straight-hocked. Without angulation; straight behind.

Substance. Good bone; on a dog in good weight; a well-muscled dog.

Superciliary arches. The prominence of the frontal bone of the skull over the eye.

Swayback. Concave or downward curvature of the back between the withers and the hipbones. Poor topline.

Team. Three or more (usually four) dogs working in unison.

Thigh. The hindquarter from hip joint to stifle.

Throatiness. Excessive loose skin under the throat.

Ticked. Small isolated areas of black or colored hairs on another color background.

Timber. Bone, especially of the legs.

Topknot. Tuft of hair on the top of head.

Triangular eye. The eye set in surrounding tissue of triangular shape. A three-cornered eye.

Tri-color. Three colors on a dog; typically white, black, and tan.

Trumpet. Depression or hollow on either side of the skull just behind the eye socket; comparable to the temple area in humans.

Tuck-up. Body depth at the loin.

Tulip ear. Ear carried erect with slight forward curvature along the sides.

Turn up. Uptilted jaw.

Type. The distinguishing characteristics of a dog to measure its worth against the standard for the breed.

Undershot. The front teeth of the lower jaw overlapping or projecting beyond the front teeth of the upper jaw when the mouth is closed.

Upper arm. The humerus bone of the foreleg between the shoulder blade and forearm.

Vent. Area under the tail.

Walleye. A blue eye; also referred to as a fish eye or pearl eye.

Weaving. When the dog is in motion, the forefeet or hind feet cross.

Weedy. A dog too light of bone.

Wheaten. Pale yellow or fawn color.

Wheel back. Back line arched over the loin; roach back.

Whelps. Unweaned puppies.

Whip tail. Carried out stiffly straight and pointed.

Wire-haired. A hard wiry coat.

Withers. The peak of the first dorsal vertebra; highest part of the body just behind the neck.

Wrinkle. Loose, folding skin on the forehead and/or foreface.

Index

This index is composed of two parts: a general index and an index of people whose names are mentioned in the text.

GENERAL INDEX

INDEX OF PEOPLE